W9-BVE-932

# THE IMPACT of the COLD WAR

## RECONSIDERATIONS

Kennikat Press

## National University Publications

Series in American Studies

*General Editor*

James P. Shenton

*Professor of History, Columbia University*

# THE IMPACT
## of the
# COLD WAR

═══════════

# RECONSIDERATIONS

Edited by
## JOSEPH M. SIRACUSA
and
## GLEN ST. JOHN BARCLAY

**National University Publications**
**KENNIKAT PRESS     //     1977**
**Port Washington, N. Y.     //     London**

*To the memory*
*of Daniel Malloy Smith (1922–1976)*

Copyright © 1977 by Kennikat Press Corp. All rights reserved. No part of this publication may be reproduced, stored in a retrieval system, or transmitted, in any form or by any means, electronic, mechanical, photocopying, recording, or otherwise, without the prior written permission of the publisher.

Manufactured in the United States of America

Published by
**Kennikat Press Corp.**
Port Washington, N. Y./London


**Library of Congress Cataloging in Publication Data**

Main entry under title:

The impact of the cold war.

(Kennikat Press series in American studies) (National university publications)
  Bibliography: p.
  Includes index.
  1. World politics—1945–1975—addresses, essays, lectures. I. Siracusa, Joseph M. II. Barclay, Glen St. John, 1930–
D843.I43        327'.09'044              76-18721
ISBN 0-8046-9158-4 (hard cover)
ISBN 0-8046-9182-7 (soft cover)

# CONTENTS

# PREFACE

The Cold War, like the series of ink-blot designs that make up the Rorschach test, has come to mean many things to many people. To the more tradition-minded, the Cold War was nothing less than, in Arthur M. Schlesinger's felicitous expression, "the brave and essential response of free men to communist aggression." To the so-called realist, it was a clash of inevitable national interests, on the one side the attempted Russian domination of Eastern Europe and penetration as far as possible into Central and Southeastern Europe, on the other the American commitment to the European balance of power. There were, of course, others. Not denying the role of the traditional concern of national security and ideology or the imperfect concern of United States policymakers to the world balance of power, New Left revisionists, emphasizing the nation's preoccupation with a freer trading "open door world," argued that the United States was more or less responsible for the *way* in which the Cold War developed. The issue was a simple one: America wanted an open door world and the Soviet Union did not. Put another way but equally succinctly by Gabriel Kolko, revisionist par excellence, "It [the United States] wished to sell," the single theme around which "American business could trade, operate, and profit without restrictions everywhere." Post-revisionists led by John Lewis Gaddis have responded to the New Left challenge by rightfully underscoring the complex interaction of foreign and domestic developments inside both the United States and the Soviet Union, concluding "that neither side can bear sole responsibility for the onset of the Cold War." Not surprisingly, then, little has been settled, historians agreeing only to disagree.

In the light of the direction in which Cold War historiography has progressed, especially in the United States, it would seem that the time has come to assess in larger measure than before the impact and consequences of the Cold War on nations and historical problems outside the traditional and parochial American-Russian perspective. In the pages that follow, scholars of various nationalities reflect on what the Cold War has meant to the countries of particular interest to them. This collection of essays is addressed to the general reading public as well as the student of history.

Within this framework, Glen St. John Barclay has written on the impact of the Cold War on Australian national and international interests; Vincent P. DeSantis, on Italy; Frans Govaerts, on Belgium; John Moses, on German Cold War historiography; I. F. Nicolson, on Nigeria; Carlos Juan Moneta, on Argentina; Phyllis Auty, on Yugoslavia; Geoffrey Warner, on great power rivalry in postwar China; and Joseph M. Siracusa, on the policies of Roosevelt and Truman in Indochina. Whatever the merits of this volume, the editors are deeply indebted to the contributors for showing the understanding and patience required for the successful completion of such a project. Finally, the editors are grateful for the cheerful assistance received from Mrs. Mary Kooyman in the typing, and, on occasion, the retyping of many of the essays.

St. Lucia

Joseph M. Siracusa
Glen St. J. Barclay

# THE IMPACT of the COLD WAR

## RECONSIDERATIONS

# 1

# AUSTRALIA AND THE COLD WAR

Cold War considerations shaped the character of Australian domestic and foreign politics to a degree probably unique among affluent, representative democracies. This was, of course, only to be expected. East-West tensions were naturally viewed in Australia, as elsewhere, primarily in terms of national security. But national security was something that Australians were unusually sensitive about. Their obsessions on this score dated from the very beginning of their history: in 1800, Governor King was convinced that the presence of two French frigates in Australian waters could only imply a design by Napoleon to swoop down on Botany Bay, raise the convicts in revolt, and annex the colony to the French Empire. There were, indeed, few periods during the next 170 years when Australia's leaders were not prepared to act as if their country were under real threat of invasion from one foreign power or another. It seemed only consistent that the people who throughout the nineteenth century had clamored for the British to annex every island in the Pacific, so that no invader could establish himself nearer than six thousand miles from the Australian coast, should have committed themselves, apparently unconditionally, to support of the American involvement in Vietnam.

But the development was not wholly predictable: xenophobia was an intrinsic and consistent part of the Australian world view; unreserved alignment with the United States was not. Australian security planning had traditionally been developed exclusively within the framework of Imperial defense, although the significance of American military cooperation had long been present in the minds of Australian statesmen. Prime Minister Alfred Deakin had recommended to the bored and disapproving Imperial Government on 27 September 1909 "a proposition of the highest international importance," for "an extension of the Monroe Doctrine to all the countries around the Pacific Ocean, supported by the guarantees of the British Empire, Holland, France and China added to that of the United States."[1] Visits by units of the United States Navy to Australian ports had been greeted in 1908 and 1925 with enormous enthusiasm and public references to Anglo-American solidarity. These demonstrations were not, however, followed up by any kind of official indication from Washington that the United States would in fact be prepared to accept any responsibility for the defense of the British Empire in the Far East. This American reticence was the more disconcerting for the Australians because of their growing doubts as to the capacity of the British to protect the Eastern Empire adequately themselves. Australian Prime Minister Joseph Lyons noted with alarm in March 1938 that British Prime Minister Neville Chamberlain had listed the defense of the overseas empire only third among Britain's military priorities, after the protection of the Home Islands and the security of the lines of communication across the Atlantic.[2]

Lyons had more cause for concern than he was aware of. Australian defense policy, like that of New Zealand, was based absolutely on the readiness of the British to send a fleet to Singapore strong enough to counter any aggressive move by Japan. But in May 1939 the British Admiralty told United States naval authorities that in the event of war with Germany and Italy in the Atlantic and the Mediterranean it might be impossible for them to send naval reinforcements to Singapore, so that the command of the Pacific would have to be assured by the United States Fleet.[3] The Australians were naturally not informed that there was a distinct possibility that they might find themselves defenseless in the Pacific. Nor were they told that there was no guarantee that the Americans would necessarily come to their help. They had, however, pretty much come to this decision unaided. Australian observers in Washington had categorized the overall mood of the Roosevelt administration at the end of 1938, unpromisingly, as one of "increased friendliness to the United Kingdom, modified by a great deal of suspicion and a firm determination not to become embroiled outside the shores of America. . . ." They also noted the very relevant factor that there was at the time not a single antitank gun in the United States that actually worked.[4]

The most that Prime Minister Menzies could suggest by way of consolation to his colleagues was that it might be difficult for the United States to keep out of a Pacific war if Japan were actually to invade Australia; and that even if this were not clearly the case, the Japanese themselves could not be positive that the United States would not come to the help of Australia.[5] It was, however, pointed out to Menzies that in 1936 President Roosevelt had asked his cabinet to consider what the position of the United States should be in three hypothetical situations involving foreign aggression against territory not part of the United States, and that his cabinet had advised that the United States could not be indifferent to an attack on Canada, nor to attacks on Mexico, Central America and northern South America, although the certainty of American intervention diminished as the distance increased; but that in the case of Australia and New Zealand, the element of distance very clearly denoted a declining American interest, and it was impossible, therefore, for the president to make any kind of guarantee to those countries, directly or indirectly.[6]

This situation had apparently not altered by the end of 1939. British ambassador Lothian reported from Washington: "There is not, I think, any particularly strong feeling in the United States for Australia and New Zealand, though they are popular as young democracies."[7] What did produce a spectacular shift in American priorities was the Anglo-French collapse in the face of the German Spring Offensive of 1940. United States involvement in Britain's struggle against the Axis had developed to the stage of a shooting, if still undeclared, war by mid-1941. However, American involvement in the Atlantic positively enhanced American unwillingness to undertake any commitment to defend the British Empire in the Pacific. Menzies attempted anxiously to confirm what American policy would actually be in the event of a Japanese assault against the colonial empires. Australian officers visited Washington secretly in plain clothes for staff talks with the Americans; still, they were unable to discover what Roosevelt's actual intentions were. The indications, indeed, were that he did not know himself. In November, he offered to lend the British destroyers to defend Hong Kong, the Philippines and the Netherlands East Indies, with a view to holding the Japanese on the line of Luzon, Malaya, Singapore and Java. This was clearly less than satisfying. The Australians, accordingly, began to press for agreement on a concerted Empire policy, regardless of what the United States might do. Menzies' successor as prime minister, John Curtin, flatly rejected a proposal by Churchill that the British Empire should simply "march in line with the United States."[8] On 5 December Churchill joyfully assured the Australians that Roosevelt had promised armed support in the event of Britain's being involved in war as a result of Japanese aggression in specific circumstances. He did not, of course, tell Curtin that Roosevelt could not constitutionally have given any such promise.[9]

Pearl Harbor got everybody off the hook. Sir Frederick Eggleston, Australian minister to Chungking, noted prematurely: "I laughed when I heard of it, for the whole of our diplomacy has been directed to getting the USA into the war in the Pacific, and here was Japan doing it for us."[10]

The Japanese attack was, however, not an unqualified blessing. By 27 December, Battle Force Pacific Fleet was out of action; Hong Kong had fallen; the Malayan front was cracking; MacArthur's strategy of defense in the Philippines was in ruins; Burma had been invaded; and the only two British capital ships in Eastern waters had been ignominiously sunk by Japanese air power, despite the conviction of the Australian chief of staff, Sir Thomas Blamey, that battleships were not really vulnerable to this form of attack. In mingled alarm and anticipation, Prime Minister Curtin published an article in the Melbourne *Herald* on 27 December 1941, in which he asserted:

Without any inhibitions of any kind, I make it quite clear that Australia looks to America, free from any pangs as to our traditional links or kinship with the United Kingdom. . . .

This was probably the most famous and also the most misinterpreted public expression of opinion ever made by an Australian prime minister. It implied, in fact, nothing remotely like a permanent or open-ended commitment to the United States. Australia looked to America because it simply was not possible in the circumstances to look to Britain. Indeed, Curtin first remarked that he was looking forward to aid from Russia, before going on to say what he was looking forward to from the United States. The crucial paragraph in his article was not the one that received the most publicity but the one that said:

Summed up, Australian external policy will be shaped towards obtaining Russian aid, and working out, with the United States as the major factor, a plan of Pacific strategy, along with the British, Chinese and Dutch forces....

But Stalin had already made it clear two weeks earlier that there would be no Russian aid for the Pacific Allies to obtain. That left the United States alone.

Nonetheless, Australian-American cooperation should have been cordial almost beyond comparison in the stormy experience of wartime alliances. The Australians themselves expected it to be so. Practically the most insulated and isolated of peoples, they had acquired a vision of the Americans as fellow Anglo-Saxons, sharing a common heritage of traditional British values, social, political and cultural. This impression survived the initial impact of the American presence. The first United States military personnel actually encountered by the Australian and New Zealand people were generally men of the United States Navy and Marine Corps, members of elite services, volunteers, superbly uniformed, rigorously disciplined and to a very great degree of Anglo-Saxon origin. The United

States Army was something else again. Here the main culture shock derived from the fact that many of its conscript members were "ethnic" Americans, of Negro or Continental European origin, sharing scarcely at all in the Anglo-Saxon heritage.

The honeymoon was over almost at once. Simple bad relations at the rank-and-file level would have been less important if there had been mutual respect or even understanding at the top. But there was not. Neither Douglas MacArthur nor Sir Thomas Blamey, the Australian commander in chief, could be described as conciliatory personalities. They could, in fact, neither tolerate nor indeed comprehend each other. Australian susceptibilities about Commonwealth and particularly Anzac solidarity were further irritated by the decision of the Joint Chiefs of Staff to divide the Pacific front into two zones, the South-West Pacific Area, including Australia, under the command of MacArthur; and the South Pacific Area, including New Zealand, under Admiral Ernest J. King. Clashes of interest abounded. Maj. Gen. Lewis H. Brereton, commander of United States Armed Forces in Australia, asked Eisenhower on 26 January to establish "a strong centralized control of internal Australian politics under American influence."[11] On 18 February the Air Force representative on the Joint United States Strategic Committee apparently recommended that Australia should actually be held with minimum forces only, in view of the difficulty of giving "depth to the defense of the line between Hawaii and Australia."[12]

By May 1942 the Australians had discovered the existence of an agreement between Roosevelt and Churchill to concentrate their main war effort initially against Germany and were denouncing it as a fundamental error. Curtin gloomily described the role of MacArthur as making Australia "subject to a form of direction by a representative of another Government" and suggested that Churchill and Roosevelt had made up their minds that if the British Empire in the Far East had to go, it had to go. He expressed his dissatisfaction with Grand Allied Strategy privately in the words: "270 planes went over Europe last night, but by Christ we can't get any here."[13] There could be no doubt that the Australian leadership was meditating a declaration of independence. The only question was when.

The showdown came understandably with the turning of the tide in the Pacific: by 1943 the Australians were far less concerned with any threat from Japan than they were with the possible consequences of United States victory. They did not mind particularly if the Americans extended their influence in the Pacific at the expense of the Japanese colonial empire. However, they were totally opposed to the idea of this happening at the expense of any of the other colonial empires. Prime Minister Curtin had become convinced that the surest way of safeguarding

British Commonwealth interests after victory was to ensure that Commonwealth military forces participated significantly in the campaigns that led to victory. He further considered that the policing of the Pacific should be a dual responsibility: the Americans controlling the North Pacific, but the British Commonwealth supervising the South Pacific. However, the British Commonwealth peoples already in the region would have to do something about this first.

The Australian and New Zealand governments accordingly conferred in Canberra in January 1944. The ensuing Anzac Pact made history as the first treaty of its kind entered into between members of the Commonwealth without British participation. More importantly, it startled both the British and the Americans not only by its public airing of Australian-New Zealand fears of American ambitions but even more by its blatant regionalism, defying as it did the global aspirations of the United Nations. Australia and New Zealand affirmed a common point of view in the South Pacific; resolved to retain the trading system of Imperial Preferences, anathema to the United States; rejected any idea of a condominium with the United States in respect of the Solomons, New Caledonia or the New Hebrides, let alone Samoa or the Cooks; insisted that there should be no change of sovereignty affecting any of the former territories that had not been sanctioned by Wellington and Canberra; and reiterated that the responsibility for policing the Pacific should be divided along the line of the Equator, with the United States keeping to the north and the British Commonwealth looking after the south.[14] Nor was this all. The Australians and New Zealanders also proposed the establishment of a regional organization with advisory powers, called the South Pacific Commission, to which would be accredited representatives of the colonial powers as well as of the United States.

American-Australian relations dived to a new low immediately. The United States was not fighting the Pacific war to keep half the ocean safe for the British Commonwealth. Cordell Hull professed to be able to understand that the Australians and New Zealanders would want to agree on things between themselves. However, he was "frankly disturbed" at the "proposal to call an early conference of powers with territorial interests in the South and South-west Pacific."[15] More emphatically, he told the New Zealanders that the Anzac Pact, "which almost shocked some of us, seemed to be on all fours, so far as the tone and method are concerned, with the Russian action towards Great Britain."[16] The State Department similarly denounced as "not a full and impartial statement of facts" the arguments on which the Australians based their defense of a preferential trading system within the British Commonwealth. The Australians, for their part, noted approvingly that the British also held different views from the United States on occasion, even though they might be still too dependent on American assistance to resist too strongly on major matters.[17]

Curtin resolved to do something about this. At a Commonwealth prime ministers' conference in London in May 1944, he again warned the United States that Australia would not be abandoning the preferential trading system; called for the establishment after victory of British Commonwealth Air Lines across the Pacific, to prevent the Americans from gaining a monopoly of oceanic air travel; and appealed for a British Pacific Force to operate, in conjunction with the Australians and New Zealanders, from bases in Western Australia. British enthusiasm was not so apparent; not for the first or last time, her Dominions seemed more concerned to defend Commonwealth interests than the United Kingdom itself. Curtin's minister for external affairs. Dr. Evatt, suggested that the prime minister remind the British that where a Dominion was acting in pursuance of its regional responsibilities, it should be able to count on British support; and that it would be serious if the United States were allowed to get the impression that Australia endorsed American views on postwar air travel.

The war ended, of course, before the plans for large-scale Commonwealth participation in the Pacific war could be put into effect. They would, in any event, have been as unnecessary politically as they were militarily. The Americans had no intention of displacing the old-style colonial empires in the South Pacific in order to introduce an old-style colonialism of their own. American victory achieved, in fact, exactly what the Australians had wanted to see happen: American arms had compensated for the deficiencies of the Commonwealth, and the Commonwealth presence had been restored to counterbalance American diplomatic or economic pressures: a perfect triangular relationship was in the making.

This situation was fostered by the deterioration in relations between Russia and the Western Allies, obvious after September 1945. Trilateralism cut perfectly across party lines in Australia: the dominant Right Wing of the Australian Labor Party distrusted American capitalism but abominated communism; the Liberal-Country Party opposition abominated communism but prided itself on being "British to the Boot-heels." The consequence was that a remarkably moderate and bipartisan approach emerged under the farrago of personal abuse characteristic of Australian political debate. The Labor Government of J. B. Chifley actively supported the Indonesian anticolonialist revolution, condemned the incompetence and corruption of Chiang Kai-shek's Nationalists, and urged that it was important to maintain satisfactory relations with whatever government controlled China, as it was by no means certain that even a Communist

China would follow the Moscow line.[18] On the other hand, they also attempted to ensure United States participation in a Pacific Security Pact, condemned the Communists as a grave menace to peace in Asia, and suggested that the most desirable situation from Australia's point of view was the presence in the Pacific of European peoples who had the support of their colonial subjects, as the Americans appeared to have in the Philippines.[19]

Nor did the change of government in 1949 to the Liberal-Country Party Coalition seriously alter this stance. Anticommunism had indeed been used actively as an election issue: the new prime minister, Robert Menzies, had accused the Labor Government of seeking to expel the white man from the Pacific, and his minister for external affairs, Percy Spender, had denounced Labor leaders for their equivocation, on the grounds that "a Government which is not totally committed to denunciation of Communism internationally must be affected by the evil itself."[20] However, once in office, Spender said that he could not see any reason why democracy and communism, as distinct from Communist imperialism, could not live together. Nor was there any doubt that Australia's primary external relationship was with the United Kingdom. Spender, indeed, suggested that Australia might seek a security arrangement with the United States even if Britain did not participate, but he hastened to insist that among the "proud objectives of our membership in the British Commonwealth ... [was] ... the special and singular interest in acting in concert with America in the affairs of the Pacific and Asia."[21]

There were, of course, certain important differences of nuance. For example, the United Nations had assumed considerable importance in the world view of the Labor Government. Australia had become the fourth-largest donor to UNRRA and had been admitted to the Central Council of that organization. Evatt had actually attained the distinction of being elected president of the General Assembly. However, the Liberals consistently denigrated the importance of the organization. Harold Holt, Menzies' heir presumptive in the Liberal Party, proclaimed in 1947 that "too much reliance is being placed upon international organisations and our part in them. . . . . For any country to accept that as the basis of its policy is fallacious and dangerous." He recommended that Australia should place its reliance instead on "strong America, a strong Australia."[22] Spender similarly warned that there was "a danger of exaggerating ... the extent to which in present circumstances [the United Nations] can exert real influence for the maintenance of peace in the world."[23]

The United Nations was, of course, not entirely without its uses, even for the Liberals: Australia was the first country in the organization to support the United States in seeking collective action against North Korean aggression in June 1950. However, the Korean War was also the last occasion on which forces from the whole of the British Commonwealth were to fight together as members of a Grand Alliance. Spender told the Liberal Party Annual Conference that "what has taken place in Korea is indicative of the close association [with the United States] which we have endeavored to create"; and he reminded the Australian people that they must "seek to revive the close working ties with our American friends which existed during the war."[24] However, Menzies took pains to inform the United States House of Representatives that the British Commonwealth was their "greatest group associate and friend in all the things that matter in this world."[25]

Later Australia participated in a meeting of Commonwealth prime ministers that produced under British guidance surprisingly conciliatory proposals to end the Chinese intervention in Korea. Menzies denied that there had even been any intention to threaten China or its legitimate interests, or to extend the war beyond Korea; and Spender openly criticized General MacArthur for recommending a more ambitious strategy, affirming that Australia actively opposed any notion of attacking China itself.[26]

Australia was clearly far from nonaligned: the ANZUS Treaty of 1952, indeed, committed Australia, New Zealand and the United States individually to regarding an armed attack in the Pacific as dangerous to their own peace. The United Kingdom was not a participant. But the role of Australia in the ANZUS situation was nonetheless pro-British rather than uncritically pro-American. Spender's successor, Casey, insisted that it was his hope merely to add "an important and intimate association with our Pacific ally, the United States of America," to "our intimate association in the British Commonwealth."[27] ANZUS was indeed conceived in a mood of intense displeasure with United States policy towards Japan: the governor-general had told Parliament in his Speech from the Throne that it had been "and will continue to be the objective of the Government, in the negotiations for a Japanese settlement, to ensure that Japan will not be able in the future to become a menace to Australian security." He had added that British migration would be in the forefront of Australia's immigration policy.[28]

Australia was certainly not following the American lead blindly. The Menzies Government failed to follow the United States in imposing a total embargo on trade with China, even though it did not follow the United Kingdom in entering into diplomatic relations with the government in Peking. Casey actually negotiated with Chou En-lai to try to forestall American intervention in Indochina; and the Australians doggedly followed the British line in insisting that the signing of the SEATO treaty should wait on the establishment of peace between France and the Viet-minh, despite accusations by Dulles that this smacked of appeasement. Menzies again insisted in 1955 that Australia had no commitment to support the United States over the defense of the Offshore Islands between Formosa and the mainland.[29]

The British line, however, was already beginning to seem tenuous. Menzies still claimed in the House of Representatives that Australia "must work incessantly for the closest collaboration between the British Commonwealth and the United States, who, between them, are exemplars of peaceful pursuits, of high ideals, and contain the bulk of the military power of the free world."[30] But the significance of the United Kingdom in American defense planning was declining. France had more men under arms by 1957. Japan and West Germany were rearming. More seriously for Australia, the notion of the Commonwealth as a military alliance was not even getting off the ground. Spender had already noted in August 1950 that some Commonwealth governments exhibited "not merely reluctance but opposition to any such conception." But Australia's own armed forces had been developed for the sole purpose of cooperating with a more powerful ally as far away from continental Australia as possible: Menzies had affirmed from the outset that

the principle purpose of an Australian army is not to repel a land invasion, but to cooperate with other democratic forces in those theatres of war in which the fate of mankind may be fought out. . . . An Australian army raised only for service in Australia would in all probability be raised for no service at all. It would be the equivalent of a wooden gun.[31]

The freedom of Australia would have to be defended "in places outside of Australia itself."[32] But the problem with this notion of "forward defence" was that one had to be sure of having allies to fight with and client states to fight over. Both these involved commitments. Menzies settled on Indo-china as providing at once an alliance and a battleground:

We would do well to consider the significance of Indo-China, not by assuming easily that the frontier of the Viet Minh is on the 17th parallel, but by contemplating that before long we may be forced to regard the Communist frontier as lying on the southern shores of Indo-China. . . . We must by armed force defend the geographical frontiers of those nations whose self-government is based upon the freedom of the spirit. . . . we must accept military commitments. . . . for us, as a democratic nation vitally at risk in these seas, to expect our great friends to accept commitments while our own attitude remained tentative and conditional, would be utterly inconsistent with the intelligence, character and record of this country.[33]

However, Indochina was very evidently a battleground in which only the United States among Australia's great friends would be likely to put in an appearance. Malaya, on the other hand, was a Commonwealth country and afforded some measure of protection by a British military presence at Singapore. Menzies accordingly decided to affirm Commonwealth solidarity by dispatching Australian forces there. This, again, involved a certain disregard of the preferences of the United States. Secretary of State John Foster Dulles favored the notion of "mobile capacity" in military strategy as against fixed garrisons. So did Casey himself, arguing that any sensible opponent would simply avoid the garrisons and go through somewhere else. Menzies insisted unconvincingly that it was necessary to be strong somewhere, rather than weak everywhere. He accordingly dispatched to Malaya a combined force consisting of an infantry battalion, two fighter squadrons, a bomber squadron, some engineers and two small warships.

This was obviously not going to deter anybody from anything. Its objective was purely presentational. As such it fulfilled two functions. In the first place, it enabled Australia to hang on for as long as possible to the rapidly dissipating concept of a united Commonwealth military presence in the East, which the Cold War might help to preserve; in the second, it enabled Menzies to continue to get all available electoral mileage out of a commitment at once ostentatious and inexpensive to the anti-Communist crusade. This was a consideration that had long been apparent to any ambitious Australian politician.

Beginning much earlier, but especially from mid-1949 onward, the Australian public had been continually reminded of the dangers to their way of life posed by both Communists within and Communists without. There is not a volume of Parliamentary Debates from 1949 that does not contain numerous and vitriolic attacks on communism and the Labor Party's attitude towards communism. This technique was made the more relevant when the Catholic-dominated right wing of the Australian Labor Party presented itself in the 1955 elections as a separate political movement, dedicated simply to keeping the ALP out of office, in pursuance of the call by Victoria's Archbishop Young to "oppose any revival of Communist influence." The significance of this right-wing thrust was twofold. In the first place, it gave an extraordinary new respectability to Catholicism: Nikita Khrushchev had replaced the Pope as the most sinister alien threat to the values of the Australian Establishment. There were also impressive electoral implications: the silvertail and the blue-collar suburbs found themselves in an odd but not unprecedented alignment; working-class votes were helping to keep an allegedly socialist party out of power. In the 1955 elections, the Liberals gained 39.73 percent of the total votes cast for the House of Representatives; their Coalition partners, the Country

Party, 7.9 percent; the ALP, 44.63 percent; and the Anti-Communist Labor Movement, 5.7 percent. The Communists, for the record, achieved 1.16 percent of the national vote.[34] Though the Anti-Communist Labor vote might not be necessary to keep the ALP out of office in the effectively gerrymandered Australian political system, it did at least perform the useful public relations function of denying the ALP a majority of the popular vote.

There was perhaps little real need for Menzies to conciliate the Anti-Communist, or "Democratic" Labor Party, as it chose to call itself: a movement that existed only to keep the ALP out of office could hardly transfer its votes to the ALP, no matter how dissatisfied it might be with the Coalition. It was, however, clearly both congenial and perfectly safe for Menzies to speak louder than anybody else in condemnation of communism, while at the same time continuing to pursue a policy that in reality was discreet, equivocal and therefore "British" in style, rather than unreservedly pro-American. Thus he gave verbal support to the United States over the defense of Formosa and the Offshore Islands in 1955, describing them as "a barrier against any new Communist aggression in the event of a great war."[35] However, he made no suggestion that Australia would actually do anything to defend the islands, and indeed made a deliberate distinction between the Offshore Islands and Formosa itself. Casey went even further, explicitly denying any Australian commitment to "assist the United States in any military action it might undertake over any of these islands."[36]

The trouble was that Australia ultimately would have to either rely on the United States to assist it or else spend more money on its own defense, unless it were to adopt the kind of neutralist stance for which Menzies and the Democratic Labor Party were condemning the ALP. Australian expenditure on defense had fallen by 1961 to 2.7 percent of gross national product, the lowest figure for any aligned country except Canada. It was increasingly unlikely that the British would be able to do much to supplement Australian weakness: the unprofitable Suez venture had shown not only the genuine difficulties of trying to run with the British and Americans at the same time but also the extent to which the British were apparently dependent on American material support. Menzies commented bitterly on Empire Day 1957:

In 1914 the English-speaking nations were the undisputed masters of the world, but they have impoverished themselves in winning two world wars.[37]

However, one English-speaking nation had very clearly done anything but impoverish itself by the experience. It was that nation to which

Australia might have to rely increasingly for supplies of defense equipment. Menzies may indeed have had the Commonwealth commitment to Malaya primarily in mind when he told the House of Representatives in 1957 that Australia's main defense role would be to contribute to the allied collective security effort in Southeast Asia.[38] However, the fact was that the equipment of the Australian Armed Forces was already standardized as far as possible with that of the United States. This situation was at least likely to raise problems if Australia were ever to become involved in a war of which the United States did not approve at the time. More significantly, it involved a total reversal of traditional Australian defense planning, a plan that Stanley Bruce had summarized before an imperial conference in 1926 as follows:

The guiding principle on which all our defence preparations are based ... is uniformity in every respect ... with the fighting services of Great Britain, in that in time of emergency we may dovetail into any formation with which our forces may be needed to co-operate.[39]

Apparently, however, the Australian people had no misgivings about the abandonment of a traditional policy of imperial defense in favor of a closer relationship with the United States, and the consequent probability of more serious involvement in the Cold War. Nobody reminded them in the 1958 federal elections of what Bruce had said in 1926 or how Australia had prepared for half a dozen imperial wars. The Liberal vote, indeed, fell to 37.23 percent of all those cast, but the ALP also declined, to 42.81 percent, and the stridently anti-Communist and pro-American Country Party and DLP registered markedly increased gains, polling 9.32 and 9.41 percent, respectively.

A more explicit solidarity with the United States may well have seemed fully congenial to the spirit of Australian domestic politics. But there was a price tag. American views on traditional colonialism were not likely to coincide with Australian views. The Australian Right had consistently lamented the displacement of Dutch colonial authority in the Indian Ocean by Indonesian nationalism. Even the Catholic, right-wing leadership of the ALP had expressed the most unbridled opposition to Indonesian claims to Dutch New Guinea. The new leader of the Parliamentary ALP, Arthur Calwell, had already claimed in 1950 that Australia could "no more let the Indonesians into Dutch New Guinea than we can let them into Darwin."[40] He had indeed argued against Australia's sending aid to Indonesia, on the grounds that "whatever assistance Australia may give to [Indonesia] may ultimately benefit the Communists which may take over Indonesia in the future."[41] Menzies' minister of external affairs, Sir Garfield Barwick, thus felt entitled to expect bipartisan support when he implied that Australia could become involved if fighting broke out between the Dutch and the Indonesians over West New Guinea.[42] However, Australia was in no shape to fight Indonesia unaided, and the United States, concerned with the containment of Communist subversion in Asia, was not looking for new enemies in the region. Unable to count on American assistance, Menzies found it necessary to reverse his policy within a month of Barwick's challenge to Jakarta. The Coalition Government accordingly acquiesced in an Indonesian takeover of West New Guinea, without even insisting that the principle of self-determination should be applied.

The Coalition had been betrayed by its own weakness and by its failure to comprehend that United States policy was in principle both anti-Communist and anticolonialist. The West New Guinea fiasco offended both wings of the Australian political spectrum. The Left rejected the undignified scramble to get back on side with the Americans; the Right denounced the sacrifice of the Dutch colonial presence in the Pacific. It was indeed hard to see how even the ALP could have handled the affair less impressively, even if its leaders had indeed been as "soft on communism" as the Coalition had long been saying they were. Australian foreign policy was in disarray. Bereft of convincing Cold War slogans with which to appeal to the electorate, the Liberal-Country Party Coalition managed to secure only 44.66 percent of the national vote in the 1961 General Elections. The ALP polled 48.68 percent. For the first time, it was reasonable to argue that the Coalition was being kept in office only by the fact that the overall Labor vote continued to be split by the DLP, which took 5.6 percent of the national vote.

One deduction was certainly reasonable: the Coalition needed the Cold War to stay in office. Marginal and ineffective changes were made in the level of defense spending in 1962. But in 1963 the prospect of confrontation between Indonesia and the New Commonwealth Federation of Malaysia offered an incomparable opportunity at once for dramatic anti-Communist action and for a reaffirmation of British Commonwealth solidarity. Nor was this all. Australia had already sent thirty army instructors to South Vietnam in 1962, to augment the twelve thousand United States personnel there, in the Military Assistance Command. The exciting possibility was emerging that Australia might find itself fighting on two distinct fronts. But for Australia to be able to fight anybody convincingly on any front, a massive increase in the numbers and efficiency of its military establishment would first be necessary. Menzies' new defense budget of May 1963 raised arms expenditure only from 2.7 to 2.9 percent of Australian GNP. However, given the miniscule nature of Australia's defense establishment, any increase at all could be made to look impressive.

The Pacific Islands Regiment guarding Papua-New Guinea against the fifteen thousand Indonesian regulars in West Irian was, for example, increased in strength by no less than 100 percent, from seven hundred to fourteen hundred. It would be just as inadequate for the purpose at its new strength as at its old, but the Government could at least claim that it was trying.

The Government's claims initially took the form of grossly misleading boasts about the quality of Australian military equipment, at the very time that Menzies and his advisers were casting about for suitable replacements for their outmoded ships and aircraft.[43] It was considered expedient that something should be done in order to be able to call a snap General Election in a favorable political climate late in 1963. But there was really only one course from which Australia could obtain the necessary hardware in sufficient quantities quickly and, it was hoped, cheaply enough. A major departure had already been made in 1961 by the decision to purchase Charles F. Adams destroyers from the United States, thereby abandoning a tradition of relying upon British equipment for the Royal Australian Navy. Two years later Australia was brought, apparently irreversibly, into the global defense network of the United States when, in May 1963, Menzies agreed to the establishment of a United States Naval Communications Station at North West Cape in Western Australia, to relay command messages to American Polaris submarines patrolling the Indian and Pacific Oceans. Then, a month before the election, Menzies announced that Australia would be buying the experimental F-111 aircraft from the United States, to provide its air strike capacity through the seventies.

This was an epochal decision, quite apart from the fact that it involved an unprecedented and as yet not fully appreciated financial outlay on an aircraft not yet built, let alone tested. The decision for the F-111 entailed setting aside another aircraft, the TSR-2, which was not only British but appeared to be mechanically more advanced than the F-111. Again the Australian public appeared to endorse the new direction: in the 1963 elections, the Coalition vote rose to 45.2 percent of the national total and the DLP vote to 7.3 percent, while the ALP sank to 44.7 percent. Whatever foreign policy the Menzies Government was following, they had a green light for it.

They responded accordingly. Australia had not yet actually made any contribution to the confrontation campaign. In April 1964 two minesweepers, an army engineer force, and four helicopters were diverted to the defense of Malaysia. In June, the new minister for external affairs, the poet and journalist-historian Paul Hasluck, insisted unequivocally on the absolutely vital necessity of defending South Vietnam. Thirty more Australian military advisers were duly sent to assist the Saigon government.

Defense expenditure was increased in November 1964 to $605 million
p.a.; and conscription was introduced, with the approval of 71 percent of
the Australian public, as indicated by public opinion polls. By February
1965 Australia had committed eleven hundred men and six warships to
the confrontation with Indonesia. The British admittedly had committed
seventy thousand men and eighty ships, but Australia literally had no
more to spare.

It was thus all the more remarkable that Menzies should have told the
House of Representatives on 29 April that Australia had decided, after
consultation with the United States and at the request of the government
of South Vietnam, to send an infantry battalion to that region as well.
Australia would thus be fighting alongside the Americans in Vietnam and
the British in Malaysia. It should have been the supreme achievement of
Australian foreign policy. Public opinion polls, indeed, indicated that 59
percent of the Australian public endorsed the involvement in Vietnam.
But the British side of the triangle was about to disappear. Confrontation
was the last military rally of the British Commonwealth. The Indonesian
counterrevolution in October 1965 that deposed Sukarno from office
effectively brought confrontation to an end. By the beginning of 1966,
the myth of the British Commonwealth was at an end too. The British
economy was floundering; India and Pakistan had gone to war with each
other again; Singapore had been expelled from the Federation of Malaysia;
Rhodesia had declared its independence from British rule; two African
Commonwealth countries had broken off diplomatic relations with the
United Kingdom; and civil war had broken out in Nigeria. The Commonwealth show was over. Australia was alone with a new prime minister and
the United States, and at war in Vietnam.

The new Australian prime minister, Harold Holt, had apparently few
misgivings about this new direction in Cold War diplomacy. It was he who
in 1947 had so cheerfully scorned the notion that the United Nations
could provide an effective safeguard against aggression. In 1965 he expressed the same sentiment, in spades, declaring, "Only a fool committed
to folly could find in the current fragile situation of the United Nations ...
a source of strength for freedom in the world at this time."[44] Not many
politicians could claim to have been so true to one idea for nearly twenty
years. It was, however, worthy of remark that he and his fellows in the
Coalition should have been so much at pains for so long to make public
their contempt for the organization. Discretion has never been one of
the legendary Australian virtues, and it was ironically fitting that the first
country to endorse the position of the Truman administration on Korea,
the first country to applaud Johnson's decision to bomb North Vietnam,
should also have been the only member of the United Nations persistently

and openly to denigrate the organization. In this, if in little else, Canberra and Peking marched together.

This, of course, was not going to disturb Harold Holt. Nor was the fact that the external situation had perceptibly changed since 1947. Holt had then based Australia's security on its relationship with a strong America, a strong Britain and a strong Holland. He was now apparently prepared to settle for the first alone.

In February 1966, a British Government White Paper on Defense had indicated that the United Kingdom would not again undertake major operations of war outside Europe without the full support of its NATO allies. British forces would be withdrawn from "East of Suez" as soon as conditions permitted. Moreover, no more aircraft carriers were to be constructed for the Royal Navy, meaning that service would presumably lose a large element of its long-range strike capacity as well. However, Holt merely dismissed the idea that the British would be abandoning a global power role in the future, while Hasluck rated the British and West Europeans for their unwillingness to become involved in Vietnam.[45] Holt did, admittedly, take sufficient cognizance of the change in British policy to ask his high commissioner in London to seek immediate clarification of British plans. He was duly informed by British Defense Minister Denis Healy that British forces

may have a useful role to play for some time in maintaining stability in the Middle East from bases in the Persian Gulf, and in the Far East from bases in Malaysia and Singapore—certainly so long as the peoples in those territories wish us to stay on terms that make sense from our point of view. If we were compelled to leave the Asian mainland the only place where we could display a major effort would be Australia. . . . [46]

The message was clear: the British would stay if Australia made it worth their while to do so. There were, of course, certain problems of logic involved: if the Australian-American alliance was as immutable as Holt and Hasluck implied, Australia could be certain of United States protection against any serious threat; and if Australia had United States protection, it would not need any help from the United Kingdom. On the other hand, if Australia could not count on the United States in all circumstances, then it would indeed make sense to keep the British in the region; but in that case one would be entitled to ask what Australia was doing in Vietnam.

It would not have been agreeable for Holt to tell the House of Representatives that Australia was in Vietnam so that the Coalition could win the next federal election. However, Holt may never have seen any logical difficulties in his way: linguistic subtleties had absolutely no place in the formulation of Liberal-Country Party foreign policy in an election year. What was apparent was that the implications of the American alliance totally overshadowed for him and Hasluck any importance that could be attributed to a Commonwealth military presence. The triangularism of Curtin, Chifley or Menzies simply went by the board. By contrast, Holt responded to a visit by United States Vice-President Hubert H. Humphrey by increasing the Australian troop commitment in Vietnam to 4,500, claiming that the whole free world was now threatened by the Chinese Communist philosophy of world domination.[47] Then in July, Holt supplied friends and enemies alike with a catch-phrase all too appropriate to the style of Australian politics of the decade: "All the way with LBJ."[48] Holt did explain subsequently that he had not intended to suggest that Australia should go all the way with LBJ to everywhere that LBJ might want to go; but Australia was certainly all the way with LBJ in Vietnam.[49]

There was one sense, at least, in which Holt's phrase was all too accurate: there were no reservations about the extent to which Australian forces had become involved in the United States defense system. Plans to develop a military relationship with the United Kingdom in Western Australia were taken up lightly in August 1966 but were allowed to die from neglect. By contrast, Holt increased the Australian commitment to Vietnam to 6,300 in December 1966 and again to 8,000 in October 1967, literally the maximum effort that Australia's resources could sustain (and also, coincidentally, the number Senator Fulbright had claimed in February that Australia should be providing if it was really serious).

Anti-Communist enthusiasm combined with the atavistic ineptitudes of ALP leader Arthur Calwell to sweep the Coalition back into power in 1966. For the first time since 1958, the Coalition actually gained a larger percentage of the national vote than the ALP, winning 49.67, as against 40.54 percent. However, perceptive—or just plain worried—commentators warned at the time that this was an election campaign with the gravest possible implications for Australian politics. The Vietnam debate had already been transferred from legislative assemblies to the streets, in Australia as well as in the United States. The prime minister had been abused, heckled and almost physically assaulted; and Mr. Calwell's public appearances had been the occasion for open brawling. One might well have some misgivings about politics that had begun to turn Australian elections into contests of gutter bravos.

There were other grounds for misgivings as well. Handsome, incredibly urbane, appealing and doomed, Australia's answer to Warren G. Harding, Holt was presiding over a policy obviously, even in its hour of triumph, all too likely to lead to chaos and humiliation. The sheer mindlessness of Australian defense policy was suddenly apparent: the American commitment had left the nation with armed forces virtually useless except as supplements to those of the United States, and without alternative sources of supply for equipment whose costs had already trebled.[50] In the meantime, Australian spending on research and development of weapons had actually declined since 1964 from 2 percent of total defense spending, a proportion about one-twelfth that considered appropriate by countries such as France, Sweden and even the United Kingdom.[51] Australia's own defense industries had received orders for only $713 million worth of equipment, in a period in which Australia had paid $1,040 million in overseas orders.[52] More painful still, Australia had received no war contracts from the United States, while industrially less sophisticated South Korea had received contracts valued at over $1 billion.[53]

Holt drowned in the sea off Victoria before the storm broke. His successor, John Gorton, reaped the harvest of a tradition of exploiting international tensions for electoral advantage and the attainment of security on the cheap. On 16 January 1968 the British spelt out unequivocally their intention to withdraw militarily from East of Suez. Prime Minister Gorton, interestingly, responded to the impending departure of the British not by a new commitment to the Americans but rather by stating at the very height of the Tet Offensive that the Australian commitment in Vietnam had reached its peak. Subsequently, at a Liberal meeting in May, he alluded to a Fortress Australia policy and suggested an Israeli-type defense posture.[54] In June he suggested that the whole notion of "forward defense by troops stationed outside Australia ... needed minute examination when the forces of that [allied] major power were to be withdrawn and the circumstances of their re-entry unknown."[55]

But the old notion of Cold War commitment died hard. On 26 May Foreign Minister Hasluck vigorously defended the United States bombing offensive against North Vietnam. His advocacy seemed a little ill-timed when President Johnson halted the air attacks five days later, without consulting the Australian Government. However, even the commencement of talks between the United States and Vietnam in Paris on 13 May 1968 did not apparently convince Mr. Hasluck that times were changing. His comments on the Czech affair implied a "cold war posture ... more inflexible and unyielding than that professed by almost any other western statesman."[56] Far worse was to follow. On 3 October Mr. Hasluck chose to deliver an address in Toronto, of all possible places, condemning the secretary-general of the United Nations for suggesting that the United States should halt the bombing of North Vietnam unconditionally.[57] On 1 November President Johnson did just that. Australia had predictably left itself aligned with a policy from which the Americans had been trying to disengage themselves at least ever since Tet.

Few governments can have been more ineptly served by their diplomatic advisers: the Australians had been caught as embarrassingly out of step as the Albanian and Rumanian hard-liners had been by Khruschchev's repudiation of Stalin, and with far less excuse. Prime Minister Gorton did his best to salvage something from the wreck of Holt's and Hasluck's policies: he advised the infuriated South Vietnamese to do as they were told by the Americans, made it clear that Australia would not try to go it alone in Southeast Asia, and repeated that the size and duration of any Australian military commitment to Malaysia-Singapore would depend upon the support and facilities provided by the host countries. By February 1969 Mr. Gorton had decided to leave an Australian force of twelve hundred men, forty-two aircraft and one ship in the region, even after the British had left.[58] There was, however, a severe limitation on their use: they would be available to be employed only against "externally promoted and inspired Communist infiltration and subversion of the kind which became familiar during the [Malayan] Emergency."[59]

They would certainly not have been much use against any serious external aggression, especially as there was no possibility of their being reinforced adequately from Australia. There was, however, the practical point that there was at the time literally nowhere in Australia to base the forty-two Mirages committed to Malaysia, as well as the sentimental consideration that Malaysia-Singapore was the last frontier where Australia and New Zealand could possibly be expected to stand on guard together. With the British disappearing over the horizon and the Americans hell-bent on disengagement, even New Zealand was better than nothing as an ally. The Commonwealth might have sunk past hope, but the Anzac flame could still raise a flicker.

Personally flamboyant, tough and deliberately indiscreet, with a beautiful voice and a battered face, an Oxford-educated brawler with a United Services tie, Gorton brought to Australian politics a brand of machismo for which his predecessors had done nothing to prepare the nation. He was also showing himself to be a diplomat more prudent and farsighted than even Menzies in his earlier days. In his first months of office, he had already taken out insurance against impending isolation by visiting New Zealand, as Harold Holt had previously done. Hasluck was kicked upstairs to vice-regal impotence as governor-general. In June 1969 Gorton made it clear that Anzac forces in Malaysia or Singapore would be available only for the defense of the Malaysian Peninsula and Singapore itself: there was going to be no chance of their getting embroiled in wranglings between Malaysia and the Philippines or Indonesia over Sabah.

Calculation of this kind was certainly far removed from the simplistic Cold War polemics that had won elections for the Coalition since 1949.

It was, indeed, all too likely to help lose an election for them, as was shown by the experience of Gorton's hapless foreign minister, Mr. Freeth, who carried the search for allies so far as to suggest that Australia might in certain circumstances consider a security arrangement with the Soviet Union. He was immediately subjected to the full fury of blue-collar Catholic reaction from the DLP, as well as to the less inhibited assaults of the League of Rights, the John Birchers from the bush, on the right of the Country Party. Gorton, who had a certain gift for verbal obscurity, left it not altogether clear whether the cabinet had actually known what Freeth was going to say before he made his calamitously farsighted speech. But the prime minister's obfuscations saved nobody: Freeth lost his portfolio right away, and his seat at the next General Election.

He almost took the Government with him. In the November 1969 elections, the Coalition vote fell to 43.35 percent of the national total, while the ALP rose to 46.95 percent. Thanks to Australia's singular method of counting votes, the new ALP Leader, Mr. Whitlam, was able to claim for four days that the issue was actually in doubt. It was not difficult to imagine why this disaster should have happened to perhaps the only Australian politician of the past thirty years who had managed to inspire genuine affection in large numbers of his fellow-citizens. There were enough reasons to suit anybody. There was the fact that Gorton's own oratorical style sometimes managed to bury his meaning so completely that his listeners simply could not tell what he was talking about. There were his incredibly inept public relations, which had inspired venomous hostility in most branches of the media. There was the open jealousy and enmity of his own cabinet colleagues. There was simple regional rivalry, evidenced in the unending intrigues of New South Wales politicians aimed at unseating the latest of a long line of Victorian prime ministers in favor of one of their own. There was the fact that Gorton's flexible and pragmatic posture in foreign affairs had left electors with little to choose between an outworn and fragmenting Coalition and a refurbished ALP. Most of all there was the fatal reality that Gorton was defying the principles of Cold War electoral strategy that had kept the Coalition in office since 1949. Gorton was prepared to offer Australia a policy of adventurous, empirical nationalism. What the Coalition had offered for twenty years had been the negation of these qualities erected into a system of government.

Gorton clearly had to go. He had already staved off one bid for power from Federal Treasurer William McMahon, a Sydneysider from the silvertail suburb of Bellevue Hill, whom Gorton had characteristically rewarded with the portfolio of Foreign Affairs, not because he had any talent for the post but merely because it would ensure that he would be out of the country as often as possible. But this was only a stopgap: faced with yet another rift in his cabinet, Gorton generously resigned and found his way out of the ranks of power to the back benches of parliament. For two years Australia lurched almost leaderless and very nearly policyless, while Defense, the Services, Foreign Affairs and even the Treasury were handed over to the care of ministers who not only were unable to provide satisfactory answers to the problems with which they were faced but all too frequently seemed not to understand what the problems were.

The bankruptcy of traditional Cold War diplomacy was not the only factor that brought the ALP crashing back into office in 1972. Possibly the major element was that Labor had at last acquired a leader with whom they were at least not certain to lose, and the Coalition, a prime minister with whom they could scarcely hope to win in any circumstances. The Liberals were simply disintegrating: it was as necessary for them to lose in 1972 as it had been for the Republicans in 1964. But it was certainly true that only the Cold War could have kept the Coalition in office for twenty-three years; and it had saddled the Coalition's successors with a foreign policy that had involved considerable expense, immense humiliation and made perhaps less real sense than that of any other allegedly independent nation involved in the Cold War. The strains it had imposed on ministerial personnel were obvious: between 1967 and 1972 Australia had four prime ministers, six foreign ministers and three ministers of defense. The last years of Coalition government presented an image of political instability unmatched by Fourth Republic France.

Yet, as a concomitant of its Cold War posture, Australia acquired the reputation of a nation peculiarly blessed with political stability. Indeed, there are few countries in which people are less likely to do violence to one another for political reasons. But this apparent virtue helped contribute to what was perhaps Australia's most serious domestic and international problem. Overseas capital found Australia the safest of all pastures for investment and exploitation. Australian Federal Treasurers, obsessed with booming stock prices and visibly swelling reserves of foreign exchange, made no attempt to control the situation. It would indeed have been illogical to have expected any action from the men who watched approvingly while sales of wheat and wool soared to their archenemies, the Chinese Communists, excusing their inaction on the grounds that "the Government doesn't sell wheat to China: it's the farmers."[60] The consequences were sobering: the net result of Australia's ideological reliability was that by 1972 foreign companies owned all of Australia's automobile industry, 70 percent of its mining, 35 percent of its manufactured exports, and about the same percentage of all Australian industry.[61]

A Cold War policy that had cultivated diplomatic subservience had brought foreign economic domination in its train. It was only to be expected that the new Labor Government of Prime Minister Gough

Whitlam would seek to introduce a few changes. They went much further than this. By the middle of 1975, Australia had virtually liquidated its commitment to Malaysia and Singapore; established diplomatic relations with North Vietnam, North Korea and China; given grounds for belief that it intended to discard traditional links with the United Kingdom almost entirely; clashed with France repeatedly over the issue of nuclear testing in the South Pacific; and locked horns with the United States on most major issues of foreign policy. The new regime condemned the United States for indecisiveness regarding the proliferation of nuclear weapons; voted against the Americans as well as the British and French on the expulsion of South Africa from the United Nations; and actively supported nonaligned Asian states in their opposition to the United States naval presence in the Indian Ocean. In June 1974 the new Labor foreign minister, Senator Don Willesee, boasted: "Australian foreign policy has, I believe, gone through a period of important and substantial change since December 1972, one result of which is that our policies are now up to date. . . ."[62] The senator was, in fact, understating the case: Australia had experienced a diplomatic revolution without parallel in the history of any allegedly Western-aligned power.

This, of course, did not mean that the new policies were necessarily more rational and appropriate than the old. Labor diplomacy was, in fact, foundering on a paradox more absurd and far more perilous than any that had embarrassed the Coalition. The simple reality was that behind its parade of independence Australia was trying to work both sides of the street, with little to offer to either. The country's fundamental defenselessness could hardly be exaggerated: in June 1973 Brigadier J. Ochiltree had told the Senate Standing Committee on Foreign Affairs that Australia possessed a combat force of only 6,000 men, which would be "a good size if our opponents had only 5,000."[63] Nobody was really suggesting that Australia could expect any military support from her new friends in North Korea, North Vietnam, China or Ceylon. There was only one country in the world to which Australia could look for meaningful aid in the event of a military threat to its interests or independence. Prime Minister Whitlam was obviously fully aware of this fact of life: it is probable that Australia was the only country in the world still insisting through 1974 and 1975 on its total fidelity to the United States alliance. What remained to be shown was that Australia had any convincing grounds for expecting these feelings to be reciprocated in Washington. Back in 1947, Liberal Party spokesmen had condemned the diplomacy of Labor leaders Ben Chifley and Herbert V. Evatt as leaving Australia "a country isolated in the world . . . lonely, and virtually alone."[64] These words had been nonsensical at the time. Twenty-eight years later, they added up to a tolerably accurate description of Australia's international position.

VINCENT P. DeSANTIS

# ITALY AND THE COLD WAR

For Italy the Second World War was perhaps a less frightful experience than for Germany. The greatest destruction was in the countryside, where mile after mile was laid waste by the withdrawing and pursuing armies. But here the people, long accustomed to pillage, took much of it in their stride. No Italian city was wrecked as Hamburg and Dresden were.

Furthermore, within a dozen years following the end of the war, the Italian nation underwent an almost miraculous recovery and reconstruction. By the mid-fifties the scars of war had nearly disappeared. Foreign visitors to Italy at that time often expressed astonishment at the rate and tempo of the country's restoration. Few nations surpassed Italy in economic recuperation in the postwar years. Her industrial production a decade after the war nearly doubled the output of 1938, Italy's peak prewar year; and her recovery from the destruction and dislocations of the war was almost as amazing as that of West Germany. Exports reached record levels and many Italian products became well known all over the world. The bridges over the Arno in Florence, blown up by the Germans, were rebuilt. The Ponte Trinita was reconstructed just as it had been in Florence's golden Cinquecento. Giovanni Gronchi, president of the Republic of Italy from 1955 to 1962 and minister of industry in the first Italian governments immediately after the armistice, wrote that "all this happened in a spirit of fraternal collaboration," because all "were convinced of the common duty to put all they had in the service of rebuilding the country.... Political discord and class struggle thus were silenced in Italy for a while, and since it was a matter of creating the bases on which to rebuild after an immense disaster, all were ready, of one mind and one heart, to go to work together—workingmen and owners, technicians and managers, rich and poor."[1] Thus, in the period of the Cold War the Italian people gave convincing proof of their vitality and their will to move along the road toward economic and political progress.

But despite the substantial economic progress of these years, some of Italy's most basic problems—overpopulation, with its attendant unemployment, and the wide gap between the standard of living of the northern part and that of the southern part of the country—remained unsolved. Though one of the main goals of every postwar Italian government was to bridge this gap, and although much progress was made in the south, greater strides were taken in the north, and the gap was widened rather than closed. The distribution of wealth and power still remained quite uneven, and the tax system did not redistribute income very adequately. Despite the economic boom of the postwar years, only a minority of Italians were enjoying a world of well-being. According to an estimate made in the mid-1960s, a mere 25 percent of the population had achieved a decent level of comfort by Western European standards, and a larger number were far below that level.[2]

And in spite of the creation of the republic and the restoration of political democracy, the main goal of Italian democracy after the fall of Mussolini—the formation of an integrated society—was not realized. To be sure, the postwar constitution assured a wide representation of the popular will, and many concrete efforts were made to eradicate the most noticeable social and economic inequalities. But the problem of national unification remained unsolved. Two principal political ideologies largely divided the country into opposing groups: Christian democracy, seeking a gradual change in the social and political system, and communism, favoring a radical modification of the system. The clash between these two parties and their allies in the postwar years intensified the historical divisions in the country and inevitably increased the difficulties of unification.

In addition, the social and political consensus necessary to make the state and its institutions important and effective did not develop. Not one of the essential elements of the emerging republic—the presidency, the parliament or the cabinet—gained prominence or influence, even though some outstanding men served in Italian public life. Italian postwar politics was almost always in a state of crisis or impotence. Yet there was a liveliness of debate and a variety of ideas and opinions, and democracy and political freedom continued to survive. And this was critically important in a country where fear was still a hangover from a stifling dictatorship of twenty years.

Italy in the postwar years suffered from being a defeated and weak country and one necessarily dependent upon the actions of others for both internal and external security. This difficulty was compounded by the heavy impact of the Cold War rivalry between the United States and the Soviet Union on virtually all European affairs and activities. The high hopes fostered by the end of the war had just about vanished within a few years. The United States and the Soviet Union, both possessing atomic weapons, were distrustful of each other's intentions and were hardening their attitudes and positions toward one another. And while the Kremlin suspected the United States was planning to "liberate" Eastern Europe from its Russian "liberators," the United States and her allies believed that the Soviet Union intended to take over all of Western Europe, by force if necessary. Mutual trust had disappeared, and mutual terror, to use the late Herbert Feis's phrase, was becoming the decisive restraint.

The origins of the Cold War have been variously explained. An early interpretation, generally accepted until recently, placed the chief blame for the Cold War upon the Soviet Union. According to this view, the Soviet leaders were determined to make the entire world Communist, by force if necessary, and for that purpose they had used the wartime alliance with the West to destroy Nazism. Once that was done, according to this theory, they abandoned the Grand Alliance to seek world revolution. They broke their promises made at Yalta by establishing Communist regimes in "liberated Eastern Europe" and awaited their opportunity to do the same thing in Western Europe, particularly in Italy and France. Finally, says this theory, the United States, in the defense of basic democratic ideals, opposed Communist expansion through the containment policy, and so the Cold War began.

A revisionist interpretation, coming mainly from the New Left historians, takes a directly opposite view by putting the principal blame for the Cold War upon the United States. These historians emphasize economic motives and regard American foreign policy after 1945 as imperialistic and counterrevolutionary. They maintain that the Cold War started when President Harry Truman, aware of the power of the new weapon, the atomic bomb, decided to compel the Soviet Union to loosen its hold on the countries of Eastern Europe and to allow them to enjoy an "open door" for an expansionist American capitalism. This, according to the revisionists, led the Soviet Union to clamp an admittedly repressive but understandably defensive regime on Eastern Europe.

Another recent interpretation, while acknowledging the materialistic motives of the United States as helping to bring on the Cold War, regards something else as the main cause. This view accepts American fears of Soviet expansionism as genuine but sees little basis in fact for such fears. According to this position, the Soviet Union was less interested in spreading communism than in protecting itself against further attacks from the West, such as the attacks by Germany in 1914 and 1941 and by Napoleon in 1812. Therefore, the Soviet leaders in the postwar years placed national security above world revolution and attempted to gain security much as the czars had done, by imposing strict control over the small countries on their western frontier.[3]

Regardless of these explanations, the suspicions each side had of the other's intentions seem to have little basis in fact. But suspicion produced suspicion, and each action taken by one side was viewed by the other as dangerous and aggressive and led to further actions. The consequence was a spiralling and an almost continuous increase in fears and in armaments. As these mutual suspicions intensified, so did the rift between the United States and the Soviet Union, and their allies. And this all-important development in the postwar years was to influence both the domestic and foreign policies of European countries, particularly those of Italy.

For many Italians during this troubled time after the war, their best and closest friends were the American people. And in the Cold War years Italy was one of the most loyal supporters of United States foreign policy. Yet a poll conducted by Doxa revealed that 12 percent of the respondents blamed the United States for the Cold War; 27 percent, Russia; and 26 percent, both the United States and Russia. Nearly 25 percent of those polled did not know who was to blame for creating the two-bloc world. Nor did most Italians agree with the traditional American view that the Cold War was caused by Soviet moves to dominate the world. Significant portions of the Italian population (from 33 percent to 52 percent), distributed among various parties, were of the opinion that both the United States and the Soviet Union wanted to control the world. Asked whether it was true that America wanted to dominate the world, 29 percent of those Italians polled said it was true, and 40 percent believed it was partly true, while only 23 percent indicated it was false. Most of the anti-Americanism, interestingly, was found among the extreme Left and the neo-Fascists, and part of this feeling resulted from Italian domestic politics. The identification of the United States with the Christian Democratic Party and the Vatican helped to make anti-Americans out of anti-clericals. And identification of the United States with big-business interests pushed left-wing Christian Democrats, who favored state-owned firms, into the anti-American camp.[4]

During the Cold War period, Italians only gradually became aware of the fact that Italy was a part of the Western alliance system. Though this was the most important development in Italian foreign policy in these years, surveys disclosed that there was no solid majority behind it. In December 1955, a representative sample of two groups was asked, "Under present circumstances which do you think is the most practical way for Italy to ensure its security?" Only 33 percent of the general public and 49 percent of the dominant political group favored continuing the current arrangement for Western defense, which was based on the alliance with the Western countries. Eighteen and 26 percent, respectively, approved a general security system including the United States, the Soviet Union and other European nations; 4 and 12 percent, respectively, wanted to form an alliance limited to Western European countries; 21 and 7 percent wished to withdraw from all alliances and take a position of neutrality; and 23 and 6 percent said they did not know.[5]

The Soviet Union sought to influence the policies of postwar Italy not only through the traditional diplomatic, political, economic, military and cultural means but also through the medium of the Italian Communist Party. The Italian Communist Party claimed the largest membership of any Communist party in the Western world and was the second-largest party in Italy after the Christian Democratic Party in the number of votes polled. Overall, the Italian Communist Party remained loyal to the Soviet Union, despite some internal opposition, and disposed of its dissidents with the use of such customary Communist charges as "dogmatism" and "revisionism." As Palmiro Togliatti, secretary-general of the party throughout the postwar period, pointed out in an address to the Central Committee in September 1957: "the tie with the Soviet Union has been our life . . . [and] this tie is put above and beyond the debate which we all want to conduct and which has always been conducted, on the way to resolve determinate problems, on the criticism which must or must not be made." But at the same meeting the party asserted the right to "the full and autonomous responsibility of each [Communist] Party for its own activity."[6]

On domestic questions the Italian Communist Party followed a somewhat independent course. Despite their close ties with the Soviet Union, the Italian Communists in the immediate postwar years acted in a way that showed they had probably learned more than any other party from their defeat at the hands of the Fascists. From the end of the war to the elections of 1948, the Italian Communists kept clear of practically every pitfall that had resulted in the Maximalist-Communist defeat of some twenty years earlier. For instance, since the Italian Communists did not accept the traditional propaganda about the impending collapse of the capitalistic system, they made an effort to keep good relations with left-wing Socialists and not to downgrade such an alliance. The Italian Communists also worked hard to improve their relations with the Catholic Church by abandoning their traditional anticlericalism and supporting some degree of collaboration. Moreover, in their efforts to conciliate the Vatican, the Communists voted in the Constituent Assembly in favor of placing the Lateran Accords of 1929 in the new Italian Constitution. And, despite strong opposition from Stalin, the Communist Party opened its membership to all adult Italians regardless of their beliefs. If the Italian Communists had followed the dictum of Stalin to restrict party membership to those who believed in and understood Marxism, the Italian Communist Party would have become a small elitist party rather than a large party with mass appeal.

The Italian Communists cooperated in the Italian resistance movement in World War II and thus were a part of the Committee of National Liberation. In this struggle the Communists faced a strong competitor in the democratic-republican socialist-colored Action Party, the heir of the cadres of the Justice and Freedom group of 1929-1934. The Action Party, by forming partisan units, prevented the Communists from having a monopoly of the Resistance. When Togliatti returned from Russia in April 1944, he abandoned the noncollaboration policy of the Committee of National Liberation and spoke in favor of resolving "the real problem: the creation of a government." In this endeavor, Togliatti favored a general coalition of the Communist, Socialist, and Christian Democratic parties. This would have been a coalition similar to those being created in Soviet-controlled Eastern European countries, where the democratic parties cooperated in government and were subsequently excluded by the Communists.

If this had happened in Italy, the communists could have paralyzed the entire party system and seized control of the country as they were doing elsewhere. But the other groups in the Committee of National Liberation had enough energy and foresight to forestall the Communists from gaining complete control of the situation. And so the political life of Italy developed as a conflict among a number of parties rather than as a program directed and dominated by the Communists. Within this framework the Italian Communist Party at once participated and cooperated, while at the same time seeking to strengthen itself throughout the country.

While the Italian Communist Party participated in the Italian governments from April 1944 until 31 May 1947, when the third De Gasperi cabinet came to an end, it was never able to secure the cabinet posts that might have given it decisive power. One must remember, however, that the government was established before the signing of the peace treaty and therefore was supervised by an Allied Control Commission in which the British and Americans had the commanding power. Togliatti himself was minister of justice, except in De Gasperi's second cabinet; but the ministries of Foreign Affairs, Interior, and Defense always eluded the Communists. As for Togliatti, he urged partisans to give up their weapons, for he wanted to demonstrate that a coalition government with the Communists was possible.

During this time the effect of Soviet policy on the Italian scene was moderate. If the actions of the Italian Communist Party represented the Soviet position, there was no revolutionary threat to Italian society. The Italian Communists followed the most conservative line of the left-wing parties until 1947 and accepted compromises, on the basis of wartime unity, that the Action and Socialist parties would not tolerate. Perhaps the Russians truly did not wish to antagonize the British and Americans during the war. Or perhaps the Kremlin wanted to keep weak and ineffective groups in power so that there would be a better opportunity later on for the Communists to seize power.

In foreign affairs, the Communist Party, while seeking the Alto Adige for Italy and the maintenance of her western frontiers, was willing to abandon Istria and the hinterland of Trieste to Yugoslavia. This position may have been in line with Soviet and Slavic policy, but it was out of line with the Italian national policy the Communists claimed to defend. Togliatti regarded Trieste as an "Italian city with a Slavic hinterland" and supported Tito's solution to this question, presumably because the Italian Communist Party at that time had to agree with the Yugoslav Communist leader. The Italian Communist position on Trieste and their later support of Tito's suggested barter of Gorizia against Trieste made the Communists appear to be little more than instruments of Soviet interests.

In 1947, the Italian Communists were excluded from the government, but they continued to affect Italian policy because they were regarded as local spokesmen for the Soviet Union. During the Cold War non-Communists assumed that the position of the Italian Communists always followed the policy of the Soviet Union. And this assumption had an important effect upon Italian politics. Since the Soviet Union was one of the great powers and could not be ignored, the Italian government usually responded in some way to the Italian Communist attitude on a question. In this way the Italian Communists, by taking a position on almost any issue, were able to force the government to take the other side to show the United States or the Vatican it was anti-Communist. Sometimes this strategy was advantageous to the government, as, for example, when it used the threat of communism to obtain more American aid, pointing out that if more aid were not received, it might be necessary to bring the Communists back into the government. For instance, when the Italian Communists opposed the setting up of American medium-range-missile bases in Italy in 1958, they proposed that in exchange for the United States' giving up these bases the Russians should give up their missile bases in Albania. Although the Italian Communists were able to convince Moscow that this was a good plan, they could not convince Rome or Washington.

The Italian Communist Party in the Cold War era steadfastly supported the Soviet position on foreign policy by opposing such major Western plans and developments as the Marshall Plan, NATO, the European Defense Community, the Common Market, and so forth. But because Italy never became a Communist country, the Italian Communist Party, for political reasons, had to have a more palatable position on Italian foreign affairs. Therefore, it formally advocated an Italian foreign policy taking a position of equal distance between the Soviet and the Western blocs. Whether or not a Communist Italy would have joined the Soviet bloc and become a member of the Warsaw Pact group was never made clear by Italian Communists; they probably preferred to keep it unclear, for tactical reasons.

The end of Communist participation in the Italian government was probably a casualty of the Cold War. In the local elections of 1946, there was a swing away from the Christian Democrats, then in a coalition government with the Communists and Socialists, toward the extreme Right. These electoral losses made the Christian Democrats uneasy about keeping the government coalition. And the heightening of the Cold War produced pressures from the United States against a continuation of the coalition cabinet. It was reported that an American condition for the loan given to Italy during De Gasperi's visit to the United States in January 1947 was the removal of the Communists and Socialists from the government. Then those Socialists who no longer wanted a coalition with the Communists followed Giuseppe Saragat out of the Socialist Party. A few months later De Gasperi resigned as premier and in forming a new government eliminated both the Communists and Socialists.

After their exclusion from the government, the Communists' opposition to major policy decisions was ineffectual. Consequently, the party adopted a more radical and activist position, as evidenced by their reaction to Italy's participation in the Marshall Plan. The Soviet Union and her Communist allies planned to offset the operation of the Marshall Plan program by disparaging it and by promoting social disorders. They put out piles of propaganda in an effort to persuade the workers of Western Europe that the program was a clever way to ensnare them with American capitalism. The Communist parties in France and Italy began large, noisy campaigns of obstruction and denunciation. In Italy the Communists and the trade unions they could control or influence struck and rioted, though with less turmoil and revolutionary fervor than in France. But the Communist campaign in Italy against the Marshall Plan could not find much support in a country so much in need of economic assistance. Moreover, the Communists wanted to keep on working terms with the more moderate Left, in the hope that in the coming elections a coalition dominated by them might gain a majority. In this way they might still secure power and the chance to govern Italy. They might lose this opportunity if they alienated too many workers, who, despite Communist propaganda, looked to American aid to provide jobs, increase wages, and allow them to eat better. The Communists never lost sight of the important fact that most Italians tend to take a practical view of life and the problems of daily existence.

Though the Italian Communists used political strikes to hinder economic aid and to reduce the advantage of Italy's participation in the Western bloc's political and defense system, they never, even at the height of the Cold War, made an attempt at direct action to gain control of the government. There were party activists, to be certain; but they never really challenged the government. Perhaps they had to reckon with the distinct possibility that the United States government was not likely to remain passive if a revolution were attempted.

If the Italian Communists could not find much support in the country against the Marshall Plan, they were able to find a greater response in their campaign against the Atlantic Pact and the new military commitments. This was mainly because many Italians believed they had repeatedly been dragged into unnecessary wars through a series of alliances, and they had a dim view of new alliances. But even in opposing the Atlantic Pact the Communist Party had difficulties. The Communists denounced the pact as an "instrument of war" and warned that its approval by parliament would result in war. Then, when this did not happen, it was not easy for the Communists to make their position believable to the Italian masses. History suggests that despite their role as local spokesmen for Soviet policy, the Italian Communists had little or no influence on foreign policy decisions and actions of the Italian government during the Cold War years.

Like the Soviet Union, the United States exerted an influence on Italian policies through all the traditional means. In addition, Italian-American and Catholic organizations played an active role, especially in their letter-writing campaigns. The American presence was felt strongly in Italy in many ways besides the military, financial, and political connections between the two countries. There was, for example, the enormous impact of American culture, in its broadest sense. American technology, movies, books, television programs, the American social system, and American political attitudes all became domestic concerns in Italy. English replaced French as the leading second language, and American idioms found their way into everyday Italian. American methods and viewpoints in the physical and social sciences and in education gained ground.

During the Cold War period, Italy was among the most loyal supporters of United States foreign policy. This was mainly because the interests of the leading groups in Italy in the postwar years corresponded with the interests of the United States in foreign affairs, and also because Italy was relatively defenseless in terms of military power. Her protection was in the hands of outside powers; and President Truman recognized this when, in December 1947, speaking on the occasion of the departure of Allied troops from Italy, he said, "If . . . it becomes apparent that the freedom and independence of Italy . . . are being threatened directly or indirectly, the United States . . . will be obliged to consider what measures would be appropriate."[7]

Italian governments, unlike others, during the Cold War did not attempt to gain advantages from the conflict by threatening to join the Soviet bloc. To the contrary, they formally committed themselves to the Western side by joining NATO and by signing the agreement for the European Defense Community (EDC). The danger for the West in these years was not that Italy might associate herself with the Soviet forces but rather that she might adopt a neutral position. The Italian Communists strongly advocated such a policy, but Italian governments in those years rejected it. The governing groups in Italy and the United States in the postwar years both wanted to keep the Soviet Union out of Western Europe and the Mediterranean. To this end the United States provided Italy with considerable aid over a number of years. Between the end of the war and 1957, the United States gave Italy $3.84 billion in grants, $744 million in loans, and $544 million in offshore procurement contracts. From 1950 to 1960, the United States furnished Italy with nearly $2 billion in military aid.[8] In addition the United States maintained two air bases in Italy, one outside Verona and the other between Pisa and Livorno, a naval base at Naples, the headquarters of the American Sixth Fleet, and guided-missile bases.

In 1958, there was some awareness by Italians that the United States might build long-range missile bases in their country and that there might also be some kind of disengagement in Central Europe. Survey opinions revealed that out of a total sample only 30 percent favored the establishment of long-range missile bases in their country by the United States and 39 percent opposed it, while 29 percent were undecided. Of Italians with a university level of education, 48 percent of those polled favored these bases and 33 percent opposed them. Those with a secondary level of education divided at 39 percent on each side of the question. Of those educated at the primary level or below, 25 percent favored and 39 percent opposed. Asked whether if Russia offered to withdraw forces from East Germany, Poland and Czechoslovakia the United States, Britain and France should accept the Russian offer and remove their forces from West Germany, out of a total sample 53 percent of Italians favored such a move; only 12 percent opposed it, while 27 percent did not know. Again, at the university level of education 50 percent of Italians favored this disengagement and 21 percent opposed it. Of those with a secondary level of education, 62 percent favored it and 17 percent opposed it; and of those educated at the primary level or below, 52 percent favored it and only 9 percent opposed it.[9] As it turned out, the Italian government allowed the Americans to build missile bases and, for some time following this opinion poll, opposed any kind of disengagement in any form, including the Rapacki plan for nuclear disengagement in Central Europe.

American money also went to the support of the Christian Democratic Party and its allies. Marshall Plan funds and AFL-CIO money were given to the CISL and the UIL, the non-Communist trade union federations, thereby resulting in increased American influence in the Italian trade union movement. The United States also sought to influence Italian elections by publicly telling the Italian people, as in 1948 and 1953, that Italy would be cut off from all economic aid if it voted for the Communist-Socialist slate over the Christian Democratic-led coalition. In 1948, the United States prevailed upon Britain and France to join in a declaration favoring the return to Italy of the entire Free Territory of Trieste. Italian-Americans and American Catholics were urged to write to their relatives and friends in Italy asking them to vote for the government parties. In Italy, some cardinals and bishops went so far as to direct their priests to deny the sacraments to those who voted for the pro-Soviet parties.[10]

The Italian elections of April 1948, coming in the midst of the Cold War, were important for several reasons, not the least of which was symbolic. It was the first election of a parliament under the new constitution; foreign political issues growing out of the American-Soviet rivalry dominated domestic issues; and the absorption of the Eastern European countries into the Communist camp, the methods used to achieve this, and the growing Soviet military buildup on the Western borders all increased the tension and the drama of this political event. The Christian Democrats were attempting to convince the voters that this election was supremely important and if the Communists were not clearly defeated, it might be the last time Italians could freely express their choice.

In February, two months before the elections took place, a coup d'etat in Prague resulted in the Communist takeover of Czechoslovakia. This event was used as an example of what could happen when a Communist party, though in a minority, succeeded in seizing power; Christian Democrats declared that the tactics used by the Czechoslovakian Communists could be employed by the Italian Communists in the event their party won the elections. Whether or not this was so, the coup d'etat in Czechoslovakia made a deep and lasting impression on the public and surely influenced the vote.

The 1948 Italian election campaign was a heated one, and it was of great concern and interest to the United States and the Soviet Union. The importance of the elections went beyond Italy itself, because the result was bound to affect the balance of the Soviet and Western blocs. A victory for the Christian Democratic Party and its allies would push Italy into the Western camp, and success for the Communist-Socialist coalition would move the country toward a neutralist role in foreign affairs, a preliminary step to joining the Soviet bloc. Therefore, the United States and the Soviet Union each supported the campaign efforts of its favored side.

As already noted, the United States used a number of economic and political weapons to defeat communism, and the Cominform, recently established, assisted the Italian Communists. The expectation of additional economic aid from the Marshall Plan, announced in June 1947, made a deep impression on the public and was warmly welcomed by the Christian Democrats, while the Communist-Socialists spurned it as "an imperialist attempt to enslave the country."[11] Whatever its intent, the aid was necessary to help Italy recover from the war, and the recognition of this necessity certainly influenced many voters. The American-British-French declaration on Trieste also influenced voters. It backed the position of the De Gasperi government and was widely used to weaken the Communist position during the campaign. And it made it easier for Italians to understand who their friends were on international matters.

The Cold War, therefore, played a leading role in the Christian Democratic victory of 1948. Though the Christian Democratic Party received only 48.5 percent of the popular vote, it had an absolute majority of the seats in parliament. De Gasperi resisted strong pressure from the Vatican to form a one-party government. Instead, he organized a coalition government of four parties, and this became the basis for future governments for the next seven years. De Gasperi also withstood heavy pressure from the United States and other anti-Communist governments to outlaw the Communist and Socialist parties.

For the next five years De Gasperi governed Italy, and the Cold War dominated the international scene. During this time a close relationship between the United States and Italy developed in foreign affairs. However, when the peace treaty was being negotiated, Italy did not openly side with the Western bloc in its growing rift with the Soviet bloc; Italy simply could not afford to antagonize one of the principal powers and thereby jeopardize a peace settlement for herself. And for a while even after the peace treaty was signed, Italy considered alternative courses for her foreign policy: to join the Western bloc by accepting the economic and defense aid being proposed by the United States; to adopt a position of neutrality and disengagement from the two great power blocs; or to play the role of mediator between the superpowers.

The neutralist position was widely supported by the general public in

Italy in 1946 and 1947. But with the intensification of the Cold War and with heavier pressure from the Soviet Union and international communism, the neutralist position gradually lost strength. Security and economic and political considerations all brought a change in Italy's attitude in 1947-48. Italy was not able to defend herself against outside aggression. She needed aid for economic reconstruction, and major foreign aid involved a political commitment. Added to these considerations were those of ideology and religion, as Italy began to align herself on the side of the West in this struggle between the two great-power blocs. Thus, when Italy accepted the Marshall Plan (July 1947) she made a political choice, considering the terms of the plan and knowing it was intended as a means of resisting communism. The 1948 elections endorsed this choice. And when Italy became a member of NATO in 1949, this action was a natural consequence of the acceptance of the Marshall Plan and the results of the 1948 elections.

In conclusion, then, while the Cold War had much to do with the Christian Democratic victory of 1948, it continued to be an advantage for that party afterward. During times of increasing tension between the Soviet and Western blocs, in such episodes as the Berlin Airlift and the Korean War, the Christian Democratic position was strengthened, and a number of previously hesitant allies and supporters closed ranks with them. Despite the violent debates on the Atlantic Pact and the Marshall Plan, the events of the Cold War offered support to De Gasperi's foreign policy.

The Cold War also made it clear to Italy that she could not remain isolated from the other nations of the West. A number of anti-Fascist intellectuals wanted Italy to avoid any alliances in the postwar period and to use her resources for moral and civic reconstruction. De Gasperi himself, at first, had reservations about making a commitment to a Western military alliance. But with the Cold War reaching its zenith and with the two opposed blocs becoming clearly delineated, Italy, like all the other European countries, was expected to make a choice. The De Gasperi government, especially Foreign Minister Count Carlo Sforza, entertained for a while the idea of neutralism, but it soon became clear that the United States could not be counted upon to continue financing Italian economic recovery and receive in return nothing more than nonalignment. Under the pressure of this argument and pressure from the United States for Italian membership in NATO, along with the realization that Italy did not have sufficient power to undertake its own defense, De Gasperi was converted. In the spring of 1949, he submitted the NATO treaty to parliament, where it was approved. Italy was now a member of NATO, and for some years thereafter her foreign policy was connected almost entirely with the function of the Atlantic Pact. Had it not been for the Cold War, this might not have been the case and Italy's foreign policy might have taken another course. But the Cold War pushed Italy into this exclusive commitment, and her adherence to NATO meant to most Italians a definitive alliance with the United States.

# 3

# BELGIUM AND THE COLD WAR

When the Second World War came to an end, the great majority of the Belgian population could certainly not imagine that a victory so bitterly won would bring security for such a short time. Indeed, the good understanding between the main victors of World War II very quickly deteriorated once the war was over. Step by step, a new worldwide conflict emerged, a conflict that never turned into a direct military confrontation but one that brought the world at times very close to the brink of all-out nuclear war. Not only did this Cold War divide the world, except for a few neutrals, into two opposite camps, but it threatened once again the war-scarred European continent. For the most part, the impact of the Cold War on Belgium was not very different from that on other European countries. The difference was rather of degree than of kind.

For historical reasons, but also for reasons of analysis, the whole Cold War period can be divided into two parts. The first was the period in which the Cold War emerged, reaching a peak with the Korean War and continuing with ups and downs until the early sixties. Though a first limited thaw in East-West relations could already be noticed during the mid-fifties, it was only after the early sixties that a second period, one of détente, set in. This détente was not without effect on Belgium's foreign and defense policies.

It is difficult to suggest one specific date as the starting point of the Cold War. One can, of course, refer to such facts as the Soviet refusal of Marshall aid in 1947 or the Communist coup in Prague on 22 February 1948. However, the first signs of deteriorating East-West relations could already be noticed as early as 1945–46, when it became clear that the USSR interpreted certain terms and stipulations of the Yalta and Potsdam agreements differently from the United States, France and the United Kingdom. There is also much disagreement among students of the Cold War with regard to its causes and development. But a critical discussion of the so-called traditionalist and revisionist views would be beyond the scope of this study. For further exploration readers should refer to the works of traditionalist authors such as L. J. Halle, A. Fontaine and N. A. Graebner, and to revisionists such as D. F. Fleming, D. Horowitz and G. Alperowitz.

Throughout its hottest years, the Cold War had four main effects on Belgium's foreign policy, internal development, foreign trade and military policy. First of all, it reduced Belgium's confidence in the United Nations and in the universalist approach that had been the basis of her foreign policy since the end of the war. Secondly, and closely connected with that loss of confidence, the growing Cold War led to Belgium's membership in both the Brussels and the North Atlantic pacts and to Belgium's firm participation in the European integration process. The Cold War and its absolute ideological gap put the country into the "Western camp," and from then onward, Belgium was expected to act accordingly. This had a deep influence on Belgian diplomacy and, to a considerable extent, on its trade policy. Thirdly, the fear of direct or indirect Communist actions against the Western world caused a quick decline of the power of the Belgian Communist Party, which had been quite successful in the years 1944–47. Finally, the Soviet threat and subsequent NATO obligations led to a very sharp increase in Belgium's defense efforts, particularly in the early fifties. It is evident that the immediate cause of these developments must be found in the widespread fear of the Soviet Union's policies and Communist ideology. The increasing reliance on US financial and economic aid in a time of recovery and reconstruction, on the other hand, certainly facilitated Belgium's political and military alignment with the United States.

The immediate postwar years were times of great uncertainty among the big powers about each other's intentions. It was a time of exaggerations and misperceptions as well. For a small country like Belgium, it was not easy to have a clear view on this rather confusing international scene. No wonder, then, that there was some hesitation on the part of the Belgian government as to what foreign policy to follow.

Belgium declared itself ready to support the UN, which was to be the great new instrument for reaching universal peace through collective security. Big power cooperation with regard to the creation of the UN, the hope that the wartime alliance among them would continue, and the general euphoria after the Allied victory undoubtedly contributed to Belgium's favorable attitude. To a certain extent, US pressure also may have played a role here.[1] However, Belgium supported the UN charter and its organization without much enthusiasm and with full awareness of its imperfections. The Belgian Parliament particularly criticized the veto right of the permanent UN members. Foreign Minister Spaak expressed the opinion of the majority in Parliament on 31 October 1945 in this way:

When I ask you to ratify the Charter and to take part in the UN, I do not do this with great enthusiasm, but with the will to participate loyally in the effort that starts. Its authors have had the wisdom to say that its actual shape could still be improved.[2]

But while the Belgian government proclaimed its support of the UN and its firm will to pursue a policy of equal friendship with all nations,[3] it also stressed on many occasions the need for regional security organizations to underpin the universal organization. The government considered this regional substructure as a more direct means for maintaining security, in case collective security should fail. Moreover, it was thought that certain problems could be solved only through regional organizations.

This interest in regional arrangements is not surprising, for Belgium had previously been a party to bilateral and broader treaties. In 1920, it had signed a secret military agreement with France and had tried, unsuccessfully, to reach a similar one with Great Britain. A few years later, in 1925, Belgium had signed the Locarno Pact,[4] which would remain the cornerstone of the country's security policy until the late thirties. Also, in the government's wartime planning for postwar security, regional arrangements had occupied a very important place, as Mr. Spaak testifies in his memoirs:

If my diplomatic activity in 1942 was particularly focused on this idea of a European entente, in 1943, 1944 and 1945, my efforts turned towards the organization of Western Europe under the leadership of England.[5]

But Belgium's wartime plans and initiatives for the creation of a Western European organization provoked a sharp reaction from the Soviet press in October 1944. Belgium was described as "the instigator and the champion of a Western bloc. . . ."[6] Foreign Minister Spaak firmly denied such intentions and gave the USSR every assurance that Belgium's plan was not the creation of a "Western bloc."[7] He told the Soviets that his concern was to organize the defense of Western Europe in the framework of collective security.[8] Spaak repeated this opinion in a speech before Parliament on 6 December 1944. He expressed the government's support of collective security through the UN but, at the same time, declared that he considered a "European alliance" and a "regional entente" as indispensable complements. In his view, any future world security system had to be built upon these three bases. For the realization of the European alliance he thought it necessary to sign "big treaties" like the existing Anglo-Soviet treaty, whereas regional ententes were to become an agency for collective security policies.[9]

Even if the Belgian government had no anti-Soviet bloc in mind, the question still arises of how far its policy has contributed to the worsening of East-West relations by arousing Soviet suspicion. After the war, as we have already mentioned, the idea of regional organizations for Western Europe's security was still present in both the minds and words of Belgium's decision makers, but no initiatives were taken, for fear that this might alarm the Soviet Union and thus endanger the mutual understanding among the big powers, which was the basis of the UN system. Even when the Treaty of Dunkirk was signed between France and Britain, on 4 March 1947, the Belgian government did not seize the opportunity to realize its own plan for a wider regional agreement. Later, Mr. Spaak explained that he had made no move at that moment because he was still waiting for a Soviet answer to a Belgian proposal for the signing of a Belgo-Soviet treaty. The answer never came.

But besides this strong will of the government to give collective security a fair chance, there were two other factors that made Belgium hesitate to take regional initiatives. There was, first of all, the Communists' participation in the government and their unusually strong presence in Parliament, which constituted an obstacle to any policy of bloc building.[10] And, secondly, in the years 1945–46 neither Britain nor France was eager to participate in a Western European organization. But later, when the Cold War grew hotter, these factors were unable to stop the growing trend toward a regional arrangement. Belgium then became one of its most active promoters.

By the end of 1947 and the first months of 1948, the Cold War had raised a wave of fear all over Europe. Most countries were struggling with heavy social and economic problems. War damage had been considerable and reconstruction required time and money. Moreover, the extremely cold winter of 1946–47 caused a dramatic shortage of foodstuffs, fuel and coal. It was an ideal background for social uprisings, strikes and Communist actions. Belgium, though better off than most other nations on the European continent, faced the same problems. This difficult internal situation was worsened by gradually deteriorating international relations. The UN system was not functioning as it had been hoped. The failure to reach an agreement on Germany or Austria; Soviet pressure on Iran, Turkey and Greece; the consolidation of Soviet power over the Soviet zone of occupation in Germany and over Poland, Hungary, Rumania, Bulgaria,

Albania and later Czechoslovakia were all frightening experiences for the weakened Western European democracies. Moreover, the USSR refused Marshall aid and established the Cominform. Finally, the Communist coup of Prague was the culminating point in this whole series of events that raised serious doubts about Western Europe's security. Even if there were no direct military expansionist intentions on the part of the Soviet Union, its whole policy was perceived as a threat. Many Belgian people feared that both France and Italy might become victims of a Communist coup. If this happened, so it was thought, it would have a dangerous effect on Belgium's security, the more so since the Belgian Communist Party had also become relatively strong. However, this Communist influence must not be overestimated; by March 1947 the Communists had left the Belgian government,[11] and by 1949 their number in Parliament had fallen from twenty-three (since February 1946) to twelve. We can agree with Ronald Steel's remark that "the defeat of the Italian Communist Party in the general election of 1948 brought an end to the fear that communism would come to Western Europe from within."[12] Nevertheless, on 28 September 1948, Mr. Spaak, in a dramatic speech before the UN General Assembly in Paris, voiced the feelings of fear and insecurity that still beset all Western European countries.[13] But by that time the Brussels Treaty had already been signed.

Against this background of increasing tension and insecurity, it is quite understandable that Foreign Minister Spaak immediately reacted favorably to the proposal that British Foreign Minister Ernest Bevin made before the House of Commons on 22 January 1948. Bevin proposed to unite against the common danger and to build up a common defense organization. His words set in motion a diplomatic process that quickly led to the Brussels Treaty. Belgium's role in shaping this treaty was quite important.[14] Spaak at once invited his Benelux colleagues for consultation in order to reach a common point of view. The Benelux memorandum, which was handed over to Britain and France on 19 February 1948, differed a good deal from the views expressed in the British and French memoranda. The three countries rejected a system of bilateral treaties and proposed instead a regional organization that would be a real community instead of a traditional alliance. Unlike the British and French memoranda, the Benelux text explicitly mentioned the danger of the expansionist Soviet Union. Finally, the Benelux nations suggested that a limited regional agreement would be an incentive for wider American cooperation with Western Europe.

The five governments started their talks in Brussels on 4 March 1948, and less than two weeks later, on 17 March, the Brussels Treaty was signed. The coup of Prague in February 1948 had only hastened this process. Belgium, together with its two Benelux partners, had had a decisive influence on certain parts of the treaty. For her, membership in this pact meant a first concrete and formal guarantee of her security. Moreover, Benelux opposition to the bilateralism of the British and French proposals and its insistence on a regional community form made the pact conform more to UN principles and to the Rio Pact of 2 September 1947. This fact, without any doubt, facilitated US support for the Brussels Treaty and paved the way for the Vandenberg Resolution and US participation in the North Atlantic Alliance. In his memoirs, President Truman refers to Spaak's positive role in the creation of the Brussels Treaty:

It was from the three small nations that a counterproposal came for one regional arrangement rather than a series of two-party treaties. Mr. Spaak, the Belgian Foreign Minister, was largely responsible for this change and it was in this form that the treaty was made. I think to Spaak goes the credit for lining up the Europeans for the treaty.[15]

It should not be overlooked, either, that the Brussels Treaty was the first important landmark on the road toward European cooperation. It created a whole range of ties among five European nations, not only in the politico-military but also in the economic, social and cultural fields. The Belgian Parliament overwhelmingly supported the government's policy in this matter. The House of Representatives voted in favor of the treaty on 28 April 1948, with a large majority of 150 as against 21 votes (all Communists); and the Senate affirmed it on 24 March 1948, with 138 as against 15 Communist votes.[16]

In fact, the Brussels Treaty was in accord with two all-important decisions regarding America's position in Europe and the world. Indeed, it was suited almost perfectly to the objectives of both the Truman Doctrine, announced on 12 March 1947, and the Marshall Plan of 5 June 1947. The Brussels Treaty had been created first of all in order to constitute a counterweight against a possible Soviet expansionist action and in order to create a firm community among like-minded democracies. But a second aim was undoubtedly to clear the way for US participation in the defense of Europe and the West as a whole. It was obvious that the Brussels Treaty nations were too weak to constitute a credible deterrent against Soviet power. For that purpose, US prestige, and the American nuclear umbrella in particular, was an indispensable counterweight. Therefore, there exists a direct link between the Brussels Treaty and the North Atlantic Treaty.

NATO was a logical consequence of the Brussels Treaty, as well as of the Truman Doctrine and the Marshall Plan. The American reaction to the

European initiative was very quick. On the very day of the signing of the Brussels Treaty, President Truman defended the initiative before Congress, where he said:

> This development deserves our full support. I am confident that the United States will, by appropriate means, extend to the free nations the support which the situation requires. I am sure that the determination of the free countries of Europe to protect themselves will be matched by an equal determination on our part to help them do so.[17]

The Vandenberg Resolution of 11 June 1948 opened the way to larger US commitment to Europe. After a short period of negotiations, the North Atlantic Treaty was signed on 4 April 1949. From then onwards, both the sword and the shield were created that gave at last a feeling of security to the Western European nations. The Soviet blockade of West Berlin between 24 June 1948 and 9 May 1949 had but hastened this process. Belgium's security was definitely embedded in a broad defensive organization that covered the whole North Atlantic area and that tied her to the strongest military power of the moment. This tie had several consequences: Politically and diplomatically, Belgium had declared itself a member of what in Cold War terms was known as "the Western camp"; henceforth, it would have to act according to this position. Consequently, the country's military policy would to a large extent be governed by NATO strategy, and its forces would find their specific tasks in the global NATO defense structure that was created in the following years.

Like the Brussels Treaty, the North Atlantic Treaty was ratified by the Belgian Parliament with an overwhelming majority. In both houses only the Communists voted against it.[18] Belgium's great dependence on US economic and financial support had undoubtedly contributed to this military alignment. To Belgian decision makers, alignment seemed more attractive, even at the expense of some loss of independence, than the alternative of remaining weak and exposed to any external or internal threat, particularly when this threat came from the strongest European power, a power whose armies had not been withdrawn from Eastern and Central Europe and whose ideology was totally antagonistic to most Belgians.

The Cold War had a decisive influence on the European integration process. This is a fact recognized by most students of the history and the dynamics of European unification. To cite only one of them:

> The movement for European unity was given a decisive impetus in the postwar period as the result of the coup in Prague in 1948 and the outbreak of the Korean war in 1950.[19]

This does not mean that the Cold War was the sole source from which the European unification movement received a new incentive. There existed a widespread conviction that the nation-state was worn out; and, most of all, the economic needs of reconstruction called for an immediate joining of means and resources. In fact, the economic sector was the one that produced the most successes in the fields of cooperation and integration, through the Organization for European Economic Cooperation (OEEC), the European Coal and Steel Community (ECSC), and still more the Common Market (EEC). In the politico-military field, things developed at a much slower pace. Belgium became a member of the Council of Europe when this was created in London on 5 May 1949. Three months later, Mr. Spaak was elected the first president of its consultative assembly. In the meantime, both the Brussels and the Washington pacts had been signed. One of their main objectives was to strengthen the cohesion among the Western European countries, and both pacts accordingly contributed to the unification of Western Europe. From the beginning, the European unification process assumed a certain Cold War character by the fact that it had the fullest support of the United States. Indeed, intensified European cooperation had been a condition for the granting of Marshall aid. Afterwards, both the ECSC and the EEC, as well as (after initial hesitation) the European Defense Community, were warmly supported by the United States.

However, the most tangible effect of the Cold War on European integration was evident in the effort to create a European Defense Community. The signing of the EDC treaty was a consequence of the Korean War, which broke out on 25 July 1950. This conflict was the most direct East-West confrontation in the postwar period. It began as a limited conflict, but nobody was sure that it would not expand. In Europe there was a general fear that another Communist attack might be launched against several or all Western European countries. Therefore, Germany asked for more US troops on its soil, and the United States willingly sent them. NATO forces were brought under a unified command, and the United States even asked for a partial German rearmament, a very frightening prospect to most people in Europe. The French Pleven plan for the creation of a European army brought a welcome solution to this embarrassing and delicate situation. The EDC got the support of the six ECSC countries and of the United States. Unfortunately, it was a stillborn child, for the French National Assembly refused to ratify the treaty in 1954. If the EDC and its complement, the European Political Community, had been realized, the Cold War would have had an even deeper and more lasting effect on the political and military condition of Western Europe, and more particularly on Belgium's foreign and defense policies. The Belgian government wholeheartedly supported the EDC, for in their view it helped realize several fundamental policy objectives: the creation of a more effective military force, the integration of the GFR in the Western community and, finally, the unification of Western Europe.[20] Parliament showed itself more reluctant. It waited quite a time before ratifying the treaty, and the majorities in favor of it were less large than for the Brussels and the North Atlantic pacts. Moreover, opposition could be found within all political parties.[21]

The signing of the EDC treaty was Belgium's most direct political reaction to the Korean War. In the military field, it responded by sending a volunteer corps and by doubling the time of the military service in March 1951 from twelve to twenty-four months. This was the longest service time in postwar Belgium and a very hard measure for the Belgian population, which has been by tradition rather antimilitarist. The Christian-Democratic government, headed by Mr. Pholien, was heavily attacked for this decision by both the Communists and the Socialists. Public opinion was aroused by leftist agitation, and after demonstrations and riots, even on military bases, the service time was quickly cut back to twenty-one months in August 1952.

A factor of less importance than the foregoing Cold War consequences was the very quick decline of the Communist Party's popularity in Belgium as a result of the growing East-West opposition. Right after the war, Communist activists and propaganda had been quite successful. From nine representatives after the 1939 elections, their number in the House of Representatives rose to twenty-three in February 1946; that figure remains the highest level ever attained by Belgian Communists. In the June 1949 elections their number fell to twelve; a year later it dropped to seven. In April 1954—after the Korean War—only four Communists were sent to the House of Representatives. In 1958 their number was even cut back to only two. Since then it has stabilized at around five seats.[22]

Another point that needs some comment is the effect of the Cold War situation on Belgium's trade pattern, particularly on its commercial relations with the countries of Eastern Europe. Statistics show that while Belgium's total imports increased from an index of 80.1 in 1950 to 104.4 in 1951 and remained at similar levels or increased in following years, imports from Eastern Europe as a whole slowed down during the peak years of the Cold War (1949–1953/55).[23] The same was true for the country's exports, though here the regression took place at a slower pace. From 1947 onward, one notices a rising trend in the export to Eastern Europe as a whole. This trend continued after 1950 for the export to the world but clearly slackened for the exports to Eastern Europe, East Central Europe and the USSR. This regression in both exports to and imports from Eastern Europe must obviously be explained by the general deterioration of East-West relations, and more particularly by the outbreak of the Korean War. However, the spontaneous reaction of fear and distrust toward Eastern Europe is not the sole explanation for the sharp decline in Belgium's commercial activities with those nations. Relations with them were already worsening in the years 1947-49. Still, this was not entirely reflected in diminishing trade. In 1947, 1948 and 1949, BLEU exports to that part of the world rose, respectively, from 52.8 to 90.1 and 131.4. A similar increase is seen in the imports from Eastern Europe, though here the regression started in 1949. Thus, it is only from 1949-50 onward, and generally until 1953-54, that the high point of regression is found.

This period obviously coincides not only with the hottest Cold War years but also with the strengthening of the ties between the United States and its Western European allies. That relationship—or, better, dependence—had grown so strong that the United States was able to oblige its allies to apply a strategic export embargo against the Communist countries. The United States had already started this policy in its foreign trade as early as 1947-48, and after the signing of the NATO treaty in 1949, pressure was put on the Allies to do the same. In 1949, an organization for joint US-European control of exports to the Communist countries, the so-called coordinating committee, or Cocom, was established.[24] However, for economic as well as political reasons, the European allies were reluctant.[25] The fact that finally all the European allies gave in to US demands was, to Gunnar Adler-Karlsson, a result of American threats to cut off aid in case of noncompliance.[26] From 1953 onward, the embargo pressure was gradually reduced, as a consequence of heavy criticism from the European allies; for various economic as well as political and military reasons, they considered the West's embargo policy a failure. The United States continued this trade restriction policy much longer than the European countries. In Gunnar Myrdal's view, the export embargo policy was "on the Western side the main economic element in the pursuance and gradual stepping up of the Cold War."[27] But mainly, according to Myrdal, it led to a consolidation of the Communist bloc, because it made the smaller Eastern European countries even more dependent on the USSR.[28] Anyway, after 1953 the effect of the export embargo on Belgium's foreign trade continuously diminished.

A last tangible effect of the growing Cold War tension was a considerable increase in Belgium's defense efforts. The increase was particularly marked in the period of the Korean War. It must immediately be emphasized that this military buildup was possible only thanks to the aid from the United States and Canada. As Britain, right after the war, had helped Belgium in reorganizing its military forces, after the signing of the NATO treaty it was particularly the United States that became the great supplier of military aid. On 27 January 1950, a bilateral treaty was signed between Belgium and the United States in the framework of the Mutual Defense Aid Program (MDAP). Between 1949 and 1957, Belgium and Luxembourg together received $1,064.5 million as military aid, which constitutes 85% of the total military aid they received from the United States between 1949 and 1965.[29] This was another means through which Belgium was tied to the United States. (The increase of Belgian defense expenditures as a percentage of the country's GNP in the period 1949–56 is shown in Table 1.) Moreover, as mentioned earlier, the length of military service was increased to twenty-four months in 1951–52. Between 1950 and 1954, the global number of Belgian forces also rose from 80,000 to some 150,000. It was the greatest military effort Belgium made in the postwar period.

The most lasting effect of the Cold War on Belgium has certainly been

**TABLE 1**

Belgian Defense Expenditure as a % of GNP

| 1949 | 1950 | 1951 | 1952 | 1953 | 1954 | 1955 | 1956 |
|------|------|------|------|------|------|------|------|
| 2.5  | 2.6  | 3.7  | 5.5  | 5.3  | 5.1  | 4.1  | 3.9  |

Source: *NATO Facts and Figures* (Brussels, 1971), p. 256.

its alignment with the United States: Belgium became one of her most reliable and faithful allies. It is obvious that in most matters of "high politics," and especially with regard to East-West relations, Belgium steadily followed the United States. The limits and possibilities of this situation became clearer in the second period of the Cold War, when détente gradually led to a closer relationship between the two superpowers and to a loosening of the ties in both blocs between the superpower and its allies. In that period, Belgium's foreign policy was aimed at maintaining a balance between loyalty to the West and bridge-building with Eastern Europe.

By 1953/54 the hottest Cold War years were over. The armistice in the Korean War, reached on 23 July 1953, and still more the Geneva armistice agreements and declarations on Indochina of 21 July 1954, might well be taken as the turning point. Two other factors also contributed to the improving international atmosphere of the mid-fifties. After Stalin's death, a new period set in for the Soviet Union. The Stalin era was followed by an internal process of destalinization and limited liberalization. With regard to international politics, this process found its complement in the proclaimed peaceful coexistence theory. However, both changes came definitely to the fore only after the Twentieth Congress of the Communist Party in February 1956. In the West this led to a new optimism that very soon proved to be premature. The suppression of the Hungarian revolt by the Soviet armies in late 1956 clearly showed that the West's optimistic expectations were not justified at all.

The first temporary thaw in East-West relations, in the mid-fifties, had an unfortunate effect on the European integration process and on Belgium's international status. Belgium, together with four of its ECSC partners, had already ratified the EDC treaty when, on 29 August 1954, the French National Assembly refused to vote on the matter. One of the motives behind this refusal was a fear that the creation of a political and defense community among six Western European nations might endanger the recently started improvement in East-West relations. For a long time, the French refusal put an end to the political integration movement. Belgium, consequently, did not become a part of a federal state, nor did her army join with the military forces of the other nations in one European army. Instead, as an alternative to the abortive EDC, the London and Paris conferences of October 1954 soon led to the membership of Italy and the GFR in the widened Brussels Treaty, which henceforth was called the Western European Union. This remained, however, without any serious effect on Belgium's foreign policy.

The years between the mid-fifties and the early sixties were a series of ups and downs in East-West relations. Among the ups must certainly be reckoned the emergence of the peaceful coexistence theory and the temporary thaw in the international field, the Spirit of Camp David during Khrushchev's visit to the United States in 1959 and, finally, the Nuclear Test Ban Treaty of August 1963. Among the downs were renewed East-West tension as a result of the Hungarian crisis in late 1956, the Suez crisis of the same year, the failure of the Paris Summit in 1960, the new Berlin crisis between 1958 and the early sixties, and the Cuban Missile crisis in 1962. In was only after the Cuban episode that a period of détente got a real chance. But it was not until the mid-sixties that the first official signs of any rapprochement between East and West were to be noticed.

The gradual easing of tension in East-West relations following 1954–56 had had noticeable effects on Belgium. The first was an increase of contacts with Eastern Europe, in the political as well as in the commercial and cultural fields. Trade developed at a much quicker pace than in the peak years of the Cold War. These developments occurred notwithstanding the very shocking effects of the Soviet suppression of the Hungarian revolt, the role of the USSR in the Congo crisis and, more recently, the invasion of Czechoslovakia by the Warsaw Pact forces in 1968. Moreover, the thaw in East-West relations gave Belgium the opportunity of assuming a specific role of bridge-builder between East and West, particularly after Harmel became foreign minister in 1966. Secondly, the East-West détente partly brought about the Atlantic crisis. This crisis had a direct effect on Belgium, for it led to the transfer of the NATO installations from French to Belgian soil. Recently, as a European nation, Belgium has also been involved in the growing difficulties between the United States and Europe with regard to such problems as the development of both the EEC and the Atlantic Alliance and the recent conflict in the Middle East. Thirdly, Belgium's defense efforts have become smaller year after year, although NATO's flexible response strategy precisely demands greater efforts with regard to conventional forces and armaments.

International cooperation, especially with the countries of Europe, has been one of Belgium's traditional foreign policy objectives. For an export and transit nation such as Belgium, economic cooperation has always been very important, if not vital, and from a political and military point of view, Belgium has always had the greatest interest in being not too dependent on one or two neighboring nations but staying in close contact with several other, particularly smaller, nations. This policy has been pursued through both bilateral and multilateral channels. Through participation in the European integration process, Belgium even tries to give a supranational framework to her international position.

The Cold War has been one of the strongest obstacles to Belgium's traditional diplomacy of openness to the whole world. Therefore, Prime Minister Van Acker and Foreign Minister Spaak immediately took the opportunity for restoring Belgo-Soviet relations when they were officially invited to Moscow in 1956. Their visit ended in the signing of an agreement for cultural cooperation on 25 October 1956.[30] But the new atmosphere of growing mutual understanding was quickly broken down by the Soviet suppression of the Hungarian revolt on 4 November 1956. This had a deeply shocking effect on Belgian public opinion. The next official visit to an Eastern European country took place in 1961. It was followed by other ones in 1963 and 1964, but it was not until 1965 that the long series of bilateral contacts between Belgium and the Communist countries of Eastern Europe began.[31] Since the mid-sixties, the list of bilateral agreements in the fields of administrative, social and consular relations, as well as that of commercial, transport, financial, economic, technical, scientific and cultural relations, has been growing.[32] Belgium's policy of international cooperation with all nations derived a new impetus from the fact that détente with the East became official NATO policy in 1967. The reflection on the future tasks of the alliance, which led to NATO's "defense and détente" policy, had been undertaken on the initiative of Belgium's foreign minister P. Harmel.[33] From 1966 until the end of 1972, Mr. Harmel pursued his détente policy in a careful and persistent way. In his view, détente should bring substantial changes in the military and political as well as in the economic sector.[34] However, in Belgium's foreign policy the widening of cultural, technological, commercial and economic contacts has occupied first place so far. For these contacts bilateral diplomatic channels have been used.

With regard to specifically political and military matters, Belgium tried to come to better terms with the Warsaw Pact countries primarily through multilateral diplomacy. It took an active part in the UN Group of Ten that was established on 21 December 1965 in order to further contacts between East and West. Like all other European nations, Belgium was also actively involved in the European Conference on Security and Cooperation (ECSC). Belgium was, however, well aware of the necessity to base détente on coordination and cooperation within the Western alliance. With most of its NATO partners it has hoped and still hopes to reach greater security and smaller defense expenses, for example, as a result of the recently started conference on Mutual Balanced Force Reductions (MBFR). Belgium has repeatedly asked for a parallelism between the negotiations in the ECSC and those in the MBFR for fear that the Warsaw Pact group might first try to get all possible advantage out of the ECSC and afterward not be prepared to make substantial concessions in MBFR. Such concessions are held very important in Belgium, because they would enable the government to reduce the country's defense effort to a certain extent. Moreover, Belgium has insisted on the aforementioned parallelism for fear that bilateral deals between the two superpowers might eventually lead to a reduced US military presence in Europe, without any serious concessions and withdrawal on the part of the USSR.

Belgium has continued to pursue its détente policy through other international organizations, such as the UN Economic Commission for Europe. It has also supported initiatives for contacts with Eastern Europe taken by the Council of Europe, the OECD and even, in some respects, the Common Market. Finally, Belgium was also the first NATO country to have official contact with Moscow after the Czech crisis of 1968, a contact that was viewed by many observers as a NATO mission to reopen the contacts with Eastern Europe. More recently, Belgium was the first NATO country to officially recognize the German Democratic Republic, followed a few days later by Luxembourg and Holland. In our view, Belgium was of all NATO partners in the best position to play an important role on the road to détente. The country already had a certain tradition of friendly relations with Eastern Europe, and, moreover, it was one of the members of the UN Group of Ten. Belgium is also a small NATO partner with a very low defense effort. These facts would tend to make the country more acceptable to the Warsaw Pact countries. On the other hand, Belgium's loyalty toward the alliance could not be doubted. Belgium is apparently more loyal than Denmark, but it is not so fervent a supporter as Holland has been under Foreign Minister J. Luns, NATO's actual Secretary-General. Belgium has proved to be a very reliable ally by consenting to the establishment on its territory (Casteau and Evere) of the NATO installations that had to leave France after the latter's withdrawal from NATO's military organization in 1966.

This balance between alliance loyalty on the one hand and a marginal defense effort, the search for early contacts with the East and the country's limited interests on the other put Belgium in a relatively favorable position to be, to a limited extent and within the possibilities offered by the international situation, an "outpost" of NATO's détente policy. Belgium turned détente into a particular function of its foreign policy and in this way found a proper role as a small nation operating on a broader framework, namely that of relations between the two politically and ideologically opposed European subsystems. The possibilities for détente have undoubtedly been favored by growing contacts between the two superpowers and by nuclear parity. Not only did these contacts set an example for the smaller powers on both sides, but a growing tendency towards disintegration in both blocs created some space for small power initiatives.

The gradually improving atmosphere in East-West relations over the last fifteen years has favored the trade between Belgium and the countries of Eastern Europe. Both import and export figures between the BLEU and the East show a clear rise after the most critical Cold War years. Whereas BLEU imports from Eastern Europe had fallen from 196.0 in 1948 to 87.5 in 1949 and 81.0 in 1952, they started rising again from 1953 onward. In 1956 they were already twice the volume of 1952. BLEU exports to Eastern Europe rose less quickly. They had fallen from 131.4 in 1949 to 92.6 in 1950 and to 84.6 in 1951. In 1953 they increased again to 100.0 and in 1956 they reached 120.5. But there were weaker years too, for example, 1955 with a figure of only 97.2, and 1959 with an export figure of 92.7 Throughout the 1960s exports have developed at an increasing rate. (See Tables 2, 3, and 4 for data on BLEU.)

During the second period of the Cold War, three international events had a negative effect on the relations between Belgium and Moscow. The first was the Soviet suppression of the Hungarian revolt in late 1956. This

**TABLE 2**

BLEU Imports and Exports[a]

| | From the World | From Eastern Europe (b) | From East-Central Europe (c) | From the USSR | To the World | To Eastern Europe (b) | To East Central Europe (c) | To the USSR |
|---|---|---|---|---|---|---|---|---|
| 1937 | 38.8 | 161.6 | 151.3 | 176.0 | 38.1 | 66.9 | 44.1 | 133.1 |
| 1938 | 32.1 | 129.2 | 93.2 | 179.6 | 32.4 | 59.5 | 43.9 | 104.8 |
| 1947 | 80.5 | 133.9 | 192.7 | 51.5 | 62.2 | 52.8 | 67.1 | 11.4 |
| 1948 | 82.3 | 196.0 | 121.4 | 300.6 | 74.7 | 90.1 | 79.3 | 121.7 |
| 1949 | 74.5 | 87.5 | 126.5 | 32.9 | 78.4 | 131.4 | 116.1 | 175.9 |
| 1950 | 80.1 | 91.8 | 111.1 | 64.7 | 72.8 | 92.6 | 82.0 | 123.5 |
| 1951 | 104.4 | 99.2 | 97.4 | 101.8 | 116.5 | 84.6 | 86.1 | 80.1 |
| 1952 | 100.9 | 81.0 | 89.7 | 68.9 | 107.8 | 91.1 | 91.7 | 89.2 |
| 1953 | 100.0 | 100.0 | 100.0 | 100.0 | 100.0 | 100.0 | 100.0 | 100.0 |
| 1954 | 104.4 | 122.2 | 90.2 | 167.1 | 101.6 | 102.1 | 87.0 | 146.4 |
| 1955 | 116.2 | 130.4 | 98.3 | 175.4 | 122.2 | 97.2 | 95.9 | 101.2 |
| 1956 | 135.2 | 166.1 | 131.2 | 215.0 | 140.1 | 120.5 | 96.1 | 191.6 |
| 1957 | 140.9 | 162.3 | 129.5 | 208.4 | 140.2 | 101.4 | 78.1 | 169.3 |
| 1958 | 129.3 | 141.1 | 134.2 | 150.9 | 135.0 | 95.8 | 92.1 | 106.6 |
| 1959 | 142.1 | 185.5 | 177.8 | 196.4 | 145.8 | 92.7 | 109.1 | 45.2 |
| 1960 | 163.7 | 193.7 | 209.4 | 171.9 | 167.4 | 148.9 | 160.9 | 114.5 |
| 1961 | 174.5 | 217.7 | 222.2 | 211.4 | 174.0 | 143.7 | 136.6 | 164.5 |
| 1962 | 188.8 | 255.1 | 239.7 | 276.6 | 192.1 | 134.2 | 127.1 | 154.8 |
| 1963 | 210.9 | 284.0 | 268.4 | 306.0 | 214.6 | 113.4 | 125.1 | 79.5 |

(a) Since 1927 Belgium and Luxembourg have constituted the Belgo-Luxembourg Economic Union (BLEU).
(b) All Communist countries of Eastern Europe as a whole (East-Central Europe + USSR).
(c) Albania, Bulgaria, Czechoslovakia, Eastern Germany, Hungary, Poland and Rumania.

Source: Gunnar Adler-Karlsson, *Western Economic Warfare, 1947–1967: A Case Study in Foreign Economic Policy* (Stockholm, 1968), pp. 260-263.

**TABLE 3**

**BLEU Imports (in 1,000 Francs)**

| | Poland | Czechoslovakia | USSR | Yugoslavia | E. Germany | Bulgaria | Hungary | Rumania(1) |
|---|---|---|---|---|---|---|---|---|
| 1938 | 283,834 | 239,000 | 783,383 | 141,846 | — | 7,892 | 37,778 | 4.1 |
| 1945 | 861 | 15,283 | 11,696 | 251 | — | — | — | — |
| 1946 | 908 | 533,016 | 52,186 | 2,011 | — | — | — | — |
| 1947 | 244,342 | 1,692,920 | 376,689 | 75,632 | — | — | — | — |
| 1948 | 346,039 | 724,364 | 2,199,216 | 380,436 | — | — | — | 0.2 |
| 1949 | 401,604 | 543,128 | 248,123 | 243,730 | 217,283 | 14,067 | 336,038 | 1.1 |
| 1950 | 347,570 | 590,533 | 544,034 | 283,279 | 122,797 | 7,976 | 219,784 | 0.2 |
| 1951 | 429,788 | 425,181 | 854,280 | 228,901 | 149,613 | 13,876 | 119,909 | 0.2 |
| 1952 | 271,926 | 401,173 | 578,667 | 229,630 | 171,255 | 31,262 | 159,119 | 0.4 |
| 1953 | 265,304 | 310,363 | 836,018 | 103,277 | 296,187 | 134,015 | 131,001 | 0.7 |
| 1954 | 223,780 | 287,223 | 1,398,302 | 156,892 | 289,187 | 91,422 | 70,531 | 1.9 |
| 1955 | 207,643 | 352,002 | 1,471,122 | 121,995 | 321,810 | 22,755 | 169,092 | 1.6 |
| 1956 | 309,547 | 543,300 | 1,791,521 | 159,533 | 373,414 | 60,094 | 143,777 | 2.0 |
| 1957 | 233,791 | 568,808 | 1,745,846 | 233,978 | 420,588 | 44,206 | 138,894 | 1.9 |
| 1958 | 296,659 | 469,656 | 1,261,735 | 281,731 | 504,877 | 65,661 | 182,118 | 1.1 |
| 1959 | 444,785 | 544,156 | 1,637,162 | 189,347 | 644,687 | 49,080 | 230,994 | 3.2 |
| 1960 | 481,404 | 646,224 | 1,432,323 | 242,457 | 782,290 | 99,909 | 250,609 | 3.7 |
| 1961 | 508,012 | 677,940 | 1,763,846 | 249,774 | 716,815 | 119,876 | 205,939 | 7.2 |
| 1962 | 630,066 | 596,908 | 2,297,761 | 290,118 | 864,095 | 158,232 | 235,079 | 6.1 |
| 1963 | 565,399 | 720,730 | 2,550,054 | 332,447 | 978,783 | 149,834 | 286,374 | 8.6 |
| 1964 | 637,951 | 747,716 | 2,484,348 | 474,999 | 1,144,876 | 126,186 | 373,105 | n.a. |
| 1965 | 678,353 | 1,038,462 | 2,314,051 | 464,983 | 1,306,678 | 124,766 | 392,062 | |
| 1966 | 750,976 | 834,989 | 3,033,653 | 444,890 | 1,314,810 | 182,779 | 451,352 | |
| 1967 | 758,998 | 764,947 | 2,975,643 | 414,052 | 1,392,541 | 149,418 | 391,168 | |
| 1968 | 941,694 | 752,765 | 3,307,107 | 575,775 | 1,469,775 | 155,258 | 603,492 | |
| 1969 | 967,148 | 905,483 | 2,939,881 | 602,307 | 1,788,146 | 248,685 | 597,951 | |
| 1970 | 1,200,530 | 970,503 | 3,899,233 | 620,384 | 1,619,826 | 253,669 | 519,560 | |
| 1971 | 1,523,941 | 1,100,253 | 5,042,281 | 1,079,089 | 1,410,644 | 316,984 | 563,144 | |
| 1972 | n.a. | n.a. | n.a. | n.a. | n.a. | n.a. | n.a. | |
| 1973 | n.a. | n.a. | n.a. | n.a. | n.a. | n.a. | n.a. | |

(1) Rumania: Trade of BLEU with Rumania in: Millions of current $ = imports c.i.f., exports f.o.b.
Source: Gunnar Adler-Karlsson, *Western Economic Warfare, 1947–1967: A Case Study in Foreign Economic Policy* (Stockholm, 1968), Appendix, Trade Matrix

**TABLE 4**
BLEU Exports (In 1,000 Francs)

| | Poland | Czechoslovakia | USSR | Yugoslavia | E. Germany | Bulgaria | Hungary | Rumania[1] |
|---|---|---|---|---|---|---|---|---|
| 1938 | 293,880 | 189,249 | 444,152 | 57,247 | — | 26,588 | 15,746 | 4.1 |
| 1945 | — | 225 | — | — | — | — | — | — |
| 1946 | 45,669 | 380,376 | 8,705 | 2,354 | — | — | — | 0.2 |
| 1947 | 217,259 | 1,092,150 | 82,074 | 119,839 | — | — | — | 0.8 |
| 1948 | 530,211 | 949,239 | 886,133 | 649,938 | — | — | — | 1.2 |
| 1949 | 543,712 | 1,275,391 | 1,312,997 | 607,859 | 182,444 | 106,668 | 505,721 | 1.5 |
| 1950 | 408,947 | 914,695 | 1,026,732 | 210,495 | 139,040 | 23,300 | 425,017 | 2.7 |
| 1951 | 527,598 | 863,507 | 668,964 | 608,145 | 175,104 | 4,990 | 382,163 | 12.1 |
| 1952 | 680,437 | 403,239 | 742,163 | 1,034,510 | 195,526 | 28,866 | 313,007 | 11.2 |
| 1953 | 867,318 | 197,368 | 826,852 | 615,680 | 351,651 | 127,070 | 307,253 | 1.5 |
| 1954 | 748,495 | 400,940 | 1,215,950 | 365,377 | 334,866 | 56,243 | 485,949 | 3.6 |
| 1955 | 771,381 | 432,089 | 846,188 | 558,097 | 381,710 | 41,052 | 518,609 | 1.5 |
| 1956 | 996,206 | 471,781 | 1,586,078 | 183,013 | 341,599 | 66,872 | 372,033 | 1.4 |
| 1957 | 764,246 | 504,559 | 1,410,042 | 234,121 | 239,356 | 90,696 | 227,482 | 1.0 |
| 1958 | 787,712 | 566,473 | 883,243 | 322,389 | 451,786 | 108,988 | 257,957 | 3.1 |
| 1959 | 712,068 | 711,712 | 375,350 | 400,294 | 418,696 | 244,523 | 385,778 | 7.7 |
| 1960 | 813,504 | 1,165,747 | 951,132 | 469,194 | 653,884 | 255,590 | 601,049 | 5.2 |
| 1961 | 533,937 | 1,261,755 | 1,367,319 | 611,640 | 598,971 | 178,813 | 458,862 | 5.5 |
| 1962 | 385,315 | 1,018,939 | 1,279,631 | 292,955 | 695,085 | 250,476 | 432,343 | 8.4 |
| 1963 | 399,992 | 829,335 | 660,359 | 612,122 | 711,177 | 184,879 | 465,920 | n.a. |
| 1964 | 716,095 | 859,380 | 735,208 | 781,354 | 421,039 | 203,081 | 610,599 | n.a. |
| 1965 | 690,091 | 1,143,144 | 1,139,426 | 766,823 | 601,632 | 234,421 | 549,883 | n.a. |
| 1966 | 750,030 | 1,104,086 | 1,322,014 | 1,033,397 | 1,469,541 | 422,202 | 568,934 | n.a. |
| 1967 | 949,167 | 781,726 | 2,014,582 | 2,007,810 | 1,251,460 | 879,637 | 539,525 | n.a. |
| 1968 | 1,141,244 | 1,039,448 | 2,371,024 | 1,018,136 | 742,243 | 435,929 | 573,060 | n.a. |
| 1969 | 1,201,770 | 903,742 | 2,557,276 | 1,727,104 | 765,015 | 224,507 | 609,067 | n.a. |
| 1970 | 1,321,419 | 1,070,742 | 2,710,107 | 2,792,353 | 797,394 | 492,407 | 970,684 | n.a. |
| 1971 | 1,381,080 | 1,201,200 | 3,235,634 | 3,087,957 | 751,215 | 396,444 | 861,057 | n.a. |
| 1972 | n.a. | n.a. | n.a. | n.a. | n.a. | n.a. | n.a. | n.a. |

(1) See Table 3, n. (1).
Source: Same as Table 3.

brutal action by the Soviet forces was severely condemned in most Belgian newspapers, and public opinion showed a great sympathy with the Hungarian people. On 6 November 1956, there was a massive students' demonstration in Brussels. Some 10,000 students, leftists as well as rightists, Walloons as well as Flemings, demanded the suspension of relations with the USSR.[35] The next day, the Senate's Foreign Affairs Committee unanimously demanded the nonapplication of the recently signed Belgo-Soviet cultural agreement and protested against the Soviet intervention. On 8 November Foreign Minister Spaak protested in a letter to Mr. Tchepilov, the Soviet ambassador. On 13 November the Belgian government announced that the Belgo-Soviet cultural agreement would remain inoperative.[36] Belgian protests had no effect at all and the hope for better relations with the Soviet Union quickly disappeared, as Mr. Spaak testifies in his memoirs:

Several years had to pass before the memory of these deplorable events faded away and before a policy of better cooperation with the U.S.S.R. and the European communist countries could be tried again with some chance of success.[37]

The only thing Belgium was able to do was to welcome some four thousand refugees to its territory.

For a second time, when the Warsaw Pact forces invaded Czechoslovakia in August 1968, Belgium could only deplore and condemn this aggression. On 21 August the Belgian government condemned "the use of coercive measures and the interference of foreign powers in the internal politics of a country." On 23 August Foreign Minister Harmel announced that all official bilateral exchanges with the countries whose forces had invaded Czechoslovakia would be suspended. Together with its NATO partners, Belgium refused to attend the festivities in Moscow on 7 November 1968 with regard to the fifty-first anniversary of the Russian Revolution.[38] But more was not to be done against a matter that the USSR—and, after a while, also the West—considered a purely internal affair of the Eastern bloc. In fact, the effect of these events on the relations between Belgium and the USSR was much smaller than that after the Soviet intervention in Hungary in 1956. In his speech before the Belgian Senate only four months after the events, on 15 January 1969, Mr. Harmel made it clear that Europe had no choice between the Cold War and peaceful coexistence and that he preferred to continue on the road toward cooperation:

We have not stopped the current of economic, technical, commercial and cultural relations with the occupying powers, whose behavior we do not understand nor approve of. We are ready to continue the dialogue . . .[39]

Indeed, a few months later, on May 27-29, Czech Foreign Minister Marko visited Belgium, and on July 23-26 Mr. Harmel went to Moscow.

In both crises the USSR was the object of strong international and also Belgian criticism. But it was the Congo crisis in the early sixties that certainly put the heaviest strains on Belgo-Soviet relations. This time, Belgium was bitterly criticized not only by the whole Communist world but also by most Afro-Asian countries, as well as by several Western allies. We will not enter into the details of this question. For our point of view only the Cold War aspect of this greatest crisis in Belgium's postwar international relations need be revealed.

The Congo, with its great natural riches, was very attractive to both the East and the West. Therefore, both sides tried to gain influence in the Congo's political and economic life. The Communist world saw this central African nation as an ideal base for enhancing its influence over Africa. The West was particularly interested in the Congolese natural resources. When Belgium used its military force in order to protect Belgian citizens and properties after the mutiny of the "force publique" in July 1960 and did not withdraw her troops immediately after a UN resolution had required her to do so, the country was severely criticized. The Lumumba regime grew more and more leftist, because it "could or would only count on the support of several neutralist countries and on that of the USSR."[40] When its leader, after a conflict with President Kasavubu, was murdered in January 1961, this again raised a wave of international protest against Belgium, particularly from the Asian countries and the neutralists. Belgium's embassy in Cairo was attacked and destroyed, and on 26 February 1961, Nasser nationalized all Belgian properties in the UAR.[41] The impact of the East-West conflict on the Congo is probably best illustrated by two persons who had an important influence on the first thirteen years of the Congo's existence as an independent nation. On the one hand, Patrice Lumumba was obviously supported by the Soviet Union and the whole Communist world; after his murder this influence diminished. On the other hand, General Mobutu assumed a vivid anti-Communist attitude and got the support of the United States and probably even of the CIA.[42] In December 1964, Belgium and the United States together were the object of new international criticism because of their armed intervention in Stanleyville at the end of November 1964, in order to free hundreds of hostages that were in the hands of the rebels. For the transport of the Belgian paratroops United States planes were used. However, the whole conflict with the Communist world and the neutralists over the Congo had no lasting impact on their relations with Belgium in the following years.

The lessening Cold War tension was one cause of the crisis that had been growing in the Atlantic alliance since the early sixties, though of course the Atlantic crisis had a much broader background. To the easing East-West tension must be added the constant decline in the defense efforts of many European allies, US uneasiness over the development of the Common Market, European fears for American-Soviet deals over the heads of the allies, and Europe's demands for nuclear sharing and for more political consultation. Moreover, the United States received little support in Europe for its policy in Southeast Asia. All these factors put serious strains on the alliance. The crisis found its most dramatic expression in France's withdrawal from NATO's military organization in 1966 and her demands for the removal of all NATO installations from the French soil. This decision had direct consequences for Belgium. After a few months it was clear that Belgium, against the will of the opposition parties in Parliament, was going to house the NATO installations. The Belgian government acted with great care in this matter but could not avoid criticism from Parliament that it had not been sufficiently consulted and informed in a matter of great importance. On 6 June 1966, after long negotiations among the fourteen NATO partners, Belgium, together with Holland and Germany, accepted, at least in principle, the transfer of the installations to her territory. The question led to an important debate in Parliament about the actual relevance of the alliance, about its future tasks, its structure, and, finally, about the transfer.[43] The government—a coalition of Christian-Democrats and Liberals—found enough support for the transfer, but the vote showed that Parliament was very divided on the question. But the greatest part of the Belgian Parliament, in fact a much larger majority than favored the transfer, thought that the alliance was still the best instrument for Belgium's security, although emphasis was also put on the fact that NATO had to become a détente-searching alliance.

But the more détente has been successful, the more the crisis in Atlantic relations has continued and even grown. Though the French example has not been followed by any of the Allies, and the alliance has been partly adapted to changed circumstances (political consultation, détente objective, Eurogroup), there remain urgent problems to be solved. The first of these is the United States-European economic and financial relationship and American uneasiness with the European defense efforts. A second source of conflict is Europe's suspicions that important deals and decisions between East and West are directly made between Moscow and Washington without any consultation of the European NATO partners. At the same time, American willingness to intervene with nuclear weapons in Europe, in case of an armed attack against one or several European allies, has become more doubtful than before, in the eyes of many Europeans. A third problem is the continual threat of the US Congress to withdraw the GI's from the European continent if the allies make no appreciably greater defense efforts. These problems will certainly not be solved by the increasing popular opposition against NATO, against defense and the military in general, which has steadily been growing in several NATO partners. Criticism of NATO is most often focused on the membership of such undemocratic regimes as those of Greece, Portugal and to some extent also Turkey.

In Belgium a public discussion of the country's defense policy started recently after student demonstrations and school strikes that were organized in reaction to the government's newest reorganization plan for the military forces. Behind the criticism of specific points of this plan, an antimilitarist tendency could be noticed that questioned Belgium's defense efforts and NATO obligations. Also, within Belgian political parties, the country's defense policy and NATO membership are being and will be discussed and reconsidered in the nearest future. All this does not mean that there will soon be an immediate switch in Belgium's foreign policy. Most probably Belgium will stay in NATO but will try to adapt the alliance more to the changed international situation and to the demands of public opinion. Belgium's role in NATO will certainly be influenced by the results of the ECSC, MBFR and SALT; by the evolution of the negotiations between the United States and Europe in matters of trade, finance and military burden sharing; by the evolution of the European unification process; and finally by the strength of internal opposition from pacifist and antimilitarist movements.

A last effect of the diminishing Cold War tension is Belgium's everdecreasing defense effort. In this respect Belgium constitutes no exception among the European allies. The decreasing defense effort has been reflected in the reduction of obligatory service time and in the level of defense— expenses, the number of men under arms, and the relative share of the defense budget in the country's total budget. The length of military service was reduced from twenty-one to eighteen months in 1954; in 1957 it was brought down to fifteen months; and finally, to twelve months in 1959. The programs of the two latest governments promise a new decrease to ten months. The Socialist Party even proposed six months in its latest election campaign, at least as a long-term objective.[44] Throughout the same period the level of defense expenditure sank at a considerable rate, as shown in Table 5.

The same downward trend was to be found in the relative share of the defense budget in the country's total budget. From 16 percent of the national budget in 1963/64, it sank to 12 percent in 1965/66 and even to 8.3 percent in 1971.[45] Also, the number of men under arms was gradually cut down, from over 140,000 in the early fifties to 110,000 in 1961/62, to 108,961 in 1967/68 and even to 97,904 in 1970/71.[46] The high defense expenditure level of the early fifties was, as we have already mentioned, a direct consequence of the Cold War and of decisions taken within NATO that demanded a quick rearmament of the Belgian forces. The decline that clearly set in after 1954 and considerably intensified in the second half of the 1960s was due to several causes. First, there was the positive influence of the relative thaw around the mid-fifties. Secondly, there was the conviction that in a time of massive retaliation strategy (NATO's strategy throughout the 1950s and early 1960s), no high defense expenditure for conventional forces and armaments was needed. However, when NATO adopted the flexible response strategy from 1967 onward, it was obvious that a large and mobile conventional force would be necessary in order to make the new strategy both credible and workable, and to put

### TABLE 5

Belgium's Defense Expenditure as a % of GNP
(GNP at factor cost—current prices)

| 1952 | 1953 | 1954 | 1955 | 1956 | 1957 | 1958 | 1959 | 1960 | 1961 |
|------|------|------|------|------|------|------|------|------|------|
| 5.5 | 5.3 | 5.1 | 4.1 | 3.9 | 3.9 | 3.9 | 3.9 | 3.7 | 3.6 |

| 1962 | 1963 | 1964 | 1965 | 1966 | 1967 | 1968 | 1969 | 1970 | 1971 |
|------|------|------|------|------|------|------|------|------|------|
| 3.7 | 3.6 | 3.6 | 3.3 | 3.3 | 3.3 | 3.3 | 3.1 | 3.1 | n.a. |

Source: *NATO Facts and Figures* (Brussels, 1971), pp. 256–57.

the nuclear threshold as high as possible. But notwithstanding continuous US warnings, Belgium, as well as most of the other European allies, kept her defense expenditure as low as before or even lower. Thirdly, Belgium's defense effort grew smaller as the result of ever-increasing demands for welfare policies and electoral promises of political parties to reduce the length of service time. Fourthly, Belgium was aware that as a small country it lacked the capacity to influence a world situation dominated by the two superpowers. Moreover, in the nuclear age, Belgium's defense efforts in the conventional field have increasingly seemed futile and a pure waste in the eyes of many people. This caused a further loss of prestige for the armed forces and growing antimilitarism, particularly because Belgium has never had a great military tradition.[47] Finally, the country's defense effort continued to be under constant pressure from rising antimilitarism, pacifism and even anti-Americanism within certain parts of the population, especially the younger generation.

Since 1959 Belgium has tried to compensate for this declining defense effort by a rationalization and reorganization of its armed forces. The theory was introduced that, instead of focusing on quantitative aspects, it was better to possess a well-organized, well-trained and well-equipped mobile smaller force. But the "quality first" theory and words like "modernization" and "reorganization" have often seemed magical terms to hide the too obvious downward trend in the country's defense efforts. The underlying philosophy of Belgian defense policy has become: Let us create a well-equipped small force that costs us as little as possible and that is still acceptable to our allies. How long this attitude will last will be clearer when a thorough discussion on matters of trade and defense has taken place between the United States and its European allies.

In order to meet US complaints, Belgium, together with its Eurogroup partners in NATO, has taken part in the European Defense Improvement Program (EDIP) that was announced in 1970. It was to be their particular effort for the realization of the Allied Defense-70 program. Additionally, the Eurogroup decided to make an extra common defense expenditure of $1 billion in 1972; and for 1973 another increase was planned, adding $1.5 billion to the 1972 figure.[48] When it finally comes to talks with the United States, the European answer to American demands will depend on a mixture of factors, the evolution of which is not yet certain: How far will détente have developed? How strong will the United States be at the international level? Will the United States have become isolationist or not? What new, still more destructive weapons will technology have produced? What will be the degree of cohesion in the Communist world? Will Europe finally speak with one voice, as one political entity with a proper foreign and defense policy? Against this background Belgium urgently needs to develop its views on what policy course to follow in the years to come. The three great alternatives seem to be: continued NATO membership, possibly under a changed treaty; membership in a politically and militarily unified Europe, nuclear or not; and, finally, a neutral Belgium, on its own or together with several other smaller European powers, that accepts the risks of its situation and relies for its security on the UN, international law and the balance of power.

# 4

# GERMÅNY AND THE COLD WAR:
## Historiographical Consequences

The impact of the ideological and power struggle between the Soviet Union and the United States on the former German Reich has been evaluated in a number of highly competent German language studies.[1] To summarize the findings of these scholars here would serve no immediately useful purpose. Instead, the intention is to focus on an aspect of the Cold War that is probably not so widely appreciated in the West—namely, the intra-German historiographical debate that was the direct reaction of academic historians in both parts of Germany to the division of their nation. The collapse of the Third Reich and Germany's elimination as both a nation and a power factor in Central Europe, as well as its subsequent partition by the rival victor powers into two "state-like entities,"[2] has understandably given rise to much historically oriented reflection about the nation's past, its present dilemma and its future prospects.

At the core of this reflection in West Germany was the question concerning the function of national historiography in a virtually nonexistent, or at least severely dismembered, German state. Whereas prior to 1945 most German historians, particularly since Ranke (1795–1886), had been of the historicist school—a trend in historical thought that has endured to the present—the obliteration of the German state compelled a radical revision of their former statist assumptions. This was because for them the state—by which was meant Prusso-Germany—was the supreme object of historical enquiry. When that ceased to exist in 1945, the Hegelian-Rankean historicists found themselves in profound difficulties. The historiographical by-products of this situation were the immediate postwar reflections of such men as Friedrich Meinecke and Gerhard Ritter, the intention of which was to explain the catastrophe that had overtaken the Fatherland

and to rescue what remained of German national consciousness.[3] As Gerhard Ritter formulated it, the historian must engage in *nationale Selbstbesinnung*—a meditation on the nation's past in order to gain clarity about the direction it should take in the future. This was the role that German historians had traditionally arrogated to themselves. They were in this sense the self-appointed political mentors of the nation. In West Germany this role was reassumed with great solemnity and, in many instances, thinly concealed bitterness, but in any case with profound concern at the plight of the once proud creation of Otto von Bismarck.

Understandably, this reaction of the professorial mind involved a requestioning of inherited assumptions about the nature of the state, a reaction that has been termed the crisis of historicism, or historism.[4] Troeltsch, Heussi and Meinecke had already in the immediate post-1918 and interwar period drawn attention to this development as a result of the German defeat in 1918. But in 1945 the "crisis" became even more profound and resulted in a repudiation, particularly by the postwar generation of academic historians, of the statism of their older professors, as well as a wider acceptance of liberal attitudes and values.[5]

This entire process has been subjected to extremely close scrutiny by historians in the German Democratic Republic (G.D.R.), who have taken a most censorious position with regard to their Western colleagues. The criticism of the latter by the Marxist historians of East Germany is, of course, nothing less than the intellectual reflection of the Cold War in Germany. It is this criticism that concerns us here; for in it can be traced the transformation of historical-political thinking in West Germany, as well as the tenor and ideological motivation of historical scholarship in the G.D.R.

To be sure, the initial postwar revisionist assessments of West German historians offered large areas for attack to their Marxist counterparts, who were not slow to move into action. Indeed, the basic general assumption in the West that the Soviet Union, its policy of Communist expansion westward, was responsible for the division of Germany virtually invited a polemical reaction from the East Germans, who, in turn, saw themselves as the spiritual champions of a democratic liberation movement against Western imperialism and resurgent fascism. With the reestablishment of "normal" academic life in Germany after 1945, most surviving West German professors of history began to take up their accustomed role as political mentors to the nation. From the outset their work necessarily antagonized the Marxists. Admittedly, they began to readjust to the changed situation, but they did not uniformly repudiate the historicist tradition and all that it implied. This was a highly conservative, idealistic, antinormative, relativist conception of national history that still concentrated its attention on the so-called state-bearing personalities by applying the "strictly individualizing method" and was thus in its essence scarcely compatible with the Marxist conception of history. German historicism, deriving from Herder, Hegel and Ranke, denied implicitly the existence of identifiable laws in the historical process and preferred to place its faith in the inscrutable workings of Almighty God through the *Volk* and ultimately the state.

The most outspoken and influential champions of historicism in postwar Germany were the above-mentioned Friedrich Meinecke and Gerhard Ritter, whose chief concerns were both to stress their anticommunism on the one hand and to try to maintain a continuity with the German national past on the other, all in the tradition extending from Herder via Hegel and Ranke, the Prussian and the Neo-Rankean schools right up to their own teachers. Seen through East German eyes, this general aim was nothing less than the historical-political-ideological underpinning of West German foreign policy aims and the consolidation of a conservative-bourgeois-antiworking-class social order. Moreover, because the West Germans, being anti-Communist, supported Konrad Adenauer's policy of integration into the West in preference to German national unity within the Soviet orbit, they were ironically described by East German writers as antinational. And the corollary to this West German attitude—namely, the claim that the Bonn regime inherited the right to be sole legal representative of the German people—was understandably provocative to the Marxist East.[6]

The point of departure of the East German critics was that after the collapse of Nazi Germany, the "official historiography" in West Germany found itself in a profound crisis. This was more serious than in 1918 because not only was the Fatherland destroyed, but there was also the necessity of confronting those social, political and ideological forces that conservative Prusso-German historiography had from its very beginnings so vehemently opposed,[7] i.e., a politically active working class and the Marxist ideology. It was claimed that the anti-Fascist democratic revolution in Germany had been planned by German Communists and in turn championed by East German historiography. For the reactionary historical ideologists of West Germany, there arose then the specter in Germany of the actual historical completion of the bourgeois-democratic revolution of 1848 and 1918 under the conditions brought about by the year 1945 in all of Germany—a prospect harboring the real possibility of the establishment of socialism. The Potsdam agreement, which was the product of the anti-Fascist-democratic world alliance, would naturally have contributed to this possibility. Its aim had been to eradicate militarism in all its forms, to which end even the imperialist Western powers were at first dedicated. This situation posed a serious dilemma for the surviving champions of traditional German historiography. However, the dilemma was not unprecedented: The aged Meinecke had already confronted it in 1918. At that time he had recognized that the salvation of Germany lay in a reorientation towards the West. And in 1945 the same concept reemerged in the speculation (by German conservatives) that the Anglo-Saxon-Russian anti-Hitler coalition would fall apart. In this event the Germans saw themselves aligned with the Western allies against the Soviets. This drive for a restructuring of the foreign policy constellation was linked with a revision of the German historical image and with a concomitant, though delayed, modification of methodological principles.[8]

Here the East German argumentation is quite skillful. The former pro-Prussian, nationalistic German self-image, which had contributed in no small way to the rise of fascism, was brought into service to effect a reconciliation with the imperialist West and to provide a historiography suitable to promoting a future alliance with them. This maneuver, of course, required a change in the basic concept of the state, which had hitherto enjoyed a primacy over society. There had to be an adaptation to the dominant Western concept of the state, which, in contrast to the Prusso-German concept, was seen as being more dependent upon social forces. Therefore, the former champions of the *Obrigkeitsstaat* (i.e., of the Prusso-German authoritarian-bureaucratic state) adjusted to the values of the bourgeois-democratic form of government in order to rescue the bourgeois-capitalist social order.[9] This process led to a restructuring of the historical image to the extent that now *Europa* became a leitmotiv of an anti-Communist West based on an interpretation of Christianity that hallowed the concept of private property and the capitalist system.

This historiographical image then projected by West German historians was attacked by the East Germans as possessing an aggressively anti-Communist spearhead, and none other than Geoffrey Barraclough, "the bourgeois English historian," was cited to reinforce this reasoning. Barraclough had commented in his book *History in a Changing World* (1955) that in the aftermath of the Second World War the old platitude about the inherited cultural tradition of the West had been transformed into a dogma or article of faith. Whereas previously it had been devoid of political implications, that tradition, according to Barraclough, had now been mobilized to become "the vehicle of organised political forces, charged with political content; it has come into its own as an ideological smoke-screen behind which the more militant upholders of 'western tradition' are preparing to manoeuvre into position the compelling artillery of the atomic bomb."[10]

West German reactionary historians were accused of operating in this sense and of incorporating the Prussian tradition into European history. Prussia was to be seen as a bulwark of the West against the Soviet Union. On the other hand, it was necessary to abandon those more compromising personalities and movements such as Hitler and fascism and to denounce them as anti-Prussian in order to accomplish the integration of Prussia retrospectively into the European tradition. In this connection the East German critics have scored some telling blows. They observed, for example, that the debate among West German historians centered around the question of what needed to be rejected from their formerly Prussian-oriented historiography in order to be able to integrate it into a more Western concept of history, or what was to be retained in order to justify historically the nationalist principle within the framework of Western "integration."

When the postwar writings of such leading German historians as Meinecke, Ritter and their older students are considered, much of the above characterization must be regarded as essentially correct. Particular attention was devoted to Meinecke and Ritter, since they claimed to be and were largely regarded as the arbiters of the genuine historical tradition.[11] The resultant analysis enabled the critics putatively to delineate a paradigm of beliefs that had come to be shared by the majority of West German historians. These were devised to emphasize the Christian, supranational tradition of medieval German history in order to stress the contrast between the civilized Christian West and the barbaric Asiatic East. In modern history, the French Revolution, particularly the Jacobin phase, was portrayed as being the source of modern militarism and totalitarianism and, as such, repudiated. The Prussian tradition was thereby exonerated from having been the mold out of which Nazism emerged.

Following this pattern of face-saving explanations, the postwar West German paradigm of beliefs accounted for the pre-1914 Weltpolitik as simply the German expression of an international political phenomenon, rather than an economic one. German imperialism was explained as being essentially very little different from that of Britain, France or Russia. Pan-Germanism was merely an extreme form and not typical of German imperialism. This argumentation is, of course, very significant in the light of the more recent researches of Professor Fritz Fischer and his school in West Germany, which does indeed emphasize the unique character of pre-1914 German imperialism and particularly the role played by economic pressure groups. Against this, the "official" historiography wanted to affirm that there could be no question of guilt for the outbreak of the First World War, since all the powers had merely stumbled into a conflict that no one really wanted. The German decision to participate had been the result of a breakdown of communication between the political and military leadership—a situation yielding tragic results that no one could have foreseen. For this reason the government of the time, especially the chancellor, Bethmann-Hollweg, was strenuously defended against all charges of aggression. The ultimate defeat of Germany was attributed to the numerically superior forces of her enemies. Indeed, the decisive factor in the outcome of the First World War had been the intervention of the United States. This defeat, together with the revolution in Russia, had begun a new era in world history. At this point the East-West confrontation began to signify the decline of Europe. Furthermore, the period of the Great War had seen the full development of the so-called industrial society (a concept dealt with below) in the imperialist countries, whereby the class struggle was seen to be overcome.[12] In treating the November Revolution in Germany (1918), these historians emphasized the policies of the right-wing social democratic leadership as having rescued Germany from communism. This interpretation paved the way for a reappraisal of the Weimar Republic as a model of German democracy, in which such personalities as Stresemann, with his Locarno policy, Brüning, and the Social Democrats, with their policies of reconciliation between the classes, were depicted in a favorable light. On the other hand, the pro-Soviet Rapallo treaty of 1922 was ignored, since there was no immediate political advantage to be gained by subjecting it to a new analysis. Communism was treated, together with national socialism, as another form of totalitarianism.

Having established these positions, West German historians could then explain the collapse of the Weimar Republic as being due to attacks from both Left and Right. Further, the roots of national socialism were demonstrated to originate in the petite bourgeoisie, the lumpen proletariat, foreign influences such as Gobineau, H. S. Chamberlain and Austrian nationalism, as well as the totalitarian tendencies of the industrial age. The German haute bourgeoisie, according to this view, allegedly played no greater part in the success of national socialism than any other section of the people. By this reasoning, the continuity in the domination of German imperialism through the Weimar period and the Third Reich to the present, as well as the class character of Hitler's fascism, was repudiated. The latter's demonic character was blamed for this phenomenon.

The historiography of the resistance to Hitler was concentrated on the high-ranking military conspirators of 20 July 1944 and their precursors; the efforts of the Communist Party were ignored, except where they were labeled as "high treason" by some writers or as an ineffectual suicidal action. In the main, the resistance motives of the conservative Carl Goedeler received the most positive evaluation by West German writers. Their chief aim was to dissociate what they regarded as the healthy German tradition from the policy errors and atrocities of the Hitler regime.

Indeed, the Prussian heritage was proclaimed to be the very antithesis of Hitlerism.

All this is essential background to an understanding of the West German assessment of the Cold War. The anti-Fascist alliance of the Western Powers with the Soviet Union was a fateful mistake on the part of Britain and the United States. This was particularly so with the Potsdam agreement. However, with the collapse of this arrangement, those forces that first appeared in 1917 finally broke through to become determining factors in world politics. As a result of the so-called East-West rivalry, the world was split into two camps. The future for Germany then lay only in a West European integration, which in turn depended upon the North Atlantic Treaty under United States leadership. West German writers always regretted the increasingly centrifugal tendencies that this alliance had shown in the course of its existence.

The responsibility for the Cold War was placed, in spite of facts to the contrary, exclusively with the Soviet Union; by a reversal of values, this power was accused of pursuing an imperialist and colonialist policy. The Western Powers were said to have practised imperialism only in the past. Indeed, in Western assessments the Soviet Union and other socialist states were generally depicted as being victims of the personality cult and its attendant evils, which were violations of genuine socialist principles. These evils were seen as causing the division of Germany and the East-West conflict; the blame lay entirely with the Soviet Union. This view led to the assertion by West German writers that the Federal Republic was the only legitimate successor state to the German Reich, a state in which the experiences of Weimar have been carefully noted and the dangers of militarism and fascism have been studiously avoided. The fact that anti-Fascist democratic forces had been violently suppressed and that the restoration of imperialistic and militaristic forces had taken place was conveniently ignored. The G. D. R., on the other hand, was denigrated as a totalitarian state under the heel of Moscow; as such it ought to be liberated and incorporated into the Bonn Republic and then into NATO.

With this critique of West German historiographical assumptions and constructions, the East Germans clearly regarded the majority of historians in the Federal Republic as functioning in the service of Bonn's official foreign policy and that of NATO. Indeed, they even went so far in their attacks as to label Friedrich Meinecke, the doyen of postwar German historians, as one of the founding fathers of the NATO historians (*ein Stammvater der NATO-Historiker*) because his background and historical-philosophical assumptions led him automatically to an ideological position in support of West Germany's inclusion in NATO. In pioneering his way from Prusso-German monarchism and nationalism to an ideology of Western European integration, said the East Germans, Meinecke was the guiding star for all other similarly motivated historians. What enabled him and them to make such an intellectual pilgrimage with so many apparent contradictions, according to this view, was a basic and constant anticommunism. This was the factor that lent unity to West German historiography during the Cold War.[13]

It is extremely instructive to observe the vehemence and skill with which the East Germans have tried to discredit the conservative leaders of West German historiography during the period from 1945 to 1965. This vehemence stems from the East Germans' belief that their tradition-bound counterparts, like themselves, had to function as the guardians of the "official" political ideology, indeed, saw themselves as the generators of that ideology. For this reason the West Germans were thought to have an in-built hostility to making any concessions to dialectical materialism; that would have been tantamount to allowing the entry of an ideological Trojan horse into the West German fortress. Therefore, the Meineckes and the Ritters of the Federal Republic were bound only to revise their basically conservative stance insofar as it was necessary to appease the Anglo-Saxon protectors of West German society. They then, naturally, fell into the role of apologists for West European integration and anti-Soviet policy. They had become, in the language of East German critics, the ideological general staff of NATO.[14] This explains the vehemence that the Communists employ when describing those German historians in the capitalist camp.

Underlying these assumptions is the Marxist-oriented reasoning regarding Western psychology: the German imperialists and their ideologists were compelled by the shock of defeats on the Volga to recognize two basic and closely interrelated factors. First, the Soviet Union had proved itself to be unconquerable. The bourgeois mind was not able to grasp that in the final analysis this was due to the laws of history, which ensured the triumph of the socialist movement. The creation of the Soviet Union itself was due to the effect of these laws. The German bourgeoisie—and not only those—understood very well that the Soviet victory and the success of the anti-Fascist movements in Europe, which were for the most part Communist-led, would enhance the attractiveness of the forces of socialism and anti-imperialist democracy to the broad masses, even in Germany. Second, the imperialist victors of the First World War, chiefly the United States and Great Britain, who allied themselves with the Soviet Union in the Second World War against German imperialism and who after 1945 occupied two-thirds of Germany as well as West Berlin, were for this reason considered by the German imperialists as saviors of the basis of German capitalism and as guarantors and promoters of its resurgence. Leading circles of German imperialism and their ideological "general staff" saw their chief role in the final stages of the war as working to eliminate the Nazi superstructure from the base of German imperialism. This was, it was argued, an adroit maneuver because Hitler's form of fascism was particularly detested by the peoples of Western Europe and North America. If German imperialists repudiated Hitler, they would win the sympathy of the Western Europeans and North Americans. Thereby they would preserve the essential basis of German imperialism; only the no longer useful Nazi superstructure had to be sacrificed. Politically, the East Germans reason, this maneuver was intended to pave the way for an anti-Soviet, antisocialist alliance with the dominant imperialist forces, chiefly the United States and Great Britain, and to detach them from the anti-Hitler coalition with the Soviet Union. As events showed, this was possible only after the total defeat of German imperialism and the beginning of the Cold War, which was inaugurated by Churchill's anti-Soviet speech made in President Truman's presence at Fulton on 5 March 1946.[15]

The question of making common cause with the Anglo-Saxon powers naturally raised certain historical-ideological difficulties for the West German traditionalists. They were forced to reassess certain key features of their historicism, such as statism (in practice, the glorification of the Prusso-German state) and the concentration on great personalities together with the concept of the amoral nature of the state. Moreover, the intuitive, individualizing method had to be modified. This was necessary in order to get into phase with the historical political thinking of the West that was derived from the Enlightenment and the liberal concept of progress. Here the key features were the idea of a natural law, of popular sovereignty, and of self-help, all of which led to a basic assumption about the "primacy of society," which was regarded as an association of individuals distinct from and aligned against the state.

The East Germans observed that in the West there existed a strongly sociologically oriented historical-political thought, one that remained, however, basically hostile to Marxist conceptions. Werner Berthold had concluded from this fact that existing bourgeois states were the outcome of earlier bourgeois revolutions and reforms and continued to be subject to the constant influence of the bourgeoisie. This fact made the so-called bourgeois democratic states just as prepared to suppress the rise of the revolutionary proletariat as was the Prusso-German capitalist junker state. For this reason, according to Marxist historians, the ideologists of the ruling classes in the West and the former German historicists were able to meet on common ground, despite their obvious differences, to confront the common proletarian enemy.

Out of this ideological armory the East German historians mounted a sustained attack on their West German colleagues. Indeed, a specialist team from the East German Historical Society was set up to investigate the "development of historiography in the two German states."[16] This group, centered at the University of Halle, produced its first collective findings in November 1962 in a symposium that was published in 1963 under the title *Anti-Communism in the Theory and Practice of German Imperialism*. As the title suggests, the intention was to present an exposé of what was regarded as reactionary West German historical ideology in all its aspects. As such, the volume is the intellectual reflection of the Cold War at that time. The title article on anticommunism, by Leo Stern, concentrated on those West German writers who in his view displayed an almost panicked fear of communism in calling for a "political general staff of the Cold War" to be set up and for a strategy of an ideological counter-attack. Such appeals showed, according to Stern, the internal insecurity of the Western crusaders against communism, "who feared the irresistible truth of Marxism-Leninism and the real economic, military and political-ideological power of the socialist world system."[17] The questionable doctrine of the "heritage of the West" would scarcely prevail against this. Such a clerical-imperialistic *Europa-ideologie* was no more than a patch-work produced from all the reactionary dross of European intellectual history, an ideology ridiculously inadequate to camouflage the reactionary character, notorious rapaciousness and brutality of world imperialism. There was no doubt, wrote Stern, that the reactionary, antirevolutionary, antihuman ideology of the Cold War would go under in the struggle against the progressive, rational, humane idea of peace and friendship among the peoples of the earth.[18]

Though this evaluation applied to all anti-Communist ideologies, it was directed particularly against the West Germans, who were characterized as the heralds and spokesmen of German revanchism. This piece of invective was typical for the period of the Cold War when the imputed goal of Western imperialism was to torpedo all efforts of young developing countries from advancing towards socialism. The posture of the United States and NATO-Germany was depicted as ruthlessly aggressive.[19] This anti-Communist policy was maintained in Germany by the reinstatement or confirmation in office of a large number of officials and academics who had been active Nazis or sympathetic to that cause. Indeed, the East Germans have expended a great deal of effort in identifying those West German personalities whose records have in this way been compromised. The presence of these "old Nazis" in high academic and administrative positions in the Federal Republic was cited by East Germans as evidence of West Germany's aggressively anti-Soviet stance. But beyond this, even younger historians, including those with no post-Nazi affiliations, have been attacked for having placed themselves willingly in the service of Bonn's imperialist-revanchist foreign policy.[20] For East German historians, then, the pronounced anticommunism of their West German colleagues was nothing more or less than what Walter Ulbricht said it was, viz., "the political weapon of the reactionary German *haute bourgeoisie* for the preparation of rapacious wars of conquest."[21] The task of East German historians was to expose this function of those in the service of imperialism and mount a counteroffensive.

Apart from the doctrinaire anticommunism of the West Germans, another central element of their attitude toward the East in the Cold War that provoked a hostile counterattack was the "doctrine of totalitarianism," by which the East Germans meant that the West classified Soviet-style regimes as totalitarian. This was incomprehensible for Marxist-Leninists, and they lamented that when Western publicists propagated this view they had a very damaging influence on West German workers by conveying to them a negative image of life under socialism.[22] The imputation that there was an essential similarity between fascism on the one hand and socialism/communism on the other was something that the East Germans found particularly offensive. They regarded the "totalitarianism doctrine" as a centerpiece in West German historical ideology and charged that the "Bonn historians" consciously applied this doctrine to canalize the hate and revulsion of peace-loving nations for the atrocities of Hitlerism towards the Soviet type of state. The West Germans, they said, tried to "prove" that fascism and socialism/communism sprang from the same social causes and were examples of essentially the same style of governmental and social system and were equally repressive in depriving human beings of their personal freedom and individual dignity.[23]

West German historians were severely rebuked for comparing the two systems in such a superficial way. Their fear and hatred of communism, which this supposedly reflected, was attributed to a reaction in the minds of imperialist ideologists against the historical dialectic currently operating, the core of which was the transition from capitalism to socialism. The "totalitarianism doctrine" was seen as a means by which the imperialists sought to disguise the essential character and basic contradictions of the present era and to divert attention from the real factors causing the conflict; thereby, the thesis that the Western world was free while the Communist was in permanent bondage could be sustained. The "totalitarianism doctrine" was essentially an expression of the general crisis of capitalism in its second and third phase.[24] The pretended rejection of fascism on the part of leading West German historians was only a means to an end. Indeed, the vociferous manner in which these men dissociated themselves from national socialism did not spring from an anti-fascist position at all, but rather from their anticommunism. But one of the chief aims here was to deny any continuity between the regime of German militarism and imperialism during the Hitler period and the present Bonn republic. So the West Germans were "conquering the past" under the banner of anti-communism and, at the same time, disguising and justifying the terrorist and rapacious policies of resurgent German imperialism and militarism, both within the country and without, as well as supporting the antinational and aggressive policies of NATO. With this argumentation, it was reasoned by East Germans that the "totalitarianism doctrine" of the West was a keystone in the ideological edifice and policies of the reactionary Bonn regime. The destruction of this doctrine was, therefore, to be regarded as an essential factor in the struggle against the enemies of the entire German nation.[25]

While the East German historians have been most assiduous in their analysis and criticism of their more traditional West German colleagues, however, they have not been blind to what they call "positive forces" among them. These would include those West German scholars who have had the moral courage and insight to repudiate the mystical, nationalist aspects of historicism such as the glorification of the state and of militarism. In the East German view, there have been very few of these, and none of them has reached the standard of the "Fischer school," which did more than any other group to unmask the true imperialist and reactionary character of the Wilhelmine state.

It is now reasonably well known outside Germany that Fischer's work unleashed a storm of indignant criticism among his own colleagues. As the British historian John Röhl commented in 1970: "The publication of [Fischer's] monumental study of Germany's aims in the First World War in 1961 aroused the greatest storm the German historical world has ever seen. Despite the initial outcry, his basic conclusions have now been widely accepted, and his influence is clearly discernible in most of the monographs now appearing in Germany. Something of a historiographical revolution has occurred."[26] It is instructive, however, to take cognizance of the East German reception of this pioneering work and to note what significance is attributed to it. The work, *Griff nach der Weltmacht*, was conceived in 1955-56, researched from 1957 to 1960, and finally appeared in October 1961. In this space of time, observed Werner Berthold, West German militarism seized the opportunity through membership in NATO to reestablish itself and reveal its menacing character to the world in typically Teutonic demonstrations of strength (*Kraftmeierei*).[27] It was against this background that Fischer was stimulated to write his book. That is to say, he was moved out of disgust for militarism to investigate that phase of it in German history that formed the immediate prelude to the Nazi era. Fischer was beginning to dissociate himself from the apologists of militarism. He even went so far as to admonish a right-wing colleague for neglecting to consider economic factors in explaining foreign policy. Indeed, Fischer's statement on this occasion (at the 1951 German historians' conference at Trier) that West German historiography would not be able to compete with that of the Soviet Union or East Germany if the economic factors were ignored had been received in East Germany very favorably.[28] Nevertheless, while Fischer and his chief assistant of that time, Imanuel Geiss, were regarded as progressive scholars who employed many concepts in common with Marxist historians, they are still regarded as essentially bourgeois, though of a particularly liberal stamp; and their views, as isolated efforts that have scarcely affected the basic imperialistic trend in West German historiography. Indeed, the vehemence of the campaign against Fischer and Geiss, which was carried out with the aid of the reactionary press and government bureaucracy, indicated to the East Germans that as a whole West German historiography stood in the service of imperialism and militarism as much as it ever had.[29]

These views were published in 1962. A more recent inventory of East German criticism was carried out in 1971 and published in East Berlin under the title of *Unbewältigte Vergangenheit.*[30] In this pretentiously produced volume a large section is devoted to a critical analysis of the social and political theory of the dominant stream of bourgeois historiography in West Germany. Overall this volume is characterized by a much more irenical tone than its predecessor. It is understandably not so overtly polemical; and the critique, much more scholarly and subtle. This change has been necessitated by the changes (advances?) made in fundamental social and political values in the Federal Republic during the intervening decade. Nevertheless, the permanently hostile basic position is always apparent. Gerhard Losek enunciated the current Communist attitude towards West German historiography as follows: The recognition of its reactionary class function and the knowledge that it is closely bound up with the policies of a state capitalism (*staatsmonopolistisches Herrschaftssystem*) form the key to an effective counterattack on bourgeois historiography in its historical ideology.[31] The view that West German (and all bourgeois) historians are the willing functionaries of a declining social system clearly persists. It is conceded by the East that their Western colleagues take some historical facts into consideration, but they are charged with frequently employing partial truths in the service of an imperialistic manipulation of popular consciousness (*imperialistische Bewusstseinsmanipulation*).[32] This is because bourgeois historians allegedly operate solely to meet the current demands of the contemporary social-political situation. They are not interested in objectively identifying the laws of social evolution and in analyzing their effect on history. This could be done only on the basis of Marxism-Leninism, a fact that illustrates that *all* historiography reflects class interests and has a militant purpose.[33] For this reason historical research involves both problems of theory of cognition and immediate political goals. This applies not only to the manner of gathering data, i.e., the criteria of selection, but also to the historiographical structuring of it.

The bourgeois historian, according to Losek, obviously writes from a historical-political conception that is determined by the current strategy and tactics of the capitalist class and as such lacks basic objectivity. It simply produces findings that are designed to serve the immediate and future policies of the monopolistic bourgeoisie. Therefore, the analysis of bourgeois historiography reveals the link between political strategy and historical thinking. And this fact presents the Marxist historians with their central task in the current debate, namely, to highlight the strategy and tactics of the class enemy in order to campaign against them. The effectiveness of this campaign will depend upon the degree to which the scientifically based strategy and tactics of the revolutionary party of the working class are understood and applied.[34]

The East Germans have in this way given their anti-Western stance an ideological rationale that imposes on their historiography an eminently militant function in the class struggle. Thus equipped they have set out to demolish the present "opposition," who had taken to adjusting to the Eastern criticism by proffering skillfully devised but nonetheless fallacious doctrines with which to defend their declining position. That is to say, West German historians have begun to borrow elements from the Marxist-Leninist theory and to employ them in the service of bourgeois historiography. Such a borrowing was the concept of the "industrial society" and the associated "convergence theory." The polemics against this have been particularly virulent, since the concept of the "industrial society" is seen by the Communists as a project that has been mounted in the advanced phase of capitalism to provide an alternative to scientific socialism, an attempt to repudiate the objective developmental tendencies of the modern era of the transition from capitalism to socialism.[35] The bourgeois idea of the "industrial society," sought to integrate all classes under the leadership of the haute bourgeoisie in order more efficiently to resist the rising pressure of the masses. In an obvious reaction to the Marxist theory of history as an inexorably advancing movement of social formations, the historically retrogressive imperialist social system was being lent the appearance of progressiveness by this theory of the "industrial society."

The roots of this theory have been traced back to the concepts of a number of bourgeois and revisionist economists, sociologists, philosophers and historians of the nineteenth and early twentieth century, the chief of whom were Max Weber (1864-1920) and Thorstein Veblen (1857-1929). Further, the prognostications of Alexis de Tocqueville (1805-1859) concerning the welfare state, the general process of embourgeoisement and of pluralistic democracy appear to be of basic significance. Not least among the spiritual fathers of the concept were such figures as Arnold Toynbee (b. 1889), with his idea of a world state as a cosmopolitan alternative to atomic war, and Karl Popper, with his pseudoscientific construction of the so-called open society.[36] All these, plus other bourgeois theorists who had vulgarized and distorted the writings of Karl Marx himself (e.g., right-wing social democrats), affected the historiographical concepts of such West German historians as Werner Conze, who published in 1957 his pioneering work on the structural history of the technical-industrial society.[37] The salient feature of the structural history of the "industrial society," which investigated the social-political processes and movements brought about by the industrial revolution, is that it assumes the possibility of a peaceful integration or cohesion of the essentially hostile components of society. From the Communist point of view, it was simply a device for disguising the internal contradictions in capitalist countries. Those bourgeois historians who persisted in assuming the validity of the concept of "industrial society" were functioning as the agents of the monopolistic bourgeoisie.

On the international level, the theory of the "industrial society" led to the so-called "convergence theory," a concept postulating that with the advances in technology in the industrial nations of both East and West, profound structural changes were taking place on the economic, social, political and intellectual levels. Because of such changes, which were common to all industrial countries, those with diametrically opposed social-political systems (i.e., capitalist and communist) found that they were becoming increasingly similar. Indeed, capitalism and socialism would in the course of this transformation process lose more and more of their originally specific characteristics and come more closely to resemble each other.

This, as Gerhard Losek observed, was a theory not so much developed by historical-philosophical and sociological speculation but rather devised for the immediate pragmatic needs of foreign policy strategy around 1960. After the failure of the "roll back" strategy and the obvious hopelessness of a frontal military attack against the socialist world, the "convergence theory" was developed to bring about a transformation in socialism by means of the long-term application of economic, political and ideological pressures to pave the way for a capitalist restoration. But this tack in imperialist strategy did not deceive East German observers. It was nothing more than a prognosis of Communist decline.[38] If capitalist societies incorporated socialist elements to give the appearance of harmony between capital and labor, the real aim was to neutralize the political strength of the working class.[39]

For all these reasons, then, the theory of the "industrial society," with its concept of integration of the classes, and the "convergence theory," along with the "totalitarianism doctrine" and the *Europa-ideologie*, form essential components of West German historiography. In addition, the emphasis in West Germany on the "industrial society" had led to an awakening of interest in West Germany in the history of the labor movement—a sector that traditionalist historians had hitherto ignored. According to East German critics, this field was now being eagerly exploited by bourgeois historians in order to show the possibility of a peaceful integration of the classes on the terms of the exploitative bourgeoisie.[40] The integration of the labor movement into the bourgeois state was regarded as a necessary precondition for the transition of the "industrial society"—a goal that the working class was presumed also to desire. Thereby the militancy of the labor movement was supposed to be dampened and the essential class antagonism overcome. In this way a dangerous threat would be laid and the working class absorbed into the "modern world" of bourgeois values.[41]

Understandably, such treatment of the labor movement by West Germans is regarded with great suspicion by those who consider themselves to be the sole interpreters of Marxist-Leninist truth. The essays of West German historians into social history were belittled as illusory means of assisting them out of their historical-ideological dilemma.[42] Such attempts were only maneuvers by the bourgeoisie to shore up their tottering sociopolitical order. The wish was the father of the idea. Thus Gerhard Losek:

So the structure-oriented "social history" reveals itself as an attempt by leading historians of the Bonn state in conscious resistance to and struggle against historical materialism to arrive at a modified theoretical-methodological tool of research which is supposed to enable the explanation of the process of social development at least from the time of the rise of capitalism and the beginning of the labour movement in accordance with the needs of the present power interests of the monopolistic bourgeoisie. This goal shows that social history and its structural historical method are practically an appendage of traditional bourgeois historiography which does not in any sense question its basic principles.[43]

With statements of such pontifical weight, it is difficult to see how any meaningful dialogue between East and West German historians could take place. The East German historians have focused more critical attention on their Western colleagues than has anyone else, with several famous exceptions. But this attention has been almost exclusively negative and could only be described as polemical.[44] Is there any change of building a bridge between the two camps? Professor Ernst Nolte of the Free University of West Berlin believes so and made this possibility the subject of his inaugural address at that institution. In first noting the differences between bourgeois and Marxist historiography, Nolte delineated the Marxists' image of their role from their own statements:

Marxist historiography investigates the "span of world history" which reaches from the classless proto-society to the communist society of the future, i.e., it understands world history as a series of class struggles, and, of course, of class alliances which emerge from the basic fact evident in all the previous history of man's exploitation of man. However, in its investigations Marxist historiography takes the side of the progressive classes and parties at a given time which in the dialectic of productive forces and conditions of production represent the future. The encompassing insight into the social character of production, which is the prerequisite for an unambiguous definition of it, is the sole possession of the advance troop of the working class, i.e., the Marxist-Leninist party, for the very reason that they stand in the forefront of a human group which is not just one historical group among others but potentially the vast majority of humanity, or at least the most progressive section of humanity, and as such occupies basically a position which is already beyond previous history as a result, due to definite laws of history, of forms of exploitation.

Nolte pointed out that if Marxist historiography was partial, then its partiality was essentially different from the partiality of any other kind of historiography. It was not in Marxist eyes a contradiction of objectivity, because the fundamental interests of the working class were always in full accordance with the requirements of objective reality. He went on to observe:

On the other hand, the fundamental interests of the middle class are incapable of coinciding with the requirements of objective reality because the time during which exploitative classes can be progressive has run out. And whatever applies to the middle class applies to its exponents in bourgeois historiography. Because it is chained to a reactionary economy and politics, it can only always veil the truth, because the essential questions which the historian puts to history are basically determined by the current interests of that class whose position he adopts. For this reason bourgeois historiography has an unscientific character even when it is dealing with remote topics. But when treating topics closer to the present, then its reactionary defensive position becomes quite overwhelmingly evident. . . . In contrast, Marxist-Leninist historiography is strictly

scientific....it contributed the intellectual armoury of the forces of socialism and peace and revealed the neo-colonialist plans of West German
militarists and monopolists, and in particular demonstrated that the G. D. R.
represented the highest point which German history had yet attained.
There is no principle difference between the leadership of the state and the
party on the one hand and the Marxist historian on the other, because the
leadership of the state is based on Marxist-Leninist historiography.[45]

Here Nolte has focused most sharply on the essential aims and self-image
of the East German historians. The essentially irreconcilable nature of the
"bourgeois" and Marxist-Leninist position is clearly recognized. However,
despite this there were certain areas in which the two camps could agree,
such as in the more mechanical aspects of historical research (*Fachmethodik*)
that were not affected by class considerations. There was, therefore,
not a total hostility between the two.[46] But beyond this, if one probed
even deeper and examined the concept of science (*Wissenschaft*) in the
work of Marx and Engels, one had to conclude that the crucial difference
between bourgeois and Marxist historiography was the former's scepticism
about the possibility of mankind's ever achieving a completely classless
society. The basic methodological postulates were essentially the same,
and certain forms of questioning, such as structural analysis, ideology-
critique, the approach to social history and even to economic history,
could be held in common.

This was the conclusion Nolte drew after examining Marx and Engels.
However, it was necessary to distinguish between their ideological edifice
as a system of thought on the one hand and the ideology of a Communist
party after it had achieved power on the other. Nolte defined these as
"Free Marxism" and "Power Marxism," respectively. When Marxism became the ideological weapon of a state it became in a sense the "science
of the state" (*eine Staatswissenschaft*), which lacked any detachment
from its own state or government. This was a situation in which objective
criticism of the state would be completely impossible, a state of affairs
that had never occurred on the side of even the most rabid champions of
bourgeois class interests among bourgeois scholars. "Free Marxism" did,
however, maintain a complete detachment by virtue of its radical opposition to the bourgeois state since that was where it could flourish. And
within the framework of bourgeois society "Free Marxism" could play an
extraordinarily positive role. However, the historical discipline within the
framework of "Power Marxism" was a factor devoid of any autonomy or
inner driving force, and it was prohibited by its very position from making
any criticism of the state. Whenever individuals attempted this by appealing to earlier tradition or were forced by special circumstances to exert
a degree of autonomy or acted spontaneously, they were warned or

forcibly silenced, as was the case recently in Czechoslovakia. And in view of the Russo-Chinese rivalry, which *Pravda* in 1964 termed "Cold War," the bourgeois historian was compelled to question whether or not Marxism instead of leading to a cessation of international conflict actually tended to increase hostility between states.[47]

Professor Nolte, in closing his sober analysis, delivered his own broadside of anti-Marxist critique over the Berlin Wall. He refused to accept that in view of the above facts Marxist and bourgeois historiography were irreconcilable opposites, as the East Germans maintained. They stood in a much more complex relationship, one that allowed some room for agreement, just as there was some measure of agreement between capitalist and communist countries. It was not a question of black and white or black and nonblack. There was a sphere of formal agreement through which both could be labeled scientific—despite the permanent central contradiction. Each stood in a unique relationship to particular social systems. Accordingly, it was possible for "Free Marxism" to exist only within bourgeois society; under "Power Marxism" no such plurality of scholarship was tolerated.[48] The West was in constant flux, in which autonomous sciences could constantly question the foundations of the society in which they existed; by doing so they justified themselves.

The discipline of "Power Marxism" in East Germany, on the other hand, had been until recently always that of a beleaguered state determined to maintain and assert itself in a warlike stance of permanent mobilization in which it was not possible to relax tension and where nothing resembling a relatively autonomous discipline could exist. This phase of postwar history had now passed, and the Cold War that in the West had been characterized by a general ideological rejection of Marxism had receded. In West Germany the Cold War era had seen a great deal of activity by "Free Marxism," which contributed to the inner tension. Nevertheless, in the present détente, Nolte declared, there was still a legitimate place for "Free Marxism," even at the universities, provided that Marxists appreciated that it was the imperfect, but for that very reason real, freedom of the bourgeois society that allowed it to flourish. It enjoyed, in Engels' words, air, light and elbow room—to a greater degree than the labor movement. The only stricture placed on "Free Marxism" was that it redefine its position as providing a peacemaking role within both social systems wherein criticism would not be directed exclusively against the bourgeoisie.

As far as "Power Marxism" was concerned, Nolte declared that it should be guaranteed the right to be heard in West Germany. However, Nolte would not go so far as to demand full reciprocal rights for West German historians in the G. D. R., although a certain amount of give-and-take ought to have been insisted upon. This West Berlin professor would have been speaking on behalf of many West German colleagues when he appealed to the East to abandon polemics and to recognize that the events of this century had shattered the assumptions of both bourgeois and Marxist historiography; for both camps should abandon the claim that right is exclusively on their side and begin to be coworkers in the same field.[49] It remains to be seen whether the East Germans will in time accept this offer of peace, which more and more in West Germany are coming seriously to desire.[50]

# 5

# NIGERIA: Wars Cold and Hot, and Lukewarm Ideas

Despite the obstacles of disparate cultures and conflicting historical records, it is nonetheless instructive to attempt to trace some of the connections between world conflict and conflict in Nigeria, between world order and order in Nigeria, and between the dominant political values exported from Europe over the years to America, to Russia, and to Africa, at different periods. Since individual men are the bearers and measures of values and of change, while the spread of both men and their values has been global and universal, the approach of this study is from the universal and general to the particular and the individual, in Nigeria. This analysis finishes with a suggestion, that one effect of Cold War in the political era of Nigeria's independence was to reinforce the tendency towards military intervention in politics. For the military could rely on logistic and diplomatic support from both sides of the Cold War in their sectional struggles that threatened to tear the new independent state apart.

A more imponderable effect of the Cold War was the impairment of truth and distortion of fact that accompanies a propaganda war and drowns the voice of reason. When, for instance, the only ideological point on which Americans, Russians and many others agreed was that imperialism was evil, accounts of good constructive work undertaken by colonial administrations had little or no chance of a hearing. Without this side of the story, the view formed of civilized men in positions of authority and power was one of a debased Marxism, an economic determinist view. When both sides in the Cold War accepted this distorted view, they were declaring a common faith in materialism, but one of a barbaric rather than a dialectical kind, and denying the values of Western civilization. (My position in relation to this matter is straightforward: having been a

member of the colonial administrative service in Nigeria from the beginning of the conventionally accepted Cold War era until two years after
independence [1947-62], I was often made aware of the fundamental
inability of many American, Russian and European [including British]
reporters of the Nigerian scene to acknowledge that colonial officials
worked conscientiously to help Nigerians towards democratic independence.)

As Winston Churchill said about Russia, Nigeria is "a riddle wrapped
in a mystery inside an enigma"—except that in the case of Nigeria the
riddles and mysteries are several, not single: societies encapsulate other
societies, mingle, overlap and colonize each other in various kinds of
diaspora, and continually draw ideas and influences from different sources.

"Influence" is a word deliberately chosen, because of the association
of its Italian form *influenza* (flu) with another sort of epidemic. The
metaphor of "flu" offers a way through the miasma of Cold War in hot
Africa: the analogy is an epidemiology of ideas, mutating through time,
spreading in slow waves from an endemic centre in Europe throughout the
world, with differing strains in different periods. Picture, then, Europe
(from Classical times, but more particularly from the Enlightenment of
the eighteenth century) as the world's main source of infectious political
ideas and values, these diseases or influenzas being caught and carried
abroad in the course of European expansion over time, and changing in
accordance with mutations brought about by ecological changes, both in
Europe and also to a lesser extent abroad. See this process as one of
successive waves continuing until we have, as at present, one world and
only one, a global system of states thoroughly infected with rather different varieties of epidemic ideas, some acute, revolutionary, some mild,
prevalent, but having lost virulence through their hosts' previous exposure
and acquired resistance. In such circumstances, it is the host population in
the European endemic center, longest exposed to the two main strains, say
A (nationalism) and B (socialism), and to their variants (capitalism and
communism being two such), who have had the best chance to build up a
general resistance, tolerance, or immunity, and even to become indifferent
to a situation of dynamic competition between the variants, in which at
times one strain is seen as disease and at other times as preventive inocu-
lation against another strain.

To continue the metaphor, the epidemics spreading the acute infections
from Western Europe to the United States, later to Russia, and later still
to tropical Africa, were very different waves at different times, inducing
very different symptoms and syndromes, different kinds of malaise, cures,
resistances, fears, even hypochondriasis or hysteria. Thus the infection of
the Enlightenment, transmitted to America, stimulated strong reaction,

aversion and resistance to kingship and monarchy, to state religion, to taxation without representation, to standing armies, hereditary privilege, aristocracy, officialdom, and so on. The prophylactic regime devised included government by laws rather than by men, faith in written constitutions, in individual liberty, in rights of property, freedom of speech and press, in private enterprise, in redemption by works rather than mere faith. Also transmitted to America, by Western European shippers mostly, and of great significance for later relations with African states, were slaves from West Africa and an ideology consonant with the peculiar institution of slave-owning.

Russia's most acute dose of ideas from Western Europe was of a much later strain. The crucial exposure, in the early twentieth century for the most part, was to the mid-nineteenth century pharmacopoeia of drastic cures for the social diseases of their day, packaged by Marx and Engels. The state was itself the disease; its chief symptom, the decay of society through alienation of its components because of the uncontrolled growth of capital, property and oppressive ruling classes. By the time the drastic measures proposed by Marx reached Russia, remedies, controls and palliatives of a more conservative, reforming, social democratic kind had come to be preferred and adopted by those in power in Western Europe, in preference to the surgery of decapitation, the removal of the patient state's head to relieve the members from oppression, and the stripping from them of private property to improve their material condition. The point is that Europe had by then tested and assimilated a good deal of socialist medicine and had begun to export it to Africa. In a sense, therefore, the civil phase of "cold war" was over for Europe, even before it moved into an international phase after 1917; the Russian cure was seen by Europeans as a worse health hazard than what it sought to remedy. The Russians, unable to accept that apparently disease-ridden capitalist and imperialist states were inoculated against international communism by long exposure to milder forms of socialism, saw Western Europe as a threat to their survival. They denounced its socialisms as sham and its imperialisms as real—as, indeed, some of them were: the nationalism and imperialism of Nazi Germany were real enough; its socialism, less convincing. The socialism of the British was real, too; the imperialism, sham.

And so, at last, to Nigeria, a country whose official date of birth, at least, is precisely known, the first of January, 1900. The first point to be made about the spread of the epidemic of European ideas to tropical Africa, and to Nigeria in particular, is that the form that was spread (apart from older strains that had gained a slight hold on the coast) was a new twentieth-century variant, combining both strain A (nationalism) and strain B (socialism). The imperial power concerned was already socialist to the extent that some, at least, of the leading advocates of expansion were Fabian Socialist—as, indeed, were some of the prominent officials in the Colonial Office. Much of the socialism in action (e.g., the various forms of government enterprise, the expropriation of the Royal Niger Company, the policy of nonalienation of communal lands, the quite stringent control and criticism of commercial firms, the public ownership of mineral resources, the steps taken by government to plan economic growth and investment) was, of course, pragmatic and done of necessity rather than by deliberate choice. But it reflected, long before Lenin, the criticisms of capitalism in action written by men like Hobson,[1] so much so that after a generation or two, the first British parliamentary delegation to West Africa in the 1920s noted with surprise what they called the socialist character of the West African colonies. Surprise on being confronted with ocular evidence refuting long-held beliefs is healthier than refusal to see, but here there was no good reason for surprise. The men who had been administering Nigeria were men of the nation, the generations, the social classes, the liberal education and intellectual traditions that had produced fairly constant adverse criticism of imperialism, capitalism, expansionism, and (after the First World War) of caesarism and profiteering. Indeed, it was often colonial officials or former colonial officials who were the main source of informed criticism, from leftist, liberal and progressive viewpoints, men such as Leonard Woolf, Joyce Cary, George Orwell and others less gifted as writers but equally representative of the cause of decolonization, independence and self-determination. That cause could be and was practically served in a colonial service career as in no other. In a West Africa without resident capitalist or settler interests to oppose and control, the close resemblance of the work to socialism in action was not surprising. What else was available as a basis for political and social advance, in the relative absence of private capital and enterprise, except such bureaucracy, state management and planning and public enterprise as inadequate resources permitted? Long before the Cold War broke out between America and Russia, with "imperialism" and "socialism," "capitalism" and "communism" as hate words, the specifically British internal debate and agonizing over what should be done with the dependent territories had eventually been resolved, by the 1940s, into a settled policy of decolonization and colonial independence. The policy was repeatedly declared, and widely disbelieved. Nevertheless, candidates for appointment to the Colonial Service were conscientiously informed by the interviewing authorities, as early as 1945, that the attainment of independence by the dependencies was the work for which they were being recruited, so there could be no guarantee of a normal life career. And pains were taken to ascertain that those selected were fully in sympathy with that policy. Consequently, there was no struggle for independence, no question of nationalists' wresting power from reluctant but weakened imperialists in West Africa—all that belongs to mythology, the mythology of Cold War reinforcing a mythology of African and other nationalisms and socialisms. The serious debate was over before the shouting really began.

Too much could be made, no doubt, of leftist, internationalist and socialist influence within the ranks of colonial administration, but the following facts are probably enough to make the point that the official carriers of political ideas to Nigeria, and the ideas they transmitted to Nigerians, fitted neither the capitalist nor the communist Cold War stereo-types of imperialism but more nearly the sort of mixture, hodgepodge, or synthesis of capitalism and socialism that has characterized British (e.g., Butskellite) domestic politics since the 1940s: the welfare state as end, and no clarity about means, beyond the avoidance of extremes. Socialist peers are one example of this. It is typical of the mixed character of British politics that of the three British colonial administrators with Niger-ian service raised to the peerage since Lugard in 1928, two (Lord Milverton and Lord Caradon) took their places on the Labor benches. Admittedly, the former soon forsook those benches, remarking that what he had taken to be a crusade had proved to be a rake's progress. But the latter, while relatively silent about black oppression, has been a consistent and out-spoken critic of anything resembling neoimperialist or white capitalist exploitation in Africa.[2] (The third, Lord Grey of Naunton, a New Zealander, is difficult to classify in United Kingdom political terms, but "unconservative" and "liberal" would certainly be correct for his period of service in Nigeria.)

Apart from the men at the top, whose influence on Nigerian political life was considerable, there were, of course, many quite zealous and con-vinced socialists and Marxists in influential posts and departments, varying from Oxbridge and London School of Economics Laski disciples to Clydesiders and South Welshmen in departments of labor. Without some such men it would have been impossible to press forward such policies as the development of trades unions, labor relations, vocational and technical education, and the cooperative movement. The writer can remember no constraints placed on them in their work—other than the practical diffi-culties of their task—that were of any significance. Certainly also there were men of more conservative sympathies, tending by a kind of self-selection to be posted for work in the Northern Region, but even for them the conventional stereotype of the Blimpish, upper-class, elitist British colonial official simply will not do.[3]

In practice, the only parts of the British political/social spectrum of

sympathies regularly missing from the Nigerian scene were the committed representative of oligarchy at one end and the committed revolutionary at the other; the voice of neither was heard in the land. What was
present, and a steady influence, in the main, was a wide representation of
predominantly middle- to lower-middle-class people, more concerned with
administration and management than with any political objectives other
than their own replacement by, so far as was possible in a volatile political
situation, an effective, apolitical Nigerian middle class of civil servants,
professional in all the accepted senses.

For the purposes of this chapter, the importance of this situation lies
in the fact that for the Nigerian growing up in Nigeria at any time after the
birth of his own country there was no obvious capitalist class, in classic
Marxian terms, within the country, that could be pointed out as the proper
focus for the politics of envy, for revolutionary nationalism, or for communism. There was no European settler class of great and wealthy land-
owners. There were a few wealthy Nigerian traders and entrepreneurs,
self-made men, potential patrons and models for emulation rather than
automatic class hostility, heroes rather than villains. There were also
wealthy emirs and chiefs, objects again of awe and reverence for most of
their subjects rather than hostility, so long as they observed some rules of
behavior. Deprived by circumstances of any more solid basis for building
up the dynamic tension of politics, ambitious politicians in Nigeria could
find for obloquy only the fact of the dominant white man, along with his
powers, salaries, houses, cars, allowances, etc. In practice, these were
mostly small and modest to the point of insignificance, and the white
men's successors found them quite inadequate for themselves, almost
insultingly so. But such campaigns served their turn and time, convincing
some who should have known better, including the owlish expert visitors
who solemnly recorded that British colonial officials were of the upper-
class elite, lived in luxury, in palatial quarters, were well paid, always
dressed for dinner, never or scarcely ever walked, and so on: all to be
found in the writings of American political scientists of the period, and all
libelous rubbish, the kind of muck that, unlike money, does no good when
widely spread. What it did, in Nigeria as elsewhere, was to represent
workers for freedom and progress as enemies of both; and for that, cold
warriors on both sides must bear some blame.

Dissatisfaction with bureaucratic domination by white men over black
was replaced at the beginning of the political era with more genuine
political tensions, the tensions based on rival nationalisms, which were
for some years taken as healthy signs of multiparty competitive politics
but eventually tore apart not only the civil polity but the army itself, and,
but for a local truce in the Cold War enabling both sides to support the

federal military, would have torn the state of Nigeria apart as well. With such excitements, issues of class conflict seemed throughout of less importance. By contrast, however, in the French territories beyond Nigeria's land boundaries on each side, participation in the politics of metropolitan France by African politicians gave a portal of entry to Communist influence immediately after the war, when the new African political movement allied itself with the French Communist Party, then part of the government of France and far stronger than its British counterpart.[4] It was natural, therefore, so long as French Communists had a share in French government, for French African politicians to ally themselves with them, and equally natural for them to break the connection once the Communists were excluded—natural, but not so successful, because for years afterwards there was a continual rumble of Communist-led rebellion to be heard across Nigeria's landward boundaries, particularly in the Cameroun. It was a development to which leading Nigerians, engrossed in their own domestic and civil politics of triangular electoral struggle between the three largest nations in the country for dominance in an independent Nigeria, paid practically no attention. Their sole arena was Nigeria. The first issue was who would be master in Nigeria once the British left; the second issue was whether that mastery could be amicably shared between rival representatives of the three main nations. Other issues were seen either as irrelevant or as expedients to be picked up opportunistically and dropped again when they had served an immediate tactical purpose.

The shape that the emergent state was taking was describable in formal political terms as federal and parliamentary, but in practice the polarization between the rival leaders and their followers had little to do with the kind of issues that can be resolved or accommodated by discussion in a national parliament, with give-and-take, ruling and being ruled in alternation; it was more primordial, "us or them," a game that could be played only once, and to a finish. If three to begin, and no one strong enough, then an alliance of two against one; and so two left, to decide the issue. And so it went, until, in the final round, the armed bystanders joined in the fight and changed its character.

Boldly oversimplifying for the sake of brevity what the writer has so far suggested but not yet proved: the Cold War raging from the beginning of Nigeria's political era until its end had no relevance to and little effect upon Nigerian civil politics. Those who governed Nigeria until then, British and Nigerian, had a shared immunity to extremes of capitalist and of communist ideology, partly because of exposure to the British mixtures of ideas on these questions and partly because of intense preoccupation with the far more pressing problems of actual economics and politics.

The political problems centered around race and nationalism, not around classes, which meant little amidst rapid change. The first problem was the creation and installation of an elite and a new middle class of black men to replace the white men (a process probably neither hastened nor delayed, merely made less straightforward, by prevailing misunderstandings arising from Cold War propaganda and prejudice). The second, more serious problem was the sharing of power between black men. That problem was resolved after bloodshed, after so-called civil war between military men, only by the complex historical accident of the existence in Nigeria of a professional officer corps formed and trained by the British in the period of Cold War for action against internal disorders. Through the exigencies of British worldwide experience for more than a generation of repeated emergency situations calling for military intervention, often begotten by ideological "cold war," ideological exacerbation of racial animosities in plural societies, the training of officers had come to be concentrated on such situations.

The Nigerian officer corps, especially after UN service in the Congo, was not different from any other professionally trained military in seeing itself, and in being seen by others, as having a part to play, in the last resort, in running the country. What Charles Malik said in 1963 of developing countries in general was already being thought in Nigeria and was proved true there also:

In practically every case the mainstay of authority and order is not any normal functioning of stable democratic institutions, but the army, and the army everywhere is western-trained and western-organized. In many instances the only native institution with which the West can still really converse is the army and from a short-run point of view this is enough. The military throughout Asia and Africa have suddenly discovered, and in my opinion correctly, that they have a role to play in staying chaos, maintaining order, cementing the national unity, and even inspiring and directing change. Rather than fight external wars, as was their traditional wont, the armies have turned inward to shoulder more creative national tasks.[5]

In the case of Nigeria, the role was endangered by a deep split in the army's own allegiances and concepts of nation, and in the "civil" war that followed. But the Nigerian army, during and since that war, has found conversation possible with both West and East. Yet Malik, from the vantage point of Lebanon and of the United Nations, was a better prophet than most. He also saw law and order in developing countries as dependent very largely indeed upon the personal character of the leaders. Every new country, according to Malik, was "stamped by the inherent character of its leaders, and the present age of many of these countries is likely to be remembered and called in the future, for good or for ill, after the name of its present leadership. This is an age of founders and law-givers of a multitude of nations."

Malik's description of the leaders' sources of ideas proceeds, unlike this chapter, from the particular to the general: "The personal character of the leader himself" comes first, "formed and determined by his own heredity, background, experience, sufferings, expectations from life, and personal embitterments"; next the national culture itself, "the systems of valuation and aspiration inherent in the native soil"; and then the influence of "the living European world of thought and organization." He goes on: "But although the amazing complex unity of this world is ultimately grounded in the Graeco-Roman-Christian-European synthesis, today it is more or less neatly polarized into 'East' and 'West'. And so the other two sources of ideas which inspire the leadership of the new countries are the Communist world and the western world, both European and American."

In this analysis, so far, the suggestion has been that such a marked polarization of "East" and "West" did not happen to be the Nigerian inheritance; that what Nigeria got was a later British mixture or synthesis together with an as yet unbroken resistance to the extremes. It now becomes necessary to demonstrate this, so far as possible, by evidence of the personal character and ideas of those who were the rulers and leaders of the emerging Nigeria in the accepted Cold War era. Part of this is based on personal recollection, much more on a study of writings by the men concerned, publications made possible, no doubt, by the interest and the market created by Cold War, and by international speculation as to which way the Nigerian big cat might jump when fully out of the bag.

"Some are born great, some achieve greatness, and some have greatness thrust upon them"—the quotation is from a letter intended to make a "contemplative idiot" of Malvolio, its recipient, but it does well enough in application to the three Nigerian leaders of the three emerging Nigerian nations, which the three could not agree to put together in one peaceful state. Ideological differences might be blamed to some extent, but such differences as there were had very little to do with the polarizations of the Cold War. It is difficult to detect anything in the leaders or their followers that would rejoice a proselytizing Marxist's heart. Their struggle for power was for power in the new state, power of one nation or following over the others, not for the domination of a class, or for a dictatorship of a proletariat, or for a classless society. In a word, each of the three, in his way, was an imperialist. Each sought to extend his power, in quite well-founded fear and distrust of the others. Only one of them ever contemplated the ideology of socialism as a tactic to regain power; it made some sense, but inevitably, some new enemies as well.

In order of their emergence on the Nigerian political scene, the first was the Ibo, the American-educated political scientist and propagandist Azikiwe, whose spur was fame and wealth rather than actual power, found wanting by his people when they later sought to thrust greatness upon him. The second was Zik's antithesis, the Yoruba, London-trained lawyer Awolowo, who early identified Zik's cloudy nationalism and Africanism as a bid for Ibo dominance and Yoruba subjection, and who achieved his own greatness by single-minded determination and persever-ance in his own ambitions for his people in a federal Nigeria, making himself the judge of the morality and legality of the means to that end. The third on the scene, Sardauna of Sokoto—the one born to greatness in the Fulani ruling class—completed the dialectic by being a synthesis or a rejection of both the southern nationalisms. It is one of the strangest things on earth that these men's struggles were taken as evidence of the emergence of a democratic, multiparty federation, the great hope for the future on "the strife-torn continent of Africa" in the early 1960s. The ruthlessness and lack of restraint of these three and their followers in Nigerian politics were not recognized in time, in the atmosphere of Cold War, for what they were. Instead, the new men were further spoiled by international flattery and opportunistic admiration, from many sources. The memoirs of the three have one thing in common—the lack of modesty, the arrogance of the *prima donna assoluta:* very stony ground for the seeds of any doctrine of universal brotherhood, including communism; much more fertile ground for ideas of acquiring and using wealth for the sake of power.

Each, of course, used to be asked by foreign interviewers for views on the Cold War and on the dangers of communism; and, like other Niger-ians, they tended to tire of the questions, which they did not find inter-esting but sometimes found insulting. Though Azikiwe's eloquent career as prominent actor-manager on the Nigerian political stage required him to assume many Protean shapes (from juvenile radical lead in the 1930s through political impresario, banker and entrepreneur in the 1940s and 1950s to governor-general, president, elder statesman and exile in the 1960s), he never made an appearance as a Marxist. He was described in Gunther's *Inside Africa* in terms such as "fanatic" and "revolutionary," and in contemporary Russian terms as "petty bourgeois." Neither descrip-tion fits. Some rhetoric of "revolution" and the "masses" and "socialism" can be discovered in his writings and speeches, but the more favored sources and allusions are from a different sort of intellectual syllabus, including Burke, Locke, Hobbes, Rousseau, Lincoln, Marcus Garvey,[6] Emerson, Talleyrand, Frank Buchman, the Old and New Testaments, and classical writings (his autobiography is titled, without modesty,

*My Odyssey*). The absence of Marx and Lenin is conspicuous and complete. Zik was certainly a man of two worlds at least, overlapping and
rather mixed, with some of the European part of his heritage acquired
from Britain, a good deal more from his American studies. Zik's range
of self-images is curious, dreamlike: sometimes he played the self-made
capitalist, the successful banker, newspaper magnate and businessman,
reveling in his cigars, his presidential railway carriage, his field marshal's
uniform, his retinue of sycophants. At other times, his vision was of
himself as an assassination victim; at still others, as Jason in search of
the Golden Fleece, as a great athlete and sporting hero, and by 1940, as
kingmaker and sage to be:

My great tomorrow, if my life is spared, should be spent in an idyllic
atmosphere, in an environment of pastoral grandeur, in a campus, where
the shades and spirits of by-gone eras, the bubbling youths of Renascent
Africa, the corps of academicians and professors of Old Renascent Africa,
shall gather round a cloistered hearth with me, firing the imagination of
African youth, steeling the spirits of African youth, and building the
foundation and superstructure of a New Africa.[7]

These are strange, mixed ideas or ideals—but always the assertion is
one of dignity rather than naked power; the implied need is that Africans
too should be admired as dignified, wealthy and wise; there is no hint of
puritanical leveling down to a classless society. There is, in rhetoric of this
kind, a divorce from reality, deliberate or not, which does not mean that
Zik ever forsook materialism for idealism; in fact, the preface to his
autobiography has this dichotomy neatly sewn together by the second
paragraph:

Since attaining manhood, I have had to fend for myself in a world where
idealism and materialism are usually opposed to each other. In the course
of my life's odyssey, I have been convinced that I must be idealistic to
justify my existence as a human being; but I must also be materialistic
to adapt myself to the concatenations of a materialistic world. To steer
between these two, it became necessary for me to be eclectic and pragmatic: to draw the best from each philosophy and make it work to my
advantage in the light of reason and experience.[8]

So much for political philosophy. Materialism wins, it is clear, but a
materialism that shows immunity to Marxian infection. Indeed, Zik
himself produced a sort of certificate of this immunity, from an authoritative record of a conversation in London before the war between himself
and a senior British administrator on leave from Nigeria, who expressed
surprise, at their first meeting, at Zik's evident loyalty to the British

Empire. "I humorously remarked: 'You must have thought that I was a Bolshie!' 'Of course not,' he said. . . ."[9]

Azikiwe's Yoruba rival and opponent, Awolowo, was from first hearing him skeptical of Zik's eloquence and motives. Just as achievement-oriented and upwardly-mobile as Zik himself (or anyone, from any society, whether modern or traditional) Awo's effortful self-improvement and self-help in acquiring an education and then, finally, a London law degree and bar qualification included jobs as uncertified teacher, clerk, typist and stenographer, bookkeeper, newspaper reporter, moneylender, taxi and truck owner, produce buyer, trader, trade union and party official. The determination reveals itself in his description of his academic attainment: "the golden objective for which I had laboured without ceasing and with unflagging perseverance for upwards of twelve years."[10] There was no question of any feeling of alienation, or of class antagonism. Awo simply set about achieving his ambition of professional status by industrious production of the necessary capital, by means of his own labor and his trading ventures, some unsuccessful. While he was away studying, his wife, like many other Nigerian women, traded and ran her business successfully. No ideological or class issue or question of left or right decided his involvement in politics. His suspicions having been aroused as to the genuineness of the Zik erudition, by 1940 he had convinced himself that Zik's policy was:

to corrode the self-respect of the Yoruba people as a group; to build up the Ibos as a master race; to magnify his own vaunted contributions to the nationalist struggles; to dwarf and misrepresent the achievements of his contemporaries; and to discount and nullify the humble but sterling quota which older politicians had made to the country's progress.[11]

Once convinced of this, he remained adamant, and there was no love lost between them.

As to Awolowo's own politics, they were (apart from his nationalism and his ambition, neither of them moderate) quite orthodox, constitutional and parliamentary—the politics one might expect from a London graduate and Middle Temple barrister of his generation—with some special admiration for the (lawyer) heroes of Indian independence and some well-developed ideas of federalism designed partly to counter Ibo unitary ambitions. Of socialism, other than "life more abundant for all," there was little trace until, after independence and for strategic reasons, Awolowo seemed driven to a radicalism of ideology as the only way left to rebuild a destroyed power base. A treason trial and prison sentence followed this undoubted aberration; and then, a remarkable turn of fortune's wheel, his release and restoration to influence as senior civil adviser to the military government. Awo, too, can be regarded as (rather inflexibly) eclectic and pragmatic, but his political inheritance of ideas—which, given a fair wind and calm sea, he would no doubt have put into effect—seems to be squarely in the British "lib/lab" tradition, complicated by a ruthlessness in ambition and in the use or misuse of public funds that has not been seen in Britain for many a year. Nevertheless, when Awo was writing from prison his *Thoughts on Nigerian Constitution,* it was Burke and Aristotle, not Marx and Lenin, and Western European institutions—party, legislative, executive, judicial and public service—that were the principal authorities and the models. He even pays a generous late tribute to "the surpassing skill in administration"[12] of the British former rulers, much pleasanter reading for them than his complaint, in the pages of Gunther's *Inside Africa* some twelve years earlier (1954), that "British administration was carried out by incompetent, inferior officials" who "did not have the true interests of the country at heart."[13] No communist this, but certainly a federalist, a constitutionalist, and in principle a parliamentary socialist. But his socialism, even if adopted, would be of a kind compatible with the capitalism, the enterprise and marketing and trading activities of Nigerian men and their wives. For centuries, it is trade and opportunities for trade that have dominated Nigerian politics and economics, for the rich, the middle classes and the poor: market values are *the* important values.

Our third man, Ahmadu Bello, Sardauna of Sokoto, lived in yet another world, with different markets and traditions. Since Wendell Willkie, at least, it has become possible to speak intelligibly of *One World,* but at about the same time it was still possible for Joyce Cary to describe one African as *A Man of Two Worlds;* and now others speak of three worlds— the two Cold War worlds and a third world, or tiers monde, which, if it existed, would certainly include Nigeria. It is therefore a pity that one is forced to speak of northern and southern Nigeria as two different worlds: it seems a complication, but in practice it is an oversimplification. It is not a question of a line somewhere between Moslem north and Christian or animist south, because there are millions of Moslems in the southwest and millions of non-Moslem northerners. There is no climatic or ethnic or tsetse belt line that can be firmly drawn, and the political map has been so redrawn as to obscure, if not to obliterate, that troublesome administrative division. Nevertheless, the Atlantic end of Nigeria was first drawn into the Atlantic or Western sphere of trade and European influences; and it was not until after the First World War that the northern states such as Sokoto and Bornu were "disoriented" from their age-old preoccupations and turned round to see and take part in the opportunities and markets and influences opening to the Atlantic by rail, road and river—a massive shift of interest that is reflected in the Sardauna's own autobiography and career. The turning round was economically pleasurable, politically painful and labored, and socially, for men of the ruling elite like the Sardauna, quite distasteful. It was eventually the economic calculations that were to prevail, and to preserve Nigeria's precarious unity.

It was a bizarre telescoping of history, by which medieval rulers were given only one generation's warning of a need to adapt, for their own survival, all at once, not to the recent British conquest and overrule, which had been advantageous to them in many ways, but to all the devilish infidel innovations since the seventeenth century, not merely industrialization and modernization and bureaucratization but democratization as well; to liberty, fraternity and equality with their own subjects, and possible subjection to southern Nigerians whose ways were anathema. The revolution from the top that followed the realization of what was required was very remarkable. The statecraft required to achieve electorally contrived dominance in a fundamentally alien system was produced. Had the strategy required conformance to the alternative modern model, that too, one feels, would have been managed with equal skill, had the task been left in the same hands, and the heads been left on the shoulders.

The task required a certain kind of man as leader, one born to greatness certainly, but also one with the education, the intelligence, and the conviction that advancing the north was "a matter of life and death to us."[14] His view of the state was simple enough: for him, Fulani government before the British had been "based on a democratic and a religious footing": "Nothing was done without consultative bodies and if at all, there is any deterioration in the system, that has been brought about by modern times.... When the British came to this country they found that we had our Chiefs, Schools, Judges and all that was necessary for civilisation."[15] And when regional self-government was established for the north, in 1957, he claimed it as "the restoration of the pre-1900 era, modernised, polished, democratised, refined, but not out of recognition.... The train, the car, the lorry, the aeroplane, the telephone, the hospital, the dispensary, the school, the college, the fertiliser, the hypodermic syringe have transformed Othman dan Fodio's world, but the basis is still there. The old loyalties, the old decencies, the old beliefs still hold the people of this varied Region together."[16] The same loyalties enabled the Sardauna to leave the rest of the country to his lieutenant, the federal prime minister, a better man, tied by loyalty to the north and powerless to prevent anything that the northern power had decided upon, the destruction of Awolowo's western region base being one of those things. It was that that set off the sequence leading to the first military coup of January 1966, in which the Sardauna was one of the first to be killed by a "radical" young major, a midwestern Ibo officer at the head of troops reported to be nearly all northerners.

A few more strokes of the same autobiographical brush are sufficient to show the proud, hubristic posture of the one "born to greatness," as he saw himself and his future in 1961, five years before his death:

I have never sought the political limelight or a leading position in my country. But I could not avoid the obligation of my birth and destiny. My great-great-grandfather built an Empire in the Western Sudan. It has fallen to my lot to play a not inconsiderable part in building a new nation.

. . . . . . . . . . . . . . . .

We have been under European direction for a long time and are under it no longer. We have had the greatest help from the British Administrative staff over the past years and we appreciate it profoundly, but the time for that has passed and we can no longer tolerate the admonitory finger of people we are paying: we will accept advice but not "grave warnings" from anyone, including the representatives of the United Kingdom and of foreign powers. We notice a regrettable tendency in this direction in several quarters.

I am sure that such advice is actuated by pure motives, but I fear that even these are tinged with some self-interest, for can anyone carry out the simplest act which is not coloured by his own personal feelings? We are frequently warned about the dangers and horrors of Communism, of which we are fully aware and against which we are fully armed. Otherwise would not all the numerous people of ours who have been to Russia in recent years have embraced Communism? And that has not been the case. When we get an active Soviet Consulate in Kaduna, I am sure that we shall be severely lectured on the grave risks, and possibly even horrors, of capitalism.

So far what we want of capitalism is to get some of the capital flowing our way.

They say that I am proud and impatient. . . . But I am not proud in the arrogant sense, for I know that I am merely an instrument carrying out God's will and pleasure. . . . All my time I give to my work: my life has been in the service of the State even from the time I went to school: for there I was learning for the future and that future has caught up with me. A new future lies ahead, into which I go, trusting in God's eternal mercy.[17]

It may seem insufficient to take three men only as fully representative of Nigeria's political and Cold War era. In practice, however, there were no major participants in Nigerian politics—apart, of course, from British administrative officials—who were not followers of one of them: without allegiance to or alliance with one of the three there was no access to regional or federal power. Changing of allegiance was often possible, though always risky, and ideological or political principles played little part. It was also a struggle in which there was little scope for foreign influence, whether from left or right. The superpowers, prudently enough, did not in fact meddle or overdo the wooing of the new state, but Cold War rivalry ensured that lavish supplies of arms were available for hot war in Nigeria, and that Nigeria's officer corps had been trained to see themselves as the mainstay of internal order in a threatening world full of subversion. It was then a matter of a cue; any cue or prompt, false or not, would have moved them from the wings to play their unexpectedly bloody part in the dénouement of the tragedy. But the tragedy itself had to do with the hot blood of nationalities and personalities rather than the lukewarm water of ideologies, with primordial rather than political attachments.[18]

The plentiful contradictions of Nigeria's apparently schizophrenic foreign policy or policies in the early years of independence were deeply puzzling to most foreign observers, including Britain's diplomatic representatives, who had perhaps less excuse for bewilderment than most. Many foreign observers expected to see some consistent ideological trend in policy, which in practice could not be achieved until the serious domestic issues were resolved. If one were pressed to say, now that the military have charge of polity and economy, what are the basic regularities and continuities of the Nigerian political system giving shape to political action, one might tentatively suggest, first, that the peoples of Nigeria are convinced, from all their experience of trade and politics, of the advantage of preserving unity in order to secure the economic advantages of access to the sea, to world trade, and to some share in the main source of wealth, the oilfields of the delta; second, that their basic idea of politics is still to accept a combination of the Sardauna's "Chiefs, Schools, Judges and all that is necessary for civilisation," Awolowo's "life more abundant," and Azikiwe's insistence upon dignity for the black man. Although the indignities of colonial rule and dependence may smart less as the years pass, the scars will remain and may be visible in policies and in strong reactions to anything representing white supremacy or patronizing attitudes. Nevertheless, a general preference may continue for the sort of admixture of capitalism and socialism, of tradition and modernity to which Nigerians' exposure to British rule, education and management accustomed them in the first sixty years of the twentieth century. It is therefore possible, given some prudence and immense effort on the part of their rulers, that political conflict may be containable to questions of a kind familiar to many of the older polities and city-states of which Nigeria has been constituted—questions of whose turn it is to rule as chief, of power sharing between civil and military lines of chiefs, of ingenious ways of controlling and getting rid of those too tyrannical, indolent, or corrupt; questions of judges and courts; questions of more equitable division of the spoils from production and trade; questions of consultation and consensus, and of settlement of dangerous disputes. Much as before, *plus ça change, plus c'est la même chose*. There is no revolutionary cure for the human condition, black or white, left or right; the prudent avoidance of revolutionary situations is a better way to health.

In the recent past, there has been on the whole a real upward social mobility and promotion. The withdrawal of Europeans and the increased military and civil bureaucratization of society have created enough opportunities to allay feelings of injustice and inferiority prompted by class rather than race. That may change, however, as uncontrolled urbanization is accompanied by pauperization and gross social inequalities. But objective noting of inequalities is one thing, and allowing them to continue beyond subjective resentment into revolution is another. In colonial times revolutionary situations could be defused by concessions and timely withdrawal by the white man. It is not so easy for a domestic regime, particularly the military one of last resort. The skills needed are many, civil as well as military, and are not all to be found in an army, however large. No army, in fact, is large enough to win a lasting victory in a class war: the poor cannot be fought off: they *may*, with luck, and plenty of oil, be bought off.

# 6

CARLOS JUAN MONETA

# ARGENTINE FOREIGN POLICY IN THE COLD WAR

Since the end of the Second World War, Argentina and the other middle and lesser powers have formed part of a global international system characterized by the existence of asymmetrical relations of power and by shifting interactions and alignments among its members. This imbalance of power has derived from the vast qualitative and quantitative differences between the superpowers and the rest of the world community in military capacity, in both nuclear and conventional terms; in scientific development; and in technological, economic, ideological and political evolution.[1]

Among the persisting but changing features of the system can be distinguished: the formation and transformation of the blocs of client states acquired by the United States and the USSR; the new opportunities for autonomy offered to the middle and smaller powers by the emergence of multipolar or plural diplomacy; the widening breach between the North and the South in the global family; the gradual displacement of the Cold War as an immediate source of international peril; the sudden revaluation of traditionally basic factors such as primary products and energy; the rifts and dissensions within the groups of client states; and the efforts on the part of some of the middle and smaller powers to establish independent cooperation with other states on the periphery of the Cold War. The distinctive stages of the postwar development may be categorized as: (a) semiflexible bipolarism, confrontation and contention (1945-57); (b) limited cooperation and the beginning of multipolarity (1957-62); (c) transition from limited cooperation to extended cooperation and multipolarity (1962-72); (d) "World Pacification," or the transition towards a new system of concerted condominium (1972-    ).[2]

In general, even in the most bitter moments of stages (a) and (b), each of the superpowers basically respected the sphere of predominance of its opponent, reserving the reciprocal right to impose sanctions against unco-operative members of its own bloc.[3] The case of Cuba was only a partial deviation from this rule, because Cuba had already sought a rapproche-ment with the USSR before the severe coercions were applied by the United States.[4] That there has been no modification in the monopoly of discipline within the respective areas of influence of the superpowers is witnessed by the action of the USSR in Hungary (1956) and Czechoslovakia (1968) and by that of the United States in Guatemala (1954) and the Dominican Republic (1965). The system was not inflexible, however, and coercions and rewards have been regulated by mutual agreement in the intermediate areas, as in the Arab-Israeli conflict. Moreover, an autono-mous course of conduct, going as far as actual secession from a power bloc, need not invariably occasion serious coercion. In the last issue, the Dominant Power may be deterred by the prospect of either provoking a nuclear war or inviting further schisms among its client states.[5] For example, armed intervention is not likely to be applied solely to defend economic interests.[6] The United States, at least, has been prepared to put up with a significant degree of autonomous action within its sphere of in-fluence, provided there is no implication of political secession.[7] Character-istically, it prefers to deal with autonomous moves by indirect means, such as supporting internal groups attempting to restore the status quo of the dependent relationship, as in the change from Allende to Pinochet in Chile.

The history of the nineteenth century and of the twentieth century prior to the Second World War reveals the following basic objectives in Argentine foreign policy: (a) affiliation to the British zone of influence; (b) opposition to the predominance of the United States; (c) relative isolationism with regard to the rest of Latin America; (d) preoccupation with the maintenance of a balance of power favorable, or at least not injurious, to the southern part of South America. The first objective was aimed primarily at providing an extracontinental balance to the pressure exerted by Spain during the struggle for independence, and by the United States after the middle of the nineteenth century. Opposition to the United States had indeed developed even before the formulation of the Pan-American policy by the North Americans. This policy was, of course, designed to institutionalize an economic and political system that would permit the United States to consolidate its influence in Latin America, so as to safeguard its commercial interests, and also to establish a strategic zone of security against European intervention. Argentina resisted the advance of North American hegemony, at first during the Pan-American conferences and later in other continental forums, while at the same time developing its own bilateral agreements with other Latin American countries, based on the principle of nonintervention. However, the shift from Dollar Diplomacy to the Good Neighbor Policy signified a change in the the North American attitude towards Latin America, particularly after the Montevideo Conference (1933), at which the United States agreed to respect the principle of nonintervention and began to pursue a policy of détente with Argentina. This phase endured until the beginning of the Second World War. U. S. policy was further modified by the extension of the global conflict. The United States was then compelled to try to safeguard its supplies of basic war materials, to counter subversive German or Italian activities through the various ethnic minority groups in Latin America, and to encourage increasing involvement in the war on the part of the Latin Americans. However, the United States continued to abstain from direct intervention. It demanded in return that the Latins adopt collective security measures, break relations with and declare war upon the Axis powers, and terminate trading links with Continental Europe.[8] Argentina opposed these endeavors throughout the war years in an attempt to defend its own vital economic interests, which involved the preservation of access to the European market.

The relative isolation of Argentina among other Latin American states was due largely to its extracontinental links with European powers. These links were ethnic and cultural, as well as political and economic. The European powers involved sought for their part to minimize Argentina's contacts with the rest of Latin America, while at the same time encouraging opposition to the growth of the predominant power of the United States. This European strategy has persisted up to the present. We also now find on the part of the Latin Americans a renewed disposition to establish forms of association with external powers such as China and the USSR, as well as with Europe, again in opposition to the United States. Naturally, the consolidation of U. S. power has made it more difficult for the Europeans to influence Latin American opposition to the United States.[9] However, we must not overlook the vast European economic interests in Latin America, especially in view of the need of the EEC to expand its markets and of the political ambitions of individual European states (such as Gaullist France) seeking to preserve their own political independence from the United States. In the case of the USSR and China, the political motivation is naturally paramount, although again their commercial interests and their economic and technological aid programs have increasing importance.

The significance of Latin American relationships varies for Argentina according to two main factors—the distribution of power in the subregion, and the organization of alignments against the United States. On the first point, Argentina and Brazil, the two most important countries of Latin America, have a long tradition of rivalry for preeminence in the subregion. Both have therefore the greatest interest in the policy adopted by the United States in allotting rewards or sanctions and in attempts to disturb the existing balance of power between them. It is most appropriate here to examine the nature of Argentine opposition to the concept of full participation in U. S. projects during the Second World War. Initially, U. S. officials attributed Argentine actions primarily to the Nazi or Fascist sympathies of the regimes of Castillo, Ramírez and Farrell. This simplistic explanation, which condemned the whole power structure of Argentina, did not take into account the complements of domestic politics and national interests. Such a condemnation of Argentine policy on ideological grounds, indeed, served mainly to rationalize and justify the maintenance by the United States of policies hostile to Argentina in the postwar period. It provided in particular an ideological interpretation for the policies adopted by Argentina during the first years of the regime of General Perón, whose government retained certain Nazi or Fascist aspects. This analysis of the heterodox position adopted by Argentina according to the formula of the "Third Position" (relations with the USSR, opposition to the United States in Pan-American and international forums, etc.) became confused with a new specter appropriate to the epoch, that of International Communism.

The neutrality maintained tenaciously by Argentina during the Second World War reflected the development of a policy aimed at safeguarding its vital national interests. This policy was concerned first of all with the need to safeguard European markets, which were essential to Argentina's economy and access to which required full freedom of the seas for peaceful commerce. Argentina also feared that the political, military and economic intrusion of the United States, aimed at consolidating North American hegemony over Latin America, would drastically reduce Argentina's freedom of action and threaten it with economic subservience under the threat of intervention. In 1942 the U. S. Department of State prepared a scheme of industrialization and commercial exchanges which would have benefited not Argentina but its traditional economic competitor, Brazil. The policy of rearmament adopted by Argentina was thus designed to compensate for its growing isolation brought about by U. S. diplomacy and to restore the balance of power in the subregion that had been altered by the massive economic, technical and military assistance given to Brazil by the United States. The Second World War, with its theaters of operations far from South America, did not itself directly endanger Argentine security. Nonetheless, anxiety necessarily arose as a result of the policy adopted by its rival, Brazil, which initially demonstrated clear sympathy for the Axis powers but then opted for alignment with the United States, actively participating in the war in order to acquire an industrial infrastructure with U. S. aid, as well as a formidable military capacity.[10] The development of Argentine defense capacity, however, evoked hostility on the part of the United States, thereby compelling Argentina to look to Germany for aid, and thus giving the North Americans an excuse to increase their attempts to coerce the military regime in Buenos Aires.

The relationship between Argentine ideology and political and economic interests was indeed complete. The oligarchic forces in power with Castillo (1941-43) displayed similar interests to those of the military regime of Ramírez-Farrell (1943-46) and even those of Perón, whose ideological alignment seemed quite distinct. A contemporary North American observer, in fact, forecast correctly that Argentina would attempt to avoid being incorporated in the U. S. system and that this struggle would unite the nationalists with the economic oligarchy. For the former, the Second World War provided an opportunity to free the Argentine economy from foreign domination. For the oligarchs, it was a matter of preserving their financial relationship with Britain.[11] For both, it was a choice between neutrality or accepting U. S. domination.[12]

Some North Americans were able to define precisely the real intentions of the United States and the implications of its policy of coercion as applied against Argentina during the Second World War and the immediate postwar years. Richard Pattee, for example, suggested four possible motivations for U. S. policy: (1) to force Argentina to declare war on the Axis; (2) to force the Argentine people to overthrow their government by revolution and replace it with one that the United States approved of; (3) to get rid of the military regime and restore civil government; and (4) to allow the unrestricted domination of the United States over the economic life of Argentina, thereby eliminating the interests of Britain and other European powers.[13] The efforts of Cordell Hull in this direction during the war were followed by the open intervention of Ambassador Braden in the elections of 1945, which gave validity to the slogan "Braden or Perón," and his later attempts to "save democracy and combat dictatorship and Fascism in Argentina."[14] The result was decisive. Perón was elected president in February 1946. Sumner Welles, in his analysis of Argentine-U. S. relations, commented: "As a result of the policy followed by the USA with respect to Argentina during the past two and a half years, this nation has received at the hands of the Argentine people the most serious diplomatic setback suffered in the Western Hemisphere, involving a loss in influence and prestige in South America which will not be forgotten for many years."[15] Welles's words are indeed an appropriate commentary on the significance of ideology in U. S. policy. Without pretending that the resemblance was total, the fact is that both the regime of Getulio Vargas in Brazil and of the military revolutionary groups in Argentina in 1943 showed sympathy for Fascist models and demonstrated certain authoritarian features in their domestic systems. Both also opposed the adoption of the U. S. system of democracy throughout South America. But so far was the United States from "ejecting anti-democratic and Fascist elements from the sub-region" that it actually assisted the designs of Vargas to extend Brazilian control over the continent.

With the rise of General Perón to power in June 1946 there was put into practice in Argentina a policy of political, social and economic development based on national capitalism[16] and characterized by the incorporation into the economic system of the vast market of the urban and rural workers, by means of syndicalizations, political involvement and the redistribution of wealth; and by the general mobilization of national resources without the traditional divisions between internal and foreign interests, with the general objective of increasing the control of the state over the general management of the economy. The adjustment of the interests of the proletariat and the bourgeoisie within the system reduced class conflicts to a manageable level. The workers, along with the army and the church, in effect constituted the basic triad of Peronismo, to which were opposed in the elections a coalition of central groups, with elements from the Left, including the Communists, led by the upper classes, alarmed by the social reforms and legislation introduced by Perón during his term as Secretary of Labor during the preceding military regime. The essence of his appeal was populist, with a direct charismatic relationship between the leader of the party and the masses, in which the role of the party structure was minimized.

In economic matters Perón amplified and institutionalized the controls developed by the Radical and Conservative regimes, as well as by the military regimes, with particular reference to exchange rates, banking and credit, wages and the marketing of primary products, meat and petroleum. Articles 38 and 40 of the Constitution of 1949 determined that private property should have a social function. Economic activity was left in private hands, except for foreign trade, which came under the control of the state, as did the public utilities, mining, petroleum, gas, coal and other sources of energy, which constituted the inalienable heritage of the nation. Perón also introduced state monopolies, such as the Argentine Institute for the Promotion of Foreign Exchange (IAPI), which controlled foreign trade; and mixed enterprises combining the private sector and the state, such as the General Direction of Arms Manufactures, which controlled the exploitation of copper, iron, manganese and other strategic metals and directed the development of the economy. These constituted the economic element of a new doctrine, the Third Position between capitalism and communism.[17]

The reform of the economic structure used the existing system of controls for a new purpose—economic independence, through the creation of a national industry, the control of national resources, and the management of finance and credit. The principal effort was always in the area of light industry, and, to a lesser extent, heavy industry. However, primary industry also came increasingly under the direction of the state, through its control of supplies of equipment.[18] The Central Bank was nationalized, national and industrial banks created, the merchant fleet increased, a national airline (Aerolineas Argentinas) formed, and a tanker fleet built. The policy of nationalization placed in the hands of the state the control of coal, iron, steel, gas, telecommunications and urban transport, repatriating the whole of the foreign debt in this sector. Argentina presented a pattern of striking economic development from 1945 to the end of 1948, experiencing thereafter a recession that reached its lowest level at the end of 1952. The factors aiding growth in the first phase were the reorganization of the resources of agriculture and industry and the improvement of prices in a world desperate for primary products, which permitted the maintenance of the high level of imports required for a program of industrialization. Further elements were the reduction of the foreign debt and the nationalization of foreign corporations.[19]

Negative factors, however, emerged with the deterioration in the terms of trade, with consequent balance of payments difficulties, compelling a reduction in imports of capital equipment. The fall in agricultural prices was accelerated by the policies of other powers (for instance, the United States diverted its own surpluses to Europe by way of the Marshall Plan). Official policy, accordingly, reversed itself, encouraging agricultural production by speeding up mechanization.[20] However, the deteriorating balance of payments situation caused a drastic decline in industrial and general economic growth, leading to a fall in the price of shares. Reserves of foreign exchange fell rapidly and forced Argentina to borrow $125 million from the Export-Import Bank in 1950, most of which ($96.5 million) was to pay for imports from the United States. The need increased rapidly the production of domestic petroleum to replace imports, while at the same time protection of domestic industrial development aggravated the balance of payments crisis. These developments decisively affected domestic political evolution. The Opposition, which found its base in the Radical groups, with their old socialist and conservative allies, increased its strength considerably during the economic crisis. An attempt to reach a compromise between Government and Opposition failed in 1953. This led to the fall of the Government, already in conflict with the Church.

The Peronist management of the economic and political process up to 1955, designed to create the bases of a genuinely autonomous future, required the existence of a solid mass support, structured and organized, and the functioning of an economic apparatus oriented towards the employment of national resources for national ends. Despite its failure, one can appreciate Perón's effort as a serious attempt to reduce significantly Argentina's dependence in the external as well as the internal spheres and to reduce the basic injustice and disequilibrium inherent in the existing power structure.

In the area of foreign trade, Argentina's position vis-à-vis the United States followed the same pattern as before the war, although the problems of triangulation and inconvertibility decidedly aggravated its problems. In 1946 and 1947 there were favorable balances of international payments, with surpluses outside the dollar area and deficits within it. The inconvertibility of the pound sterling in 1947 prevented the transfer of funds to pay for imports from the United States. The situation was stated clearly in the Report of the Central Bank: "Two-thirds of Argentine exports are destined to countries with which we maintain bilateral trading relations, while most of our imports have to come from the USA, awaiting the slow recovery of the European countries."[21] The balance of payments remained favorable until 1949. However, Argentina had serious deficits in 1950, 1951 and 1952, due to the failure of export prices to rise and due to the growth in imports of fuel and industrial raw materials.

Argentine trade has been characterized by bilateralism, envisaged by the government as a contractual arrangement to secure supplies of basic materials[22] and conflicting necessarily with the multilateralism favored by the United States. Equally important until 1949 was the attempt to maintain a preferential commercial and economic link with Britain and Europe in general, based on bilateral arrangements with most European countries, as a means of strengthening Argentina's position against the United States. This also encouraged the "economic unions" and bilateral accords with Chile, Bolivia, Ecuador, Nicaragua and Paraguay, which represented a genuine effort to organize progressive economic integration in the subregion, based on bilateral accords. Commercial triangulation was imposed because "Argentina was obliged to ensure, through bilateral accords, the sale of its export surpluses and the acquisition of its basic requirements."[23]

Negotiations with Europe were based on the Eady-Bramuglia Treaty with Britain in 1946, involving arrangements for payment, the sale of meat and iron and the negotiation of a commercial convention; and the Andes Convention of February 1948, which sought to regularize the sale of nationalized iron products and the position of Argentine funds deposited in London before the inconvertibility of the pound in the previous year. In 1949 a commercial agreement worth 129 million was concluded with Britain for five years, terminable at a year's notice. By this agreement Argentina undertook to supply meat, grains, cereals, oil and primary products, receiving petroleum, coal, steel and manufactured goods in exchange.[24] This agreement, essential for the policy of extracontinental relationships, caused grave concern in the United States because it reaffirmed bilateralism, signified a serious obstacle to U. S. sales of petroleum and manufactures to Argentina, and impeded the strengthening of U. S. influence in Buenos Aires. The United States accordingly applied pressure on Britain, threatening to cancel aid to that country, to compel London to introduce substantial changes in the Andes Convention.[25] Afterwards, Argentina effected other alterations to obtain better prices for its imports of fuel and nonessential items.[26] A new commercial treaty was concluded with Britain in 1955.

Argentina's postwar activities in the global, regional and bilateral arenas were all influenced by the new configuration of the international bipolar system, by the remodeling of the Pan-American subsystem proposed by the United States to adjust to the needs of the new situation, and by the evolution of the new distribution of world power. Argentina sought in its foreign policy to improve its national welfare; to strengthen its sovereignty; to assist its development in the economic, social, scientific, technological and cultural fields; and to increase its capacity for effective participation in the international system. The methods chosen, of course, differed according to whether Perón or the Liberal Revolution was in office. It is nonetheless possible to identify certain objectives sought by all the postwar regimes. These were the amelioration of the distribution of subregional power, the strengthening of the national frontiers, and the preservation of extracontinental links of support. In the case of Perón, there was also what may be termed a policy of heterodox autonomy, i.e., a policy seeking to increase autonomy progressively through limited and selected confrontations with the Dominant Power.[27]

The defense of Argentina's national frontiers involved the intensification of the conflict with Britain over the Malvinas; the scientific exploitation of the Argentine sector of the Antarctic and the defense of sovereignty in the political as well as in the juridical and diplomatic fields; the accords with Chile; and the declaration of sovereignty over the Argentine sector of the continental shelf. In addition to reorganizing the National Commission of the Antarctic (1946), creating the Antarctic Institute, installing new permanent bases and sending numerous expeditions to the area, Argentina claimed in the Inter-American Conference on the Maintenance of the Peace and Security of the Continent that the "Zone of American Security" should cover the Malvinas, South Georgia, the Sandwich Islands and the Antarctic sector. In the General Assembly of the UN, the Legal Commission of the UN, OEA and the World Meteorological Organization, the diplomats of the Palacio San Martin similarly reiterated their defense of national rights over these territories.[28] The defense of Antarctica precipitated confrontations with both the USSR and the United States. In June 1950 the USSR presented a note to the Argentine government referring to "the pretensions of certain countries and the Antarctic problem in general."[29] In a secret memorandum to the U. S. State Department that noted the reservations of the United States respecting the affirmation of Argentine sovereignty in Antarctica, Buenos Aires claimed that its national rights did not admit of any compromise.[30]

The interrelation of these diverse elements and the use of the confrontation of the Cold War to increase the freedom of action available against the United States generally characterized the conduct of Argentine foreign policy in this period. For example, Perón had intended to ask the United States to support the position of Argentina against Britain over the Malvinas. However, in the Conference of Bogotá (1948) Argentina had strongly opposed the acceptance of the principle of intervention in a proposal for collective security that would have given a supranational capacity to the central organ of the OAS. Similarly, Argentina opposed a plan by the United States, Chile and Brazil to eradicate all subversive Communist and totalitarian activity. In a long conversation with Ambassador Bruce, in April 1948, during which he discussed extensively the relations between the two countries, Perón exhibited his suspicion of communism and his desire to oppose its penetration in South America. He also referred to Foreign Minister Bramuglia's opposition to the U. S. proposal for anti-Communist cooperation at Bogotá: "Speaking frankly ... Argentina wants the Malvinas and you [USA] want an anti-Communist pact; we were playing a little poker at Bogotá."[31]

Argentina's relative isolation in Latin America was transformed into a systematic and coherent program aimed at solidarity. Through the commercial accords and "economic unions" Argentina attempted to modify the structure of international trade in Latin America, hitherto directed towards the United States and Europe, attributing new importance to intraregional commerce. This policy helped to resolve the economic problems of Argentina and other countries of the region by increasing their power relative to that of the United States and favoring a stronger political relationship, which was put in practice with limited success. In the area of Latin American action on continental problems, one can point to Argentine diplomatic activity in numerous Pan-American conferences in defense of adequate prices for primary producers, the liberalization and expansion of the North American market, the erection of protective measures, the importance of increasing Latin American production, and the need for economic and social change. Argentina in particular condemned U. S. techniques of surplus disposal, which provided impossible competition for the less developed countries of Latin America, and put forward its own program of technical and financial aid. For example, in the Fifth Inter-American Conference (Caracas, 1954), Argentina openly and explicitly attacked U. S. surplus policies and the legalisms invoked to defend them. It accused the United States of having used Marshall Plan funds to finance programs of agricultural development in European colonies in Asia and Africa in competition with Latin American producers.[32] The Argentine foreign minister affirmed that "in the sphere of the national communities, the despair of the masses indicates everywhere the disparities and injustices of capitalistic individualism; in the field of international relations we assist at a process by virtue of which two-thirds of the world, which represents deprived humanity, seek to obtain relentlessly a more equitable share of the goods created by their efforts."[33] Elsewhere emphasis was placed on foreign investment and on the need to assure markets for the exports of Latin America. Argentina especially insisted on the need to provide technical assistance for the development of the continent.[34] In the Third Extraordinary Meeting of the Inter-American Economic and Social Council in Caracas, in February 1953, Argentina presented specific proposals, including one referring to regional economic integration, recommending that the American governments establish organizations of this nature in Latin America. Argentina also asked for assistance for the industrial development of the American countries and for improved opportunities for trade in primary products. The Fourth Meeting of the IESC evoked a bitter attack by Argentina on the Bretton Woods Agreements, "which did not satisfy the real needs of developing countries."[35]

Perón clearly saw that a policy of heterodox autonomy in Latin America required, besides a certain measure of power, skillful utilization of capacity to influence international, regional and internal developments; a firm political base with a strong national economy; and a favorable regional environment, providing support for autonomous measures by other powers of equivalent status. Apart from the organization of domestic support, the aggregation of power in Latin America should offer means for a viable autonomous policy by Argentina. However, in Perón's case, as in that of other leaders who have sought to execute autonomous politics (e.g., Frondizi), these policies proved in large measure actually incompatible. Thus Perón's efforts were limited in their effects and Frondizi's nullified.

In the still famous conference called in November 1953 at the National Military Academy, Perón spelled out the lines his country should follow in international politics. He indicated the opportunities and problems of the year 2000: conurbations of vast magnitude, overpopulation and a tremendous scarcity of grain and primary materials. He forecast that the struggle for their possession would be violent and that the future of nations would be determined by their reserves of basic foodstuffs. Latin America, and particularly the subregion, possessed these riches and open spaces. Their development and defense demanded "the real and effective union of these countries" and the organization of a common defense of their resources.[36] For this purpose, the permanent union of Chile, Brazil and Argentina would provide the nucleus for the progressive union of Latin America.

With these objectives, Perón delineated a program of continental union after 1946. As has already been seen, this was in large measure a continuation of the efforts of the military regime of 1943. Brazil, with its resources, population and space, necessarily continued (as it does up to the present) to provide a fundamental element in such a project. Perón accordingly discussed his projects with Getulio Vargas (Brazil) and with General Ibáñez (Chile). "Getulio Vargas was totally and absolutely in agreement with this plan and attempted to apply it when in office. . . ."[37] Space does not permit a full account of the Brazilian-Argentine interaction, which has lasted up to the present day. It is important to note that a cycle of confrontation and cooperation manifested itself in these years. The basic goals of cooperation were shared by the more nationalistic group in the government of Vargas, before his fall in 1945, and by the Argentine military regime. Perón revived them with Vargas in the fifties, but without success, due to certain internal and external factors influencing Brazilian politics. Most important of these were the activities of the economic groups linked with the United States and the nationalists, who now feared that an accord with Buenos Aires might lose them a chance of predominance in the subregion. (It should be remembered that the book *Geopolitics of Brazil*—the basis for an actual Brazilian geopolitical concept—was written in those days.)

Among the external elements was the factor that Brazil and Chile both had governments that sought to play an independent role. This was fully appreciated by the U. S. State Department. For example, as early as 1948 a memorandum prepared for Assistant Secretary Armour declared: "It seems unlikely that Argentina will have much success in creating an austral bloc, particularly if we succeed in strengthening the inter-American system. . . . We should not permit an exaggerated fear of an austral bloc to obscure our objectives in strengthening the inter-American system."[38]

The government of the Liberal Revolution of 1955 nonetheless attempted to create an atmosphere favorable to an accord with Brazil. However, the idea of Joao Goulart linked with Kubitschek as a competitor for the Brazilian presidency alarmed the Argentine military leaders. Goulart was doubly suspect in their eyes; his political speeches had earned him the reputation of a Marxist-Populist. In October 1955, on the eve of the Brazilian elections, Buenos Aires declared that Goulart had had contacts with Perón during his reign, seeking arms for a workers' militia in Brazil.[39] This broke the Kubitschek-Goulart front. It may be supposed that this political maneuver was intended to evoke a reaction by the Brazilian armed forces, who might then install in Rio a military regime of the same type as that in power in Buenos Aires; or, the maneuver might at least incline the balance to the Tavora-Campos combination. In either case, it was hoped to obtain an atmosphere favorable to close political accord between the two governments.

An Argentine-Brazilian accord contemplating the extension and liberalization of economic, cultural and political relations between the two nations and "the realisation of permanent consultations of all matters of common interest and the coordination of policies in the continental and global spheres" did indeed form the "Convention of Friendship and Consultation" arrived at by Jânio Quadros and Arturo Frondizi in Uruguay on 21 April 1961. But a new factor was the opposition to this accord manifested on both sides of the frontier. The crisis provoked by the accession of Quadros and the strong opposition of those groups favoring a position of privileged dependency for Brazil, as well as the apprehensions felt by those Argentines with a limited strategic view, together with the actions of groups linked with the United States, all constituted obstacles that could not be overcome. Thus was lost an opportunity to unite the two most important elements on the continent in a movement towards a combined autonomous policy.[40]

The coup of 1966, which displaced the radical government of President Illía and installed the military regime of the so-called Argentine Revolution, was concerned above all with the growth of Brazilian power. Onganía attempted to strengthen Argentina's position in the subregion and to reach a modus vivendi with Brazil. This set off a dialectical interaction between the forces seeking a position of privileged dependency with the United States and the growing geopolitical and economic problems arising from the use and conservation of natural resources and the control of the avenues of transport and communications in the River Plate Basin. With Brazil fully embarked upon the path of expansion and subregional predominance adopted after 1964, looking forward to augmenting the difference in power between Argentina and itself and extending its influence over the less developed powers of the continent, the necessity for seeking an accord with Buenos Aires assumed progressively less importance. The similarity in the ideological stance of the two regimes towards communism led to certain coincidences of policy without leading to any effective schemes of cooperation. Hence, the ineffectiveness and vagaries of the attempts of Onganía to reach an accord with Brazil based on a similarity of ideologies.[41] The prospects of an entente diminished rapidly while tensions rose on both banks of the River Plate.

The collapse of Onganía's strategy led to a significant change of policy under the regime of General Lanusse, who attempted an alteration (more apparent than real) in Argentina's position with regard to the United States and the rest of Latin America. Officially, the new line was based on a regard for the concept of "political pluralism in the international community." This principle was enunciated in the Declaration of Salta, reached between President Lanusse and Allende of Chile, outlining a policy of full cooperation and economic exchanges between regimes of differing ideology. Compared with the rigid line pursued by Brazil, the acceptance of a moderate flexibility in this area (although the permissiveness of ideological heterodoxy did not go so far as to include Cuba) favored a political and economic alignment between Argentina and countries and groups more autonomous, like the Andean Group. Such a development would have strengthened the position of Buenos Aires in Latin America and permitted the adoption of a stronger attitude towards Brazil. But changes of regime occurred in both countries, causing political instability, all at a time when Brazil was seeking to strengthen its own relations with the rest of Latin America. "Political pluralism" dissipated itself in rhetoric, without concrete results. Lines of communication—not put into practice—were indeed officially established with Chile. However, it was not possible to effect the desired changes in the policies of Brazil, Paraguay or Bolivia.[42] The Agreement of New York, which theoretically was to provide for the development of Paraguayan-Brazilian enterprises in the Plate Basin, soon demonstrated its ineffectiveness. The government of Dr. Cámpora, who assumed office with massive popular support in May 1973, attempted to revive Perón's project to commence strategic works in the area, to increase the possibility of an autonomous policy.

These examples indicate the permanent importance of the subregion in the formulation of Argentine foreign policy. The governments of these countries, whatever their political aims, necessarily are concerned to maintain good relations with Brazil. It is nonetheless possible to attempt to strengthen the links between Buenos Aires and La Paz, Asunción, Montevideo and Santiago, or at least to try to neutralize or reduce the effects of similar policies pursued by Brazil. The preservation of subregional equilibrium in the face of Brazil's determination to achieve predominance remains a constant factor in Argentine external policy. Argentina's own relationship with Brazil reveals differing motivations, depending on whether the government in Buenos Aires seeks to be autonomous or dependent. In the first case, good relations are sought basically as a means of uniting forces against the Dominant Power. In the second, they are sought as a means of reducing competition between the two countries, in order to achieve greater privileges from the United States. However, since even dependent regimes wish to preserve some degree of autonomy, they will seek to combine their forces to some extent (e.g., the project of the Liberal Revolution in 1956 for a joint defense of the South Atlantic with Brazil and Paraguay).

An examination of Argentine conduct during the postwar period reveals the importance of extracontinental relationships. The Third Position was, in fact, largely an attempt to increase freedom of maneuver vis-à-vis the United States. For a time, Britain provided one base for external support, but its efficacy declined rapidly after the forties. Argentina could not openly oppose the United States in fundamental issues, for fear of the ensuing imbalance of power. It would, for example, have been impossible to avoid siding with the United States in the case of conflict with the USSR. The government of Perón could not effectively alter this situation, but the skill with which its external policy was developed permitted some degree of flexibility.[43] Unfailing awareness of the limits imposed by circumstances, concentration on increasing the margin for maneuver, and an unfailing sense of opportunity all helped to extend Argentina's area of autonomous action.[44] The following examples show this policy in action.

The doctrine of the Third Position implied a new ideological alternative to the polarization of the Cold War. It also suggested an alternative relationship between man and society. According to the Address of the President to Congress on 1 May 1952, this doctrine would seek to avoid the evils of both capitalism and collectivism. As Perón told Ambassador Bruce, who complained that "these statements usually created a bad impression in other American countries," he himself did "not believe in a Communist or Socialist state or any form of totalitarian economy . . . but . . . the purely capitalist countries frequently have trusts or monopolies which cause abuses."[45] Public utilities, for example, should be owned and operated by the government. In the international field, however, the Third Position did not imply a rigid neutrality that would free Argentina from capitalism only to let it fall into the other extreme. Perón assured the ambassador that Argentina would not seek to adopt a neutral position between the United States and the USSR in the case of conflict; in such an event, Argentina would immediately take the side of the United States.

The fact was that Argentina was in a difficult position. The shortage of armaments remained acute. The United States did not recognize the new regime until it had accepted the obligations of the Act of Chapultepec and the San Francisco Treaty.[46] Congress applauded shortly afterwards when Foreign Minister Bramuglia declared publicly that Argentine sovereignty had not been infringed or even compromised by these undertakings. The UN Charter and the Acts of Mexico and Chapultepec did not, in fact, supersede national sovereignty. Accepting them was merely a matter of adopting a policy acceptable to the United States in order to obtain arms and improve Argentina's position in the new global organizations, without renouncing vital Argentine interests.

Although the government was able to obtain weapons from Britain in 1947, this problem continued. Argentina was experiencing a serious dollar crisis, which could not be compensated for by sales to Europe, thanks to the operation of the Marshall Plan. The situation was described in a note from U. S. officials in Buenos Aires to the secretary of state: "Several of these officials have remarked in private conversation that unless a remedy is found for Argentina's dollar shortage it will be necessary to change this country's entire foreign policy. . . . The administration would like to show us that it can get along without dollars, but both the President and the Foreign Minister admit that it is impossible to obtain what they desire from Russia and the satellite countries. . . . Industrialization has become almost a mania with Perón and some of his Cabinet and they realize that the industrialization programme cannot be carried out without American equipment, machinery and technical know-how. If the dollar shortage continues, Argentina will have to abandon a good part of its Five-Year Plan."[47] The need for capital and equipment became even more serious in the years following. The links with Britain collapsed; the internal political and economic situation deteriorated; but Perón continued with industrialization and the repatriation of the foreign debt in the hope that the situation arising from the Korean War might result in improved markets for Argentina. Limited support was given by the United States; the visit of Milton Eisenhower provided the occasion for an official display of goodwill; agreement was reached on the purchase of the Kaiser automobile works; contracts were made with California Argentina and with Royal Dutch Shell and Standard Oil of New Jersey for petrochemical development.

The strategic vision was thus complete. Perón's analysis foresaw the possibility of war between the United States and the USSR, and his clear perception of the intentions of the United States towards Latin America and his vision of the bipolar world and the Third World provided the technique for the full application of the Third Position in the international arena. However, the Third World was in a state of gestation between 1945 and the opening years of the next decade. One could discern some potential foci of power (e.g., India, Yugoslavia), but the greater number of the Afro-Asian countries were still struggling for independence and had not emerged from the status of colonies. Perón proclaimed his Third Position to these peoples, but the Third World was incapable yet of comprehending it. The system never became a nucleus capable of combining the powers and the potentials of the Third World. With bipolarity at its most severe, bids for autonomy in the zone of influence of either Dominant Power were likely to be dangerously penalized (witness Yugoslavia in Eastern Europe). If one looks at the conduct of India, one of the leading forces in the intermediate zone, one notes that even Nehru, a bitter critic of bipolarism, conceded in Parliament that in the event of war between the United States and the USSR, India would support the United States, as the lesser of two evils.

Perón had to consider too the serious problem of what might happen if Argentina were to persist in a refusal to become involved in a new war. The advances in technology meant that this war would differ radically from any other. The European theater of operations would be wiped out; it would be more difficult to maintain lines of communication than during World War II; and the economic devastation in Europe would be far greater. The United States would want to acquire stocks of primary materials from Latin America in return for arms, of which it would be the sole provider. Could Argentina allow these factors to contribute to a new aggrandizement of Brazilian capacity, breaking the balance of power permanently? How would Argentine security be affected by taking an active part in the war? Would the USSR and Eastern Europe come to represent important markets, and would it be possible to gain access to them? There was also the ideological element to be considered. Perón had repeatedly indicated his anti-Communist position and had denounced the Soviet regime as a form of imperialism, albeit of a form different from that of the United States. This authentically expressed his position. But it did not necessarily entail his being anti-Soviet and therefore pro-American in a Cold War sense. The doctrine of the Third Position was quite explicit in this regard. In any event, the "organized community" of Peronismo was a variety of national capitalism and not a model for socialism. Perón had therefore told Ambassador Bruce in 1948 that Argentina's position "had been planned over two years ago and there had been no deviation from this determination and there would be none."[48] Bruce decided himself that "in the President's mind there is little or no doubt that war is inevitable between the United States and Russia."[49]

Argentina's attempts to provide guarantees in extreme situations and simultaneously maintain independent positions elsewhere contributed to the uncertainty and confusion over Argentine policy that troubled many officials of the U. S. State Department, whose thinking was understandably influenced by the legacy of the Second World War and the concept of "all or nothing." The capacity for negotiation that Argentina was attempting to gain by this policy and the way in which it was influenced by the methods of the Dominant Power itself were never correctly evaluated. It was nonetheless early appreciated that a hard line against Argentina would positively delay the formation of the anti-Soviet bloc desired by the United States. Ambassador Bruce took these factors into account in his recommendations to Washington: "We are convinced that if we carry out a wise and realistic policy towards Argentina, we can have this country on our side in the event of real trouble with Russia. . . . There are strong nationalistic elements in Perón's Government which are opposed to any form of cooperation with the United States. [However] Perón . . . is coming more and more to the realization that cooperation with the United States is desirable. . . . We cannot hope to accomplish anything worthwhile by a policy of unilateral condemnation and turning a cold shoulder to Argentina. . . . We cannot hope to have real American unity unless our relations with Argentina are on at least a reasonably friendly basis."[50]

The basic objectives of the United States in its policy towards Argentina included, essentially: the incorporation of that country in Washington's scheme of active Pan-American anticommunism; the surety of being able to count on Argentine support in the event of war; the introduction of certain changes in the political structure and domestic economy of Argentina; the obtaining of agreement to the installation of military bases (an objective applicable to all Latin America); condominium in the Antarctic; and the prevention or frustration of any attempts by Buenos Aires to achieve economic or diplomatic unions that might conflict with intentions, or to acquire an extracontinental basis of support that might strengthen Argentina's capacity for autonomy. There was, naturally, some difference of ideas in the State Department as to how these objectives should best be attained. For example, it was believed that Argentina was seeking some kind of Marshall Plan for Latin America "to gain greater international influence and concomitantly to attain a greater degree of industrialization with the attendant assured markets in South America." However, on the question of whether this Argentine objective should be opposed or assisted: "We should not be disturbed by this. The more Argentina is involved in over-all Latin American cooperation, the less possibility there is of an austral bloc. Argentina's neighbours can be trusted not to deliver themselves fully into that country's power. We should strongly encourage Argentine economic cooperation in inter-American matters."[51]

It is easy to see the apparatus of domination at the disposal of the Dominant Power: political and economic coercion, and intrusion into the military, scientific, cultural and technological subsystems. Examples abound:

If we should have a war in the future, we want Argentina on our side. There is no better way to do this than by increasing our influence with the armed forces. By supplying Argentina with the arms and technical knowledge it is requesting we would not be making that country a military threat to the U. S. or to any other country in the hemisphere . . . we would not permit that country to attack another American republic. . . . Our cultural activities should be directed to a very practical end. We can encourage the Argentines to look to the United States for scientific, engineering and other knowledge, to buy U. S. books and to look to us for technical assistance and other help in developing their country. . . . A cultural program for culture's sake should not give us any great concern for the moment. . . . If the European Recovery Program is put into effect we should not permit large amounts of dollar exchange to be paid Argentina unless the latter adopts a reasonable policy with regard to the price of wheat and takes certain measures which would substantially improve our relations. . . . We should stress inter-American unity and avoid unilateral condemnation of Argentina. In all inter-American conferences and meetings we should emphasize freedom of the press, free enterprise and free elections. . . . We would waste our time preaching principles to the Perón Administration. We should make that Administration see that certain advantages will accrue to Argentina under given conditions.[52]

With respect to bases, the United States sought these by either bilateral or multilateral accords. Defense Secretary Forrestal repeatedly attempted to convince Secretary of State Marshall that it was expedient for the United States to raise during the Ninth International Conference of American States at Bogotá "the availability of bases and facilities during time of emergency to forces of the American states in the defense of the Hemisphere. . . ."[53] Marshall, however, replied:

It is extremely doubtful whether the Conference at Bogotá will provide an appropriate opportunity in which to negotiate a reciprocal, multilateral agreement on this subject . . . [It] is likely that the introduction of bases into the Conference would result in extensive and widely publicized political debate, with a poor prospect of this Government's being able to achieve the conclusion of an agreement such as the National Military Establishment desires. A failure on our part to succeed in our initiative would, I believe, seriously hamper rather than facilitate the acquisition of rights for the United States on a bilateral basis.[54]

During the first decades of the century, Lenin assigned to Argentina the character of a semicolonial country linked to the British imperial system.[55]

Subjection to Britain did, indeed, seem to hinder the attainment of relations between Argentina and the USSR in 1927. In that year Britain attempted to prevent the establishment of diplomatic relations between the two countries. The situation continued uncertain through 1928, before Irigoyen's return to power, with both a Soviet commercial attaché at Buenos Aires and the ambassador of the Tsarist regime. In that year, however, the USSR concluded that the extension of North American economic and military influence over Latin America, displacing the British presence, would "transform the Continent into one of the most important arenas for conflict within the imperialistic colonial system."[56] In 1931 Argentina expelled one of the officials of a Russian trading organization, charging him with dumping products below their market value and with promoting communism. Then in 1936, in the Council of the League of Nations, the Argentine delegate Ruiz-Guinazu reversed his policy of seeking an understanding with the USSR, claiming that the Argentine delegation to St. Petersburg had been attacked and that apologies had not been received. He took the opportunity to make clear that "the Argentine Government does not recognise the Soviet Government and for the moment does not maintain diplomatic relations with it."[57] Three years later, Argentina proposed the immediate expulsion of the USSR from the League for having violated its principles by attacking Finland.

These examples show that the development of relations between the USSR and Argentina had been characterized by conflict long before the Second World War. The role Argentina had played in achieving the expulsion of the USSR from the League was not forgotten. Another important occasion for conflict was provided by the attitude Argentina adopted during the war. The USSR denounced the pro-Nazi and pro-Fascist leanings of the military regime of 1943, "amongst whom the War Minister, General Perón, is the most conspicuous."[58] Nonetheless the USSR observed that a permanent characteristic of Argentine foreign policy was to oppose the advance of North American domination over Latin America. April 1945 saw a characteristic clash between the United States and the USSR over the participation of Argentina in the San Francisco Conference. Molotov objected that "Argentine policy during the past years has not been friendly to the United Nations."[59] The United States opposed this view steadfastly, and finally the USSR accepted Argentine entry. The USSR considered the U. S. position evidence of bad faith, because Roosevelt had promised at Yalta that he would not support the admission of Argentina to the UN.[60] The North American press criticized the action as "reminiscent of the policy of appeasement adopted towards Hitler before the Second World War."[61] The entry of Argentina into the UN thus caused one of the first confrontations between the superpowers in the new world organization. However, a year later Buenos Aires and Moscow established full diplomatic relations, exchanging ambassadors. The Soviet press commented favorably, claiming that the establishment of relations with the USSR would help Argentina to affirm its independence.[62] This turnabout in Argentine-Soviet relations, of course, suited the objectives of both parties. The establishment of relations with the USSR occurred at a time of serious tension between the United States and the USSR, when the Soviets refused to withdraw their troops from Iran. It thus demonstrated the Third Position, affirming a policy significantly independent of the United States. This position served to increase Argentina's bargaining power with the United States and to limit seriously the options open to that power in dealing with the USSR. For the Russians, the relationship with Argentina formed part of a new policy towards the middle and smaller powers within the context of the Cold War confrontation with the United States.

The Cold War thus had a marked influence on Argentine strategy. The United States' extreme sensitivity to the danger of the subversive penetration of "international communism" was manifested many times during the reign of Perón. In August 1947, before the Rio Conference, Foreign Minister Bramuglia informally mentioned to Bruce that Argentina wanted an agreement with the United States and the other nations of the continent to combat Communism.[63] On this occasion, Bramuglia was told that the United States was not interested.[64] A year later, at Bogotá, Argentina opposed a North American proposal for joint action against communism. How to reconcile this change of front? The fact is that tactics varied but the strategy remained the same. It is possible to believe that Perón genuinely shared the North American concern about communism. But it was not his top priority. In the international field, Perón strengthened his ties with Tito after his breach with Moscow; he modified Argentine policy towards an actual alliance with the United States in case of war; and he deferred indefinitely a final decision on an approach for closer relations from North Korea.[65] He explained his establishment of relations with the USSR by saying that "at the time the policy of the United States was definitely unfriendly toward Argentina and so was that of the Soviets. . . . He said he thought at the time that it was better to establish diplomatic relations with the Soviets and 'get them at least off his neck.'"[66] The proposal for an anti-Communist agreement at the Conference on the Inter-American Treaty for Reciprocal Assistance was thus simply a ploy in the diplomatic game. Argentina did not want the ITRA to become a reality. When Washington reversed the original idea of the conference, both countries agreed to improve their exchanges of communication and information concerning Communist activity.

Another example of the effect of the Cold War on Argentina is the use made of the political conflict in Colombia during the Bogotá Conference. Perón told Bruce that "recent happenings in Bogotá should be a lesson to all of us as it [sic] demonstrated how easily civil war could break out in many Latin American countries and only after one side or the other won would it be known whether the government would side with the United States or with Russia . . . [T]here would be little real danger from the Communists in the United States and Argentina because of their high standards of living," but "we must not forget that there are 19 other American Republics where the Communists have fertile fields for their propaganda and organisational activities." At the same meeting, Perón criticized the North American strategy for combatting communism. In his view, Washington tended to approach the problem "Government to Government" instead of establishing direct relations with the people. Argentina offered here to use its influence in syndicalist circles in Latin America. However, the United States regarded this offer as yet another attempt by Argentina to develop an autonomous policy in Latin America.

Elsewhere, in the case of the Greek conflict, Argentina voted with the majority of the General Assembly in favor of inviting Bulgaria, Albania and Yugoslavia to stop helping the Greek rebels and establish relations with the Greek Government. However, Argentina abstained from intervening in favor of either the Western Powers or the USSR, to the extent that the Greek affair was viewed as a Cold War conflict.[67] Argentina similarly adopted a mediatory role in the Berlin Blockade.[68] In Korea, fearing that this might indeed be the start of a new World War, Argentina again voted with the majority of the Assembly in favor of the U. S. position. However, its participation was limited. Argentina did not send troops. On the question of the admission of Communist China to the UN, Argentina, which had voted against this proposal before, now abstained from voting, claiming that abstention was in accordance with the principles of international law, as recognized at the Bogotá Conference, and that the problem of China was really a reflection of the differences between East and West.[69] In essence, Argentina always maintained to the greatest possible extent its independence of opinion and action regarding the confrontation between the United States and the USSR.

However, Argentina permanently confronted the United States, and other industrial powers, on economic questions. It proposed in the UN the creation of an International Commission of Primary Products, in an attempt to safeguard the interests of the middle and smaller powers. It also frequently criticized the work of the IBRD and the IMF, organizations to which Argentina did not then belong. Argentina similarly attacked as self-seeking the aid programs of industrial powers towards the underdeveloped world. In the Havana Conference, 1947–48, Argentina defended the principle of state control of the economic sector; accused the North Americans of attempting, through tariff liberalization, to impede industrialization in Latin America so as to retain their domination of the continent; and announced its own program of exports to Europe and aid for Latin America. Argentina also supported programs to finance the development of the middle and smaller powers, explained its own concept of economic integration, emphasized the reality of the gulf between the rich and the poor nations, and insisted on the importance of technical aid and foreign investment, under appropriate controls, for the acceleration of economic development.[70]

In sum, the basic principles of Argentine foreign policy in the decade 1945–55 were spelled out by Foreign Minister Remorino as: the freedom and rights of peoples; the dignity and social welfare of individuals; freedom of self-determination for states; integration of the American territories occupied by foreign powers; fair prices in commodity trade; continental solidarity in America; the abolition of war; and the solution of international problems by due process of law. Argentina accordingly sought to strengthen its influence in Latin America, moving away from its relative isolation. It adopted a strong policy in defense of its national sovereignty and territorial rights. It sought an accord with Brazil that would strengthen the capacities of both nations. And it maintained its opposition to the United States and its own links with Britain, according to the strategic vision of a heterodox autonomy. The former extracontinental axis with Britain was, however, replaced by a slight alignment with Moscow in the confrontation between the United States and the USSR. Argentine foreign policy was thus both practical and consistent in its objectives, although it suffered certain reverses in practice. These derived largely from the problems facing Perón in the last years of his regime. On the one hand, he could have sought to extend his revolutionary program, occasioning vast social and economic changes and moving from heterodox autonomy to open secession in foreign affairs. Or he could have tried to apply the concept of national capitalism in as moderate a form as possible. This, in fact, is what he attempted.

In the largest sense, the strategic vision that guided Argentine foreign policy looked forward to a drastic change in the structure of world power, in which "the rich of today will be the poor of tomorrow." Supporting this vision is the fact that the underdeveloped countries, rich in primary products and minerals and relatively uncontaminated by the excesses of postindustrial society, possess very significant springs of political and economic power, which will enable them to bargain effectively with the industrial powers that depend upon them for their supplies of raw materials.

The Third Position, the democratization of the international system, the moves towards greater integration and concentration of power, the attempts to alter the rules of the power struggle all combined to present a foreign policy that united everywhere ideology and pragmatism, linking contemporary problems with the process of historical evolution.

# 7

# YUGOSLAVIA AND THE COLD WAR

Yugoslavia's attitude toward the Cold War passed through a number of different phases in the period 1945 to 1973. These phases varied with the different stages of the relations between the two superpowers—the United States and the Soviet Union, and with the different phases of Yugoslavia's own relations with the Soviet Union. Her relations with the United States always took second place, though this does not mean that they were unimportant. Another factor that exercised a permanent but varying influence on Yugoslavia's policy was that throughout the whole period Yugoslavia was a Communist state with a communist—or socialist, as they preferred to call it—ideology, which always played an important part in determining policy, even though pragmatic considerations often took first place.

For Yugoslavia, the first phase of the Cold War lasted only from 1945 to 1948 and ended with her break with the Soviet Union. The second phase started after an interim period of isolation and lasted from 1955 to 1962; a third phase lasted until 1970, after which it might be said that the Cold War moved towards détente, which for the superpowers was another means of attaining the same objectives as those of the Cold War. This third phase held special dangers for Yugoslavia, for at that time she could expect little help from the United States and consequently had to accept the friendship of the Soviet Union.

During the first phase of the Cold War, Yugoslavia's attitude was determined by her position as a new Communist state. Her government had recently come to power as a result of the revolution brought about by the Partisans under the leadership of the Communist Party's general secretary, Josip Broz Tito, during the Second World War. Yugoslav Communists were very proud of the fact that they were the first Communist party since the Bolsheviks to achieve power. But they were unprepared for the gigantic tasks involved in setting up a Communist government in a war-destroyed country and in an international atmosphere of increasing hostility to communism. Tension between Eastern and Western wartime allies had escalated after the opening of the second front by the United States and Great Britain made clear the imminence of major decisions about territorial divisions in Europe. This issue revealed the latent hostility between the United States and Great Britain on the one hand, with their ideology of democracy, open frontiers, and capitalist economies, and the USSR on the other, with its Marxist ideology, its fear of invasion from the West, and its old-fashioned expansionist foreign policy. In 1945, Yugoslav leaders had to choose between the two.

When the Cold War first began to take form in 1944, Tito and his associates were in a somewhat ambivalent situation. They needed Western aid but were basically in opposition to the West, partly for ideological reasons and partly because they realized that Great Britain and the United States would not support their claims to Trieste, Venezia Giulia and parts of Carinthia. By the end of 1944, the Tito government knew that these areas were to be incorporated into the Allied Military Government-occupied territory, whose fate was to be decided at the peace conference. They feared—and with some reason—that the disputed areas would be assigned to Italy and Austria for political, anti-Communist reasons. They felt that any Western aid such as UNRRA supplies would be used to infiltrate political spies under the guise of administrators.

At that time the Yugoslavs still had strong hopes that the USSR would, for ideological reasons, supply material aid and political support for their territorial claims. They also expected no less a reward for their heroic achievements during the war. But they were soon to be disappointed. For the Soviet Union was not primarily motivated by ideological reasons in its foreign policy and was neither grateful for nor particularly pleased by the Yugoslav revolution.[1]

Early in 1945, the Yugoslavs found that Soviet support for their desire to keep troops in Trieste and Venezia Giulia was lukewarm at best, and certainly not strong enough to prevent Britain and the United States from enforcing Yugoslav military withdrawal behind the Morgan Line—much deeper into Yugoslav territory than Tito wanted. They also found that their relations with the Soviet Union in economic and political fields were highly unsatisfactory. Yet, in spite of this, the Yugoslav leaders believed that their loyalty belonged chiefly to the Soviet Union as the leader of all Communists, that they must bear with what they believed to be temporary difficulties with the Russians, who were their only possible ally and the only example of how to run a Communist state.

The Tito government requested from the Soviet Union—and received on most disadvantageous terms—experts in various technical and military fields. At the same time they tried to demonstrate their support for Soviet Cold War attitudes and policies. They refused UNRRA aid until they were assured that the head of mission in Belgrade would be a Russian; later they refused Marshall Plan aid because of its capitalist origins. They had repeated difficulties in their relations with the United States—and the difficulties were by no means one-sided. In 1947, after repeated Yugoslav complaints about flights of U. S. military planes over their territory had been ignored, orders were issued to Yugoslav ground defense to fire on offending planes. Two U. S. planes were shot down, creating a very tense international incident. The Cold War atmosphere at this time was exacerbated further by Yugoslavia's aid to Communist rebels in the Greek civil war. The Soviet Union was at least aware of this support, though it seems likely that it did not encourage this Yugoslav policy, and the aid eventually had to be withdrawn when Yugoslavia was herself in trouble with the Soviet Union in 1948.

This early period of the Cold War coincided with the most difficult and insecure period of Tito's regime. Yugoslav leaders were fairly sure of sufficient support from ex-Partisans, but they were also aware of increasing opposition in the countryside to their harsh measures of nationalization of industries, both large and small, and their measures against private landholders, whose holdings had in any case been strictly limited. After nationalization came centralized planning and the Five-Year Plan for rapid industrialization, based on the example of the Soviet Union. Following the principles of the Cold War, Yugoslavia was to use only internal resources and such aids and credits as she could get from the Soviet Union and the satellite regimes in Eastern Europe. Foreign trade with capitalist countries was to be reduced to a minimum. These ideas, combined with lack of economic expertise and experience, proved unworkable. Yugoslavia did not have enough basic resources to industrialize rapidly without aid from and trade with the West. She lacked fuel and power, industrial experts, capital equipment and certain minerals; and although such essential resources as nonferrous metals and water for electric power were in abundant supply, these could be exploited only by modern techniques and machinery. In spite of her efforts to operate within the Soviet sphere, by 1948 43% of Yugoslavia's imports and 48% of her exports were with countries outside the Communist bloc. The fact that the targets Tito set for industrial development under the Five-Year Plan were far too high and that the centralized planning was inefficient and unrealistic cannot be attributed to Soviet influence, since the Russian leaders never approved of the Yugoslav plans for industrialization; they would have preferred Yugoslavia to function as a controlled satellite in the Soviet orbit.

In the field of agriculture, the Yugoslavs followed an independent line contrary to what Soviet leaders would have liked. Their policy was to allow peasants (who had been the backbone of the Partisan movement and who provided essential food for the industrial and town-dwelling population) to keep their farms as private property. But holdings were limited to forty-five hectares (only twenty-five to thirty-five hectares of this being arable land). At the same time, the government forced peasants to sell their produce to the state at artificially low prices and put pressure on them to join cooperatives. This policy antagonized the peasants, who composed seventy percent of the total population at the time, and it did not appease the Soviet leaders. In 1947, the Soviet Union created an association of Communist parties called the Cominform, whose—but not proclaimed—aim was to control and discipline the Yugoslav Communist Party and its leaders.

In this difficult period, the Yugoslav government feared that a counter-revolution might be organized from abroad with help from the United States and Great Britain, whose troops were stationed at that time near the Yugoslav frontiers with Italy and Austria. Today, with hindsight, it is possible to see that the exaggeratedly hostile Cold War attitudes shown by Yugoslav leaders at this time, may have been caused by their knowledge that they stood virtually alone, without allies. By this time they had begun to realize that they could not count on Soviet support for the new Communist regime that Tito had established.

The expulsion of Yugoslavia from the Cominform was announced to an astonished world on 28 June 1948. The reasons behind it were revealed only slowly, over succeeding months. Very soon, however, it became clear that this event marked the end of Yugoslavia's attempt to emulate Soviet policies. It also marked the beginning of the end of the first phase of the Cold War as it affected Yugoslavia.[2] Tito and his associates had been too independent to please the Soviet Union. At the same time, Cold War policies of the Soviet kind had been unpopular with the great majority of Yugoslavs and had brought little benefit to their country, either politically or economically. The reasons for Soviet hostility to the Communist regime in Yugoslavia were not entirely clear to Yugoslav leaders at the time and are still arguable. However, if the Cold War was due to Stalin's fear that the West—including a resurrected Germany—would soon unite for a concerted effort to overthrow Communism in Russia, then Yugoslavia, with its key strategic position between Central and Eastern Europe and with its important seacoast on the Adriatic giving access to the Mediterranean, was a vital link in Stalin's western defense. Stalin may well have felt, after the explosion of the atomic bomb had brought about the unexpectedly sudden collapse of Japan, that the Soviet Union was wide open to attacks from both East and West. The United States at this time seemed to be supremely powerful—strengthened rather than destroyed by the war and with strategic bases and forces all over the world. If the Cold War was also due to rivalry between the two great powers over division of land in Central and Eastern Europe, then Yugoslavia's position between the two was still important. This Cold War context would explain why Stalin continued his hostile policy against Yugoslavia long after it became clear that the expulsion from the Cominform had failed to bring Yugoslav Communists into line.

Stalin made every effort to get rid of Tito and replace him with leaders who would accept subjection to the Soviet Union. When this failed, he resorted to an economic boycott by Communist countries aimed at causing disruption and starvation, which he hoped would result in popular discontent and force a change of regime. Although this boycott did not bring a change of regime, it did produce a dramatic slump in trade (exports were halved, imports fell by three-quarters), and the dire emergency created by this slump and subsequent disastrous internal harvests forced the Yugoslav leaders to devise new policies.

Reversing her earlier anti-Western attitude, Yugoslavia now looked to the West for food to prevent starvation, and for the necessary aid and credits to pay for it. As in later stages of Yugoslav development, economic necessity was to lead to subsequent political change. But first, major political obstacles had to be overcome, both by Western nations and by the Yugoslavs themselves. Leaders in Great Britain, the United States and France had first to be reassured that the plight of Yugoslavia was genuine, that the improbable story of the Cominform break was not a put-up job. Once convinced of this, they were prepared to go to considerable lengths in economic and later military aid in order to "keep Tito afloat" and prevent Yugoslavia from falling to the Soviet bloc. The Yugoslavs, on their side, could not execute their political somersault without misgivings; they feared that aid would have political strings, making them the capitalist lackeys that Soviet propaganda already described them as.

Aid started in 1949 as a trickle—at first from Great Britain, the U. S. Export-Import Bank, the International Monetary Fund and Holland; later from France, Belgium, West Germany and others. Early loans were given on short-term credit at low interest rates, varying between 3.5 percent and 7 percent. From 1951 long-term loans were given; between 1951 and 1957, Great Britain, the United States and France financed a huge program of industrial and agricultural development in specified areas worked out by the Yugoslavs in consultation with Western experts. In addition to the capital goods necessary for basic industrialization and agricultural materials (including stock and seeds), on a much smaller scale the Yugoslavs received large imports of grain from the United States. They also received quantities of military aid to modernize and equip their army in case of a Soviet-supported invasion from the Communist enemies who surrounded Yugoslavia on all frontiers, except those with Italy and Austria. The industrialization projects were virtually completed by 1961. Total aid can be calculated in various ways but was considered by Western officials to have been in the region of $2.4 billion. The transformation of Yugoslavia into a modern industrial state, with town development and infrastructure on a par with the small countries of Western Europe, had begun.

Aid from the West had been given without political strings, and Yugoslav leaders maintained their independence in all internal political matters. In the international field, the suspicion and truculence of the early postwar years gradually gave way (on both sides, it might be said) to more cooperative and positive attitudes, which led to the removal of the outstanding issues that had earlier caused trouble between Yugoslavia and the West. In 1949 Yugoslavia stopped all aid to the Communists in Greece; by 1951 she had accepted the peace treaty frontiers with Austria; and by 1954 she had made a bilateral agreement about disputed frontiers with Italy, allowing Italy to keep Trieste and the greater part of Zone A (Venezia Giulia) but giving Yugoslavia the whole of Istria and Zone B. The compromise was followed by an exchange of populations in areas that changed hands and led to fruitful economic and relatively peaceful political relations for the next two decades.

The impact of the changes that took place in Yugoslavia between 1950 and 1960 was enormous. A virtual industrial revolution created major economic changes, which were inevitably accompanied by social and political changes of equal magnitude. Stalin died knowing that he had failed to subdue Tito, but before the full import of Yugoslavia's Western-orientated independent communism had been revealed. It is significant that Khrushchev and other Soviet leaders made great efforts as early as 1955 to placate Tito and win Yugoslavia back to their side by offering friendship and brotherly Communist cooperation. The visit of Khrushchev and Bulganin to Belgrade in November 1955 did not result in Yugoslavia's joining the Soviet side in what was then a new phase of the Cold War; but it did result in the resumption of relations between Yugoslavia and the rest of the Communist world. This development was to have a lasting effect on Yugoslav policies, which from this time onward tended to move in a fluid central position between East and West, oriented sometimes toward one, sometimes toward the other.

In 1955, when Khrushchev offered apologies and hearty friendship, Tito remained cold and aloof, but he did sign an agreement that accepted friendship with the Soviet Union providing that the Soviet Union explicitly recognized the right of Yugoslavia and other Communist states to deal independently with their own internal affairs. This stipulation was repeated and written into all political agreements with the Soviet Union in the next twenty years. However, the true value of this Soviet promise was shown by the brutal Soviet invasion of Hungary in 1956 and the even more savage invasion of Czechoslovakia in 1968. The lesson of these incursions was not lost on the Yugoslav leaders and had deep effects on the evolution of their policies in all fields—political, social and economic.

The evolution of Yugoslavia's doctrine of separate roads to socialism was the most far-reaching result of the Cominform split. It was the first crack in Soviet solidarity in the Cold War; and the visit of Khrushchev and Bulganin did not restore the previous solidarity. The Soviet leaders were aware that Stalin had miscalculated the reaction of the West to Tito's adversity; yet, they also had an exaggerated idea of their own capacity to heal the breach with Tito and to restore Communist solidarity at a time when Soviet relations with China were deteriorating. In spite of the agreement that Khrushchev managed to make with Tito in 1955, the breach was never fully mended. Tito's brand of nationalist communism, his doctrine of separate roads to socialism, proved to be more popular in Yugoslavia, and in some other parts of the Communist world, than anyone in the Soviet Union—or indeed in the West—had foreseen. Tito's independent communism had its roots in the solitary struggle of the Yugoslav Partisans during the war—without Western aid until 1943, without Soviet aid until 1944. It was also nourished by the unpopularity in Yugoslavia of the Stalinist and Cold War measures undertaken immediately after the war. By 1955, when Khrushchev and Bulganin naively tried, and failed, to bring Tito back into the Communist fold, Yugoslavia was well launched into an independent course of action and a new ideology to justify that course as essentially Marxist, if not strictly Leninist. This ideology, and the pragmatic changes that went with it, brought an entirely new element into the Cold War. It confirmed Yugoslavia's isolated position between the two groups of allies—the Soviet bloc in the Warsaw Pact, and the United States and its Western allies in the NATO alliance.

The basis of the new Yugoslav communist ideology was the belief that there can be different roads to socialism, varying with the conditions and experiences of each country and each revolution. The idea was that each Communist country must be able to evolve its own forms of economic and social life suited to local conditions within the wide framework of Marxism. The first basic Yugoslav contribution to the new ideology was the idea of Workers' Self-Management.[3] When it was first introduced by law in 1950, the idea applied only to workers in industry; during the fifties and sixties the doctrine was gradually widened until it included most aspects of social, economic and political life. Self-management—that is, decision making by all members of any given enterprise or unit of work— was even introduced into the Communist Party. Whether or not the doctrine has been effective in introducing workers' control is difficult to estimate. Its success in industry and elsewhere has varied with place and time, but one thing has been clearly demonstrated: the inclusion of all people in some forms of decision making has introduced an element of participatory democracy into the fabric of Yugoslav society that is characteristic of the Titoist era, and it has produced an entirely different society from that in other Communist countries. It is quite different from the hierarchical authoritarianism, the centralism, or the Stalinist mode of socialism inherent in Soviet concepts of state.

The twenty years that saw the evolution of self-management also saw an economic development in Yugoslavia that amounted to an industrial revolution. In this period Yugoslavia was transformed from a mainly agrarian (75 percent of workers) to a mainly industrial (63 percent of workers) urban-living population. As workers flowed into industry and became more sophisticated town dwellers, they came to demand more real autonomy in their industries. Self-management in enterprises worked at first only in a very restricted field. Workers' Councils did not have control of policy, which in the fifties was still in the hands of central planning authorities; they could not dispose of profits, organize investments or appoint important personnel. Gradually this was changed. From 1958 onward, they were gradually given more autonomy, and this change was accelerated after 1965—especially after the fall of Rankovic in 1966.

A whole series of economic reforms was introduced to give Yugoslavia a market economy that would lead to greater participation in world markets, to liberalized trade and to much greater productivity. From 1967 foreign capital, under certain restrictions, was allowed in Yugoslavia to help in the modernization and expansion of industry. The whole program of liberalization was accompanied by many features that gave Yugoslav economic life more in common with Western economies than with those of the Communist bloc. Apart from the autonomy of enterprises and the liberalization of trade, economic change brought a huge increase in consumer goods, both imported and home-produced. On the negative side, was a big increase in unemployment that came when enterprises were forced to be efficient and profitable or go into liquidation. Between 1965 and 1971, unemployment figures doubled to 400,000; this figure does not include the large numbers of Yugoslav workers (more than 700,000) who sought employment abroad. While the dinar was devalued (twice in 1971) to bring it in line with world values, the cost of living rose by 11 percent in 1970 and even more in the following two years. These developments were simultaneously occurring in Western countries with market economies.

Important changes occurred in Yugoslavia as economic expansion and development affected both the backward regions of the country and relations between the different Yugoslavian republics. Changes in the latter area were of the utmost importance. Liberalization of economic life led to liberalization in the political field. Accordingly, republican autonomy and freedom from central interference followed the abolition of central planning and the achievement of autonomy for banks and enterprises. Once the republicans had responsibility for their own development, it was found that the position of backward regions in relation to the more developed areas of the country had not improved despite planned investment in backward regions over the past two decades. Republics began to complain about the size of their contributions to federal investment, about their share of earned foreign currency and a host of other issues—political, cultural and linguistic. The liberalization of political life and removal of restrictions on the communications media allowed arguments and complaints to be carried on in public in a most heated atmosphere. One remarkable feature of these developments was that the Yugoslav Communist Party, which had become decentralized in the 1960s, became so embroiled in arguments between republics that it appeared Yugoslavia had not one but six Communist parties; it was evident that regional loyalties, even for party members, had begun to outweigh loyalty either to the party or to the Federal Republic of Yugoslavia.

By 1970 both the economic and the political situations were deteriorating rapidly. Conditions were such as to arouse speculation as to whether Yugoslavia was heading for economic collapse and whether this would be preceded or accompanied by a breakup of the federal state. The situation aroused great interest in the Soviet Union and in the West, since neither side in the Cold War wanted Yugoslavia to become a power vacuum or to fall into the sphere of influence of the other. In fact, neither of the gloomy prognostications was realized. Several factors combined to save Yugoslavia from collapse. A major factor was Tito's stern action in reasserting the authority of the Yugoslav Communist Party over local republican parties that had gone too far in supporting extreme nationalist causes. In Croatia, where the party leadership had made a demagogic appeal for popular support for nationalism, those responsible—and that meant the top leaders of the party—were forced to resign from office and all positions of influence. Later the attack spread to Serbia, where the party leaders were accused of failing to take action against nationalist centers of power. The purge of any who could be accused of having fostered separatism or local nationalism spread gradually throughout the

Yugoslav League of Communists and throughout the country. Simultaneously, in the cultural field and mass media there was a movement away from the liberalism that was thought to have facilitated the propagation of extreme nationalist views. Tito appealed for a return to communist virtues of earlier days. He strongly advocated a middle way, and in this he had the support of the majority of the people, who were not strongly politically committed but were interested in a higher standard of living and the availability of consumer goods for a comfortable life.

The crisis in internal affairs in the early 1970s underlined the difficulties and importance of Yugoslavia's relations with the United States on the one hand and the Soviet Union on the other. By this time, relations between the United States and Russia had changed from those of the Cold War, through tolerant coexistence, to a form of détente that was positive in character despite the United States' overtures for friendly relations with the People's Republic of China. Détente between the United States and Soviet Russia held dangers for Yugoslavia, for it meant that she was unable to exploit the Cold War by using one side as a protection against the other—a policy Yugoslavia had used profitably in the years since 1955.[4]

Relations between Yugoslavia and the Soviet Union had been subject to sharp fluctuations during this period of the Cold War. The main cause of these fluctuations was the Soviet Union's obstinate opposition to the Yugoslav concept of the independence of small states and to the new Yugoslav ideas of socialism. From time to time during the period 1955-70, the Russian leaders tried to regain the support of Yugoslavia. At such times they were prepared to make concessions; and the first concession always demanded by Yugoslavia was the recognition of her independence and integrity. The first agreement on these lines was signed when Khrushchev and Bulganin visited Belgrade to apologize for the Cominform break.

The 1955 Belgrade Declaration was signed, on Tito's insistence, between two equal heads of state, President Tito and President Bulganin. The declaration contained the Soviet Union's specific recognition of Yugoslavia's independence and right to develop her own forms of communism or socialism without Moscow's interference. This recognition appeared to put relations between the two socialist countries on a sound basis. After this, for a brief period it looked as if relations between the two countries would improve. Tito made his first visit to Moscow in ten years. But the honeymoon was brief. Friendly relations were shattered by the brutal Soviet invasion of Hungary in direct contravention of the Belgrade Declaration's doctrine of independence for small Communist countries. From this time on, relations between the two countries deteriorated and then remained at a low ebb for five years. During this time, Yugoslav ideologues were working out their new theories of socialism. They began with Workers' Councils and moved on to self-management as a way of socialist life. In 1958, these doctrines were reaffirmed at the Seventh Congress of the Yugoslav Communist Party, and the party's name was changed to the League of Yugoslav Communists to mark the change in doctrine about the party's role in society. Henceforth the party, or league, was to play a guiding rather than a leading role. These moves only exacerbated the Soviet bloc's campaign of vilification against Yugoslavia. This campaign was accompanied by a trade boycott (as was the period of the Cominform break) and the suspension of small investment credits negotiated in 1956.

During these years of cool relations with Russia, Yugoslavia's economy was expanding, unaffected by the Soviet boycott. Investment credits, loans and free gifts were flowing in from the West—from England, France, Germany and especially from the United States. These were the years when the Yugoslav armed forces were being modernized. The invasion of Hungary had shown that a small Communist country must be ready to defend itself, and Yugoslavia intended to be prepared. By this time it was admitted that the real threat was from the Soviet Union and not from any Western powers. However, Yugoslav leaders were careful to emphasize that Western aid would be accepted only as long as there was no Western interference in Yugoslavia's internal affairs, no attempt to exact some form of quid pro quo. It was also stressed that Western ideas and capitalist ways of life would not be acceptable in socialist Yugoslavia. In fact, such influences entered Yugoslavia imperceptibly with consumer goods, with heavy industry, and with the technical experts and expertise that flowed in from many Western countries. It may be that the rising standard of living, the emphasis on consumer goods and the easier way of life for all, which was so welcome to Yugoslavs after the terrible years of suffering and deprivation that had lasted almost fifteen years, would in any case have separated Yugoslavia further from the Soviet Union. Certain it was that Western contacts of all kinds appealed to the essentially Western character of most Yugoslavs, who for centuries had had more in common with their Western neighbors—Catholic or Byzantine—than with their enigmatic and often brutal, or brutalized, neighbors in Russia—Czarist or Communist. Yugoslavia reaped full Western benefits from this phase of the Cold War, which reached its points of sharpest conflict in 1961, first in the confrontation between the Western allies and Russia in the Berlin Wall crisis, later in the Cuban missile crisis. Yugoslavia remained isolated but was oriented more toward the West than toward the Soviet Union in these years.

The U. S.-Soviet situation began to change in 1962. The existence of a military stalemate in spite of political crises and confrontations opened up the way to bargaining and compromise. Moreover, Sino-Soviet hostility in the early sixties made the Soviet Union more approachable in its relations with the West. These changes in the Cold War situation, and especially the changes in the Soviet attitude toward the West, had an inevitable effect on Soviet-Yugoslav relations. Improved relations were welcome to both sides (for, however much Yugoslavia proclaimed her indifference, a boycott by Communist countries was neither comfortable nor profitable); but it seems probable that the initiative for friendlier relations came from the Soviet Union. The Soviet leaders realized that their freeze had done little harm to Yugoslavia, had not intimidated Yugoslav Communists and perhaps would harm Soviet interests in the long run. By 1963 there had been a substantial improvement in relations between the two countries, marked by the exchange of high-level visits (Tito visited the USSR unofficially in 1962 and officially in 1965 and January 1967, while Khrushchev visited Yugoslavia in 1963, and Brezhnev made an unofficial visit in 1966); there were also cultural and economic missions.

The basis of improved relations was a considerable identity of views on a number of international issues and the recognition on both sides that bad relations were unprofitable. For the Soviet Union there was always the hope that Yugoslavia could be lured back, by one means or another, to the Communist bloc, a hope bolstered by a persistent Soviet misinterpretation of the mentality of Yugoslavs in general and of Tito in particular. On the Yugoslav side there was the realization that Yugoslavia's expanding trade needed to find markets in the East as well as the West and that Soviet cooperation was essential before this could be achieved. The way was therefore open to some form of rapprochement, provided the Soviets would treat Yugoslavia as an equal independent state and reaffirm the basic tenets of the Belgrade Declaration.

Negotiations took place in unofficial visits (Gromyko to Yugoslavia in 1962 and Tito to Moscow in December of the same year; Khrushchev to Brioni the following year). Trade and cultural cooperation were initiated, and in 1965 Tito made an official visit to the USSR, after which a joint communiqué was issued in which the Yugoslav principles for independence and noninterference were restated and guaranteed by the Soviet Union. This, again, opened the way to better trade relations, including a long-term agreement for the years 1966–70. From 1955 to 1966, trade between the two countries had remained very limited, in spite of a slow increase in total volume from $40 million in 1955 to $118 million in 1957, which dropped again in 1961 to $82 million. By 1968, with improved relations, it increased to $400 million, and from this level it was to be further increased in the 1970s.

Improvement in political relations did not keep pace with those in the economic field, and the Yugoslavs were particularly wary of close party relations, for they realized that these were the means by which Soviet leaders hoped to lure the Yugoslavs back under their authority. The Yugoslavs did not send party delegates to the meeting of Communist parties held under Soviet surveillance in 1967—though Tito had made another official visit to Russia earlier in the year. Tito was too wily to be caught in the Soviet trap of organized parties again, and he was aware that trouble was brewing in Czechoslovakia that would arouse Soviet reprisals of which he could not approve. On an unofficial visit to Moscow in April 1968, he warned the Soviet leaders that any use of force by them would have serious consequences. Though Tito dared to speak to Russian leaders as a leader of an independent state, his opinions were not treated like those of an equal, as the Soviet invasion of Czechoslovakia in the summer of 1968 clearly demonstrated. This invasion resulted in a renewed deterioration in relations between Yugoslavia and the Soviet Union; Tito declared that "the use of force in the settlement of disputes is unacceptable notwithstanding the aims and motives which have tried to justify it.... the sovereignty of a socialist country has been violated and trampled upon and a serious blow has been inflicted on socialist and progressive forces throughout the world." He knew it was useless to complain but the fear of an invasion of Yugoslavia was present in enough minds for Tito to warn the Soviet leaders that Yugoslavia would fight if her territory were invaded by any power whatever.[5]

This time the deterioration of relations did not last so long as before. Soviets faced continuing trouble in Czechoslovakia and potential opposition from Rumania, Hungary and possibly Poland. Their eastern frontier with China was in permanent danger from a regime that regarded the Soviet Union as ideologically unsound, just as the Soviet Union regarded Yugoslavia as unsound. Russia could no longer afford the luxury of long drawn out enmity with Yugoslavia and started to woo her once again. And as before, the Yugoslavs set out their minimum political terms for considering resumption of improved relations. For the Yugoslavs the basic principles were unchanged: Soviet recognition of Yugoslavia's independence; equality in international relations; and Yugoslavia's right to develop her own kind of socialism, based on self-management, without being attacked or boycotted by the Communist bloc. "All countries have an equal and inalienable right to full sovereignty and independence, equal treatment in international relations, and a free choice in the ways of internal development and the forms of international relationships and cooperation." Trade and cultural relations were gradually resumed, but, as in 1967, the Yugoslav League of Communists again did not send a fraternal delegation to the Moscow meeting of eighty-one Communist parties in June 1969. However, the situation was not the same as before. Yugoslavia was in need of help—especially in the economic field. The Soviet Union, meanwhile, needed Yugoslavia's friendship. She wanted a period of peace and détente to aid her drive for arms limitation and at the same time needed allies in her support of Arab policies in the Middle East. This led the Soviet Union to give more attention to Yugoslavia's economic needs and to adopt an entirely new attitude toward Tito's policy of nonalignment, which the Soviet Union up to this time had either ignored or treated with lofty contempt.

The doctrine of nonalignment was one of the new policies worked out by Yugoslavia after the break with the Cominform.[6] It was first conceived as a position in foreign policy that would afford protection for Yugoslavia during her years of isolation from the Communist bloc. The idea was that by associating herself with other small or weak nations, Yugoslavia would have potential allies—at least in the United Nations—in case of Soviet aggression. At the same time, it allowed Yugoslavia to demonstrate her independent position and underlined that she had not sold out to the capitalist, imperialist West.

Other general ideas of nonalignment were evolved during succeeding years. In 1964 it was described as a movement based on the equality of nations and the widest possible international cooperation. The movement, it was stated, stood for active coexistence, for common action in support of common interests shared by states that might have different social systems. The principles of nonalignment were carried further by some of its adherents, especially by some Arab and African states: they endorsed the need for the liquidation of colonialism, neocolonialism and imperialism and for the success of national liberation movements. As the years passed, the nonalignment movement gained more members, until in 1973 it was said to represent more than half the population of the globe. At the same time, its purpose appeared different to different members. It sometimes seemed that for some nations the concept of nonalignment was worth supporting only as long as it could be made to serve their own causes; many members were mainly interested in local (e.g., African or Arab) issues. By the 1970s, the movement seemed to have shifted a long way from an agreement among friendly nations to take a nonaligned position in a Cold War world.

Yet Yugoslavia did not relinquish her leading position as originator of the movement. In the early years the movement was dominated by world figures—Tito, Nasser of Egypt and Nehru of India. By the late sixties the only outstanding personality left was Tito. Nasser, Nehru and Nkrumah were dead; Sukarno had disappeared from the scene. Both the passing of these great personalities and the increase of many small new states with an interest in nonalignment showed up the difficulties involved in trying to give strength and purpose to the movement. Yet Yugoslavia did not give up the idea of nonalignment as a basis for foreign policy. President Tito traveled tirelessly throughout the sixties and early seventies in efforts both to gain support for nonalignment and to show himself as a leader of international status. He made many visits to countries of the Middle East, Far East and Latin America. He visited Great Britain, the United States and France. He addressed a session of the United Nations at almost the same time as Nikita Khrushchev. Although nonalignment did not seem to have achieved much world influence, except in affecting some voting at the United Nations, it had certainly allowed Tito to be seen as a leader of something more than Yugoslavia; it showed that he had enlarged his position from an isolationist in the Cold War world to the defender of security of an international group.

The showpieces of nonalignment were its four conferences, initiated and organized to a large extent by Yugoslavia. The first was held in Belgrade (1-6 September 1961) and was attended by twenty-eight nations, including three observers; the second was held in Cairo (5-8 October 1964) and was attended by fifty-seven nations, including ten observers. The third, held in Lusaka (8-10 September 1970), increased its attendance to sixty-four, of whom ten were observers. And the fourth, held in Algiers (13-15 September 1973), had an attendance of eighty-four states, of whom nine were observers. All conferences revealed a lack of cohesion and unity of purpose among the attending nations.

In spite of its leaders' calls for world support, the movement for a long time aroused little interest from the great powers. The United States was indifferent; Great Britain, lukewarm; and the Soviet Union, almost hostile. On the first day of the conference in Belgrade, the Soviet Union demonstrated its lack of respect for the principles of peace being announced at the conference by exploding an atom bomb at the time of the opening session. When Brezhnev assumed the role of Soviet leader after the fall of Khrushchev, he was openly antagonistic to nonalignment, and other Communist states were encouraged to take the same attitude. "Nonaligned countries can play the game of nonalignment only because of the existence of the armed forces of the Warsaw Pact," was a typical gibe from Poland. Then, in 1968, the Yugoslav leaders were accused of taking a position "not of nonalignment, and not with socialism, but rather with antisocialist forces in the Czechoslovak Republic and with the whole imperialist chorus."[7] This accusation made clear that any Yugoslav policy different from that of the Soviet Union was condemned and that nonalignment could be accepted only as long as it took no line opposed to that of the Soviet Union.

There were, however, many areas in international relations in which the policy of the nonaligned nations, especially Yugoslavia, differed little from that of the Soviet Union. In the Korean War and the crises in Cyprus they took an anti-U. S. and anti-British point of view. In the Middle East they supported the Arab cause; indeed, Tito went so far in 1957 as to break off relations with Israel unilaterally, even before getting the agreement of his ministers to such a policy. This made it impossible for him to be accepted as a mediator between the two sides in the Middle East conflict. Yugoslavia and other nonaligned nations also took the same view as the Soviet Union toward the war in Vietnam and American intervention in Cambodia; and it was noticeable that whereas U. S. policy was the subject of frequent criticism, no criticisms were offered against the policy of the Soviet Union. It was some time before the Russians saw that this was a situation that could be exploited to their own benefit.[8]

The fourth conference of nonaligned nations, in Algiers in 1973, seemed to show nonalignment principles as unchanged. The movement was proclaimed as "not only a resistance to blocs, but also a struggle against force in general." "We cannot permit the big powers to decide the course of events—particularly when they affect our own destiny—by their agreements, even though they may be motivated by the best intentions." At the opening of the Algiers conference Tito claimed nonalignment as the voice of the conscience of mankind. He claimed "substantive results in strengthening independence of peoples and relaxation of tensions throughout the world, and an even broader affirmation of peaceful coexistence." Yet, at the same time, he drew the attention of the conference to the change in the Cold War situation, which had particular importance for nonaligned nations, especially for Yugoslavia. "If in the meantime [that is, since the first nonalignment conference, in Belgrade in 1964] the Cold War has lost its intensity," Tito told the conference, "if in relations among the great powers, negotiations and agreement have replaced confrontation in many ways, if the situation in some parts of the world has been considerably improved—our efforts have also been woven into this progress." It was soon to become clear, however, that the nonalignment movement still did not play much part when it came to major conflicts. The Arab-Israeli war of 1973 broke out soon after the end of the Algiers conference. In this conflict the sympathies of Yugoslavia and many of the nonaligned countries were, like those of the Soviet Union, with the Arabs; but the weight of influence that eventually forced a ceasefire came from the two superpowers working together, not from Tito or the nonalignment movement.

Between 1970 and 1973, the international situation had been changing and with it Yugoslavia's relations with world powers. By this time, harsh

Cold War attitudes had virtually disappeared, to be replaced by an atmosphere of positive détente. Moscow was worried about China's increasing respectability (President Nixon visited China in 1972 and Great Britain reestablished diplomatic relations with her, while China herself began to open up her trade to the West). Russia was also worried about the growing Westernization of Eastern Europe. After peace had been reached in Vietnam in 1973, the Soviet Union was interested in strengthening her position in the Mediterranean and Eastern Europe before the United States had time to reestablish her peacetime strength. The Soviet Union seemed to realize that her earlier Cold War policies and harsh attitudes toward the West and toward Yugoslavia had brought little harvest in international relations, that a policy of détente might be more likely to forward her aims. It was in this spirit that the Berlin Agreement was signed, a visit of President Nixon to Moscow was broached, and the Soviet leaders began to cultivate the friendship of Yugoslavia once again. This time they offered more, both economically and politically, than in any previous period of friendly overtures.

The wooing of Yugoslavia started in earnest in 1971, when Brezhnev visited Belgrade "after twenty years' polemics." Before Tito would engage in talks, Brezhnev had to confirm that relations between the two states were based on the Belgrade Declaration of 1955, while Tito stressed Yugoslavia's full independence and the inviolability of her frontiers. The visit was successful in a limited way, and it led to further cooperation between the two countries in all fields and to the signing of a long-term economic agreement the following year. Kosygin visited Yugoslavia at the end of September 1973 and had talks with President Tito about long-term economic cooperation. He tried to flatter the Yugoslavs by references to "brotherhood and unity" that had been "cemented during the heroic struggle for freedom and independence." But his speeches still contained allusions that showed the old Soviet iron hand in the velvet glove. He spoke of the Soviet Union's "solidarity with the initiative of Comrade Tito"—a reference to Tito's strong internal measures against liberalism. He also mentioned "eliminating national egoism." "The Soviet people," he said, "want socialism in Yugoslavia to be consolidated and to be increasingly closely connected with the socialist community." This showed what many Yugoslavs thought was an unhealthy interest in their internal affairs. Many people thought that economic arrangements, which were part of the purpose of Kosygin's visit, were also part of a wider Soviet plan to gain some new means of influencing Yugoslavia's policies, both internal and external.

A long-term economic agreement between Yugoslavia and the Soviet Union had been signed in November 1972. It provided for a $540-million credit from the Soviet Union for thirty-eight Yugoslav industrial projects. By September 1973 the process of taking up these credits had already run into difficulties, which Mr. Kosygin hoped to eliminate. Yugoslavia again found it necessary to insist the cooperation must be based upon full voluntarism and equality. Relations, it was stressed, were between "equal countries with different characteristics and following different paths and with different international positions...." There was still a feeling in Yugoslavia that the Soviet Union was trying to exploit its strong position at the expense of an economically weakened Yugoslavia. How far the economic difficulties had been straightened out by Kosygin's visit it was difficult to tell.

One change, however, was certain. It became clear shortly after Kosygin's visit that the attitude of the Soviet Union toward nonalignment had changed. In 1971, when Brezhnev visited Belgrade, he was still opposed to nonalignment, saying that it had its limitations and adding that Yugoslavia's system of self-management was unacceptable to Moscow. By 1973, though self-management was probably still unacceptable, the Soviet leader thought it better not to mention it, and there was no denunciation of nonalignment. With the outbreak of the Arab-Israeli war in October, the nonaligned countries were seen as potential allies in the Soviet policy for support of the Arab cause. President Boumédienne, who had acted as host to the fourth nonalignment conference, held in Algeria, went to Moscow to canvass big power support. On this occasion aid or mediation from Yugoslavia was not considered of any importance. The nonalignment movement, or at least that part of it that supported the Arabs, was in danger of being taken over by Moscow.

At this juncture, there were many reasons that Yugoslavia was prepared to accept some form of friendship with Moscow. Because of the détente between the Soviet Union and the United States (which persisted in spite of the Middle East war), Yugoslavia could no longer play one superpower off against another. It was dangerous to be on bad terms with the Soviet Union unless Yugoslavia could be sure of other allies, other sources of economic aid. The United States at this time was experiencing turmoil in domestic politics and in the international field was anxious to be on friendly terms with the Soviet Union and China.

A hidden element in Yugoslavia's relations with the Soviet Union was the unknown factor of the succession in the event of Tito's death or resignation from active political life. Having reached the age of eighty-one in 1973, it was inevitable that Tito would disappear from the political scene before too long. The Soviets were interested that the succession, whenever it came, should not be the occasion for any more liberal experiments or for the possibility of a counterrevolution. It is probable that at this time they preferred stability in Yugoslavia, with a regime that was neither extreme right nor extreme left, though they would certainly have preferred a regime likely to be obedient to Moscow to one showing independence. It seems that Brezhnev and Kosygin had decided that they could win more influence in Yugoslavia by friendly means than by hostile pressure. The Yugoslavs, on their side, desired Soviet friendship for a number of reasons: in a period of economic weakness, they were facing increased competition from the Common Market countries before they had established themselves in Western trade; they were experiencing their own political troubles among different nationalities and with the League of Communists; and the future was uncertain because of the age of their president. At this time friendship with the Soviet Union was seen as a protection against Soviet interference and a means of getting economic aid and increased trade, at least for an interim period.

In spite of the Soviets' repeated recognition of Yugoslavia's right to independence and her own form of socialism, it seems unlikely that the Soviet Union had abandoned all the reservations she had had about Yugoslavia since 1945. What is more likely is that once the Cold War had disappeared from the international scene, it seemed inappropriate to use Cold War methods in a campaign against Yugoslavia. In the 1970s more sophisticated methods of winning Yugoslavia over to the Communist bloc were being used.[9] Perhaps for the time being the USSR had abandoned her attempt to dominate Yugoslavia as being virtually impossible. One thing that usually worked in Yugoslavia's favor remained unchanged: her geographic position firmly fixed between East and West, between the Danube in Central Europe and the Mediterranean. It seemed unlikely in the 1970s that either of the superpowers would allow Yugoslavia to be engulfed by the other, with all the strategic advantages that this would bring. That fact in itself appeared to give Yugoslavia some guarantee of independence, regardless of whether the superpowers were in a state of Cold War or of détente.[10]

# 8

# AMERICA, RUSSIA, CHINA AND THE ORIGINS OF THE COLD WAR, 1945–1950

One does not have to be a New Left revisionist to argue that a major objective of United States foreign policy during the Second World War was to lay the foundations for American predominance in the postwar world.[1] In the Far East, Chiang Kai-shek's China was an important element in the American vision. Large and populous, it could be a significant factor in the balance of power after the defeat of Japan. Antiimperialist, it could be relied upon to second American opposition to European colonialism. Anti-Communist, it was most unlikely to align itself with the Soviet Union, the only rival for global hegemony after the collapse of the Axis powers. Economically backward, it would have to rely heavily upon American aid and assistance. In sponsoring China as one of the "big five" postwar powers, therefore, the United States was sponsoring what it thought would be a very dependable ally, not to say a satellite.

Unfortunately, there was a major obstacle in the way of the realization of this vision: the very real possibility of civil war in China between Chiang Kai-shek's Nationalists and the Chinese Communists, led by Mao Tse-tung. Not only would civil war prevent China from assuming the role envisaged by the United States; it might also tempt outsiders to fish in troubled waters, with potentially dangerous consequences. As early as September 1943, President Roosevelt told one of his advisers that "what he feared most of all was the flaring up of civil war in China after Japan's defeat. The danger there was that the Soviet Union would intervene in behalf of the Communists, and the Western powers would be tempted or forced in their own interests to back the anti-Communist side. We would then see . . . very much the same situation that we had witnessed in Spain during her civil war, only on a far greater scale, and with graver dangers inherent in it."[2] It therefore became the principal short-term aim of American policy in China to prevent this contingency from materializing. This aim was to be achieved externally be securing pledges of noninterference from the Soviet Union, and, internally by promoting a coalition between the Nationalists and the Communists. This was the policy embodied in the Yalta agreement on the Far East in February 1945 and in the ambassadorship of Maj. Gen. Patrick Hurley.

By the end of 1945, however, this policy seemed to be in a state of almost complete disarray. Political talks between the Nationalists and the Communists were deadlocked, and armed clashes between the two sides were increasing in frequency and intensity. By transporting large numbers of Nationalist troops and some of its own marines to north China, the United States had, in the view of the American commander in China, General Wedemeyer, incurred the displeasure of the Communists without greatly advancing the object of the exercise, which was to assist Chiang to take over control of the area from the Japanese. In Manchuria, which had been occupied by the Soviet army during its brief August campaign against the Japanese, the Russians were not only preventing the Nationalists from taking over the administration of the region, but were also said to be stripping it of industrial equipment and to be arming the Communists with weapons captured from the Japanese. "If the unification of China and Manchuria under Chinese National Forces is to be a United States policy," Wedemeyer cabled the chief of staff of the army on 23 November, "involvement in fratricidal warfare"—which was explicitly forbidden in his orders—"and possibly in war with the Soviet Union must be accepted and would definitely require additional United States Forces far beyond those presently available in the Theater to implement the policy." Wedemeyer did not believe that American public opinion was prepared to accept such risks and advocated dumping the problem in the lap of the fledgling United Nations.[3]

The secretary of state, James F. Byrnes, told a high level policy meeting in Washington on 27 November that he "doubted whether the United Nations Organization, which is not yet established as an organization, could make a contribution in time to help in the present difficulties." He felt "that taking everything into account perhaps the wise course would be to try to force the Chinese Government and the Chinese Communists to get together on a compromise basis, perhaps telling Generalissimo Chiang Kai-shek that we will stop the aid to his government unless he goes along with this. It might be as well . . . to tell Russia what we intend to do and to try to line them up with this policy."[4] Byrnes himself sought to "line up" the Russians at the Moscow conference of foreign ministers in December. The task of implementing the policy in China was entrusted by President Truman to the prestigious and recently retired chief of staff of the army, Gen. George C. Marshall.[5]

In an important sense, the Marshall mission was a colossal piece of bluff, for the U. S. administration realized that, however much pressure it applied to Chiang Kai-shek in order to make him conform to its plans, it would always have to back him in the last resort against the Communists. This emerges very clearly from the record of a meeting between Marshall, President Truman, and Byrnes's deputy, Dean Acheson, on 14 December:

I stated [wrote Marshall] that my understanding of one phase of my directive was not in writing but I thought I had a clear understanding of his [i.e., the president's] desires in the matter, which was that in the event that I was unable to secure the necessary action by the Generalissimo, which I thought reasonable and desirable, it would still be necessary for the U. S. Government, through me, to continue to back the National Government of the Republic of China—through the Generalissimo within the terms of the announced policy of the U. S. Government.

The President stated that the foregoing was a correct summation of his direction regarding that possible development of the situation.

The Under Secretary of State, Mr. Acheson, confirmed this as his understanding of my directions.[6]

Ostensibly the umpire, the general was really playing for one of the teams.

Initially, Marshall scored what appeared to be some outstanding successes. He presided over a truce agreement between the Nationalists and the Communists on 10 January 1946, a series of political agreements between the two sides later in the month, and, most important of all, an agreement on the basis for military reorganization and the integration of the Communist armed forces into the national army on 25 February.[7] But this framework for cooperation began to crumble almost at once. Was there every any real prospect of a lasting accord? Communist attitudes will be examined later, but those of Chiang Kai-shek, as outlined in a conversation with Marshall on 10 March, indicate that he placed little reliance upon the agreements so painfully negotiated. "He is convinced," Marshall wrote, "that the Communist Party is loyal to Soviet Russia and, in the final test, on the side of the Russians. He thinks that their intention is to infiltrate into the Government positions primarily for the purpose of gaining control of foreign policy in order to play the Soviet hand. He considers that the Communists look on General Marshall as, in effect, their protector while building up influence in the Government and reorganizing their armies. He feels that their acceptance of the demobilization and reorganization plan is largely for the purpose of obtaining well-trained, organized and equipped 18 divisions. In other words, he is unalterably of the opinion that the Communist Party is for the Communist theory of life and the Soviet Russia regime."[8]

Given these views, it is small wonder that Chiang and his supporters resolved that the best way to deal with the Communists was not to enter into a coalition with them, but to destroy them by armed force. But this, of course, precipitated the very civil war that the Marshall mission was designed to avoid. Marshall did put considerable pressure upon the Nationalists to moderate their policy of armed confrontation. Negotiations for a $500-million loan from the United States to China were suspended in April. In July, Marshall counseled delay in the passage of the China aid legislation, which was designed, among other things, to establish a permanent basis for the provision of military advice and assistance to the Chinese government. In August, he initiated an embargo upon the supply of ammunition to the Chinese army and warplanes to the Chinese air force. In September, he requested the suspension of the program of assistance to the Nationalist forces in their reoccupation of Manchuria.[9]

Right-wing critics of American policy in this period have charged that these measures positively assisted the Communists in their bid to gain control of China.[10] Their arguments are unconvincing, but it should in any event be emphasized that the purpose of the sanctions against Chiang was quite the reverse. Both Washington and Marshall believed that a military solution to the Communist problem was unattainable and that the only way in which the Generalissimo could maintain his position was to outmaneuver the Communists within the framework of a political settlement. The philosophy was well outlined by John Carter Vincent, the director of the State Department's Far East office, in a conversation with the Chinese minister-counselor in Washington on 9 September:

I expressed the view [Vincent recorded] that a reduction in the influence of the Communists might be more readily achieved if the Government "took them in" (in more senses than one) on a minority basis rather than try to shoot them all. I felt, and I was sure General Marshall felt, that a National Government moving ahead with American support in the job of rehabilitation and reconstruction would have a better chance to cut the ground out from under the Communists, even though they were in the Government, than it would have of doing so by keeping them out of the Government and endeavoring to eliminate them by force. I reminded him [i.e., the minister-counselor] that 15 years' intermittent efforts to eliminate them by force when they were receiving no support from Russia had certainly not proved successful.[11]

The sanctions, in other words, were designed to make Chiang see sense. They seemed to be the only way. As Marshall explained in exasperation to an American adviser of the Generalissimo's, "If you let this bunch know you are for them, you can't do anything with them."[12]

Marshall's pressure tactics were not, however, successful. His account of one of his last conversations with Chiang, on 1 December 1946, shortly before his return to the United States to become secretary of state, shows only too clearly how little he had been able to achieve:

I summed up the situation [he wrote] with the comment that the Communists were too large a military and too large a civil force to be ignored; that even if one disregarded the brutality of the inevitable procedure they could not be eliminated. Therefore, it was imperative that the efforts to bring them into the Government should continue and the greatest care should be taken to avoid having military action disrupt the procedure of negotiations.

The Generalissimo . . . expressed again his firm conviction that the Communists never intended to cooperate with the Government; that they were acting under Soviet influence; that their purpose was to disrupt the Government and to influence its foreign policy. . . .

The Generalissimo stated that he felt it was necessary to destroy the Communist military forces. If that were done there would not be great difficulty in handling the Communist question. He estimated that some eight to ten months would be required for this purpose.[13]

Although Marshall never fell for the line that the Chinese Communists were not Marxists but "agrarian reformers," he originally believed, unlike Chiang Kai-shek, that they were independent of the Soviet Union. It was their failure to condemn Russian actions in Manchuria that first led him to have second thoughts; and by the end of October 1946, a U. S. embassy assessment, in which he presumably concurred, referred to their growing tendency to follow a Soviet line. "This is manifested most obviously," the assessment ran, "in Yenan statements which follow automatically Soviet releases and statements concerning specific problems in the Far East and events in other areas of the world. . . . Foreign correspondents and other observers are still searching—but thus far without success—for a Chinese Communist who is in any state but one of complete agreement with all Soviet actions." Although not even the Nationalist government had been able to provide "substantive proof" that the Russians were actively supporting the Chinese Communists, "such proof . . . is not important. What is important is that the affinity should not be misunderstood and underestimated."[14]

This brings us to the problem of what Russian and Chinese Communist policy really was. Were Stalin and Mao Tse-tung working in tandem, and were the Chinese Communists any more inclined to put faith in a political settlement than Chiang Kai-shek? Both of these questions are answered in the negative if we are to believe one of the most famous quotations in the history of the Chinese civil war. Thus, early in 1948, Stalin is reported to have told a visiting Yugoslav delegation that "after the war we invited the Chinese comrades to come to Moscow and we discussed the situation in China. We told them bluntly that we considered the development of the uprising in China had no prospects, that the Chinese comrades should seek a *modus vivendi* with Chiang Kai-shek, and that they should join the Chiang Kai-shek government and dissolve their army. The Chinese comrades agreed here in Moscow with the views of the Soviet comrades, but went back to China and acted quite otherwise. They mustered their forces, organized their armies and now, as we see, they are beating Chiang Kai-shek's army."[15]

What is wrong with this version of events is that it ignores the fact that the Chinese Communists did pursue the policy advocated by the Russians, at least until February 1946. On the first of that month, Liu Shao-ch'i, one of the top-ranking Chinese Communist leaders made an important speech, the text of which has only recently become available. China's revolutionary struggle, Liu argued, had already changed to a peaceful, parliamentary and legal struggle. The party must therefore adapt itself to the new situation and develop debating skills and election techniques. It would participate in the government alongside the Nationalists, and Liu made it clear that this meant Nationalist participation in the government of the "liberated," or Communist-controlled, areas. The Communist armed forces would be integrated into the national army and party committees and political commissars abolished. In return, Communists would share in the running of the defense ministry. Liu criticized the left-wing deviation of "closed door-ism," whose exponents were unwilling to adopt new methods and did not believe that Chiang would not attack the Communists or that he was capable of carrying out reforms. This tendency was dangerous and must be overcome.[16]

It is impossible to overemphasize the importance of this speech. Hitherto, the Communists had steadfastly refused to merge their army with that of the Nationalists, or to give up the autonomous status of the liberated areas, but here was Liu Shao-ch'i advocating both. It is true that, during and after the Cultural Revolution in China, systematic attempts were made to portray Liu as an inveterate "revisionist" and "capitulationist" and that the speech in question was produced as evidence of these sins. But it is inconceivable that Liu would have spoken in favor of concessions of such magnitude without the support of the party leadership as a whole, and it is significant that Mao Tse-tung has evidently chosen not to put any of his internal policy speeches for this period on the public record.[17]

Of course, the Communists subsequently realized that a peaceful strategy for the conquest of power was not going to work and reverted to armed struggle. This was followed by a noticeable change in the Soviet attitude towards the situation in China. As Charles B. McLane has written: "During the last ten days of June [1946] . . . there began to appear in *Pravda* and in other organs what must be considered, in comparison with previous months, a virtual deluge of news dispatches from or concerning China. In the writer's opinion, the sudden interest in Chinese affairs expressed in these dispatches signified a definitive turn in Russia's policy toward China. The editorial comment which presently followed confirmed the change. It was the most decisive observable development in Soviet Far Eastern policy since the end of the war." McLane noted that criticisms of American intervention in China became markedly sharper, that General Marshall was directly attacked for the first time, and that the activities of the Chinese Communists, which had been virtually ignored since August 1945, began to be detailed. "From this time on," he concluded, "readers . . . need not necessarily have inferred that Moscow would immediately underwrite the Communists' further efforts in China or support them with material aid. They could, however, safely assume that, barring unforeseen developments, the Chinese Communists could count on Moscow's political, diplomatic, and moral support. . . ."[18] In sum, far from diverging sharply, Russian and Chinese Communist politics seem to have kept quite closely in step.

This does not mean that the goals, and still less the priorities, of the two parties were necessarily the same. While we may safely assume that the Chinese Communists wanted to gain control over the whole of China, we simply do not know what hopes the Russians entertained. We cannot even deduce them for their actions, for these were frequently ambiguous. In Manchuria, for example, the Russians helped the Communists by supplying them with large quantities of captured Japanese weapons,[19] by turning over local government to them, by helping to suppress the "Kuomintang Underground," and by obstructing the landing of Nationalist troops.[20] But, at the same time, it seems that the prolongation of their occupation of Manchuria was prompted more by a desire to extract economic concessions from the Nationalist government than to consolidate Communist control over the area.[21] Despite their refusal publicly to condemn Soviet actions in Manchuria, there is evidence that the Chinese Communists, like Chiang, were irked by the tardiness of the Russians in withdrawing. "After all these years this is too much!" Chou En-lai bitterly complained to a member of the U. S. embassy in February 1946.[22] Then there was the wholesale plundering of Manchuria's economic resources. President Truman's reparations expert, Edwin Pauley, contrasted Soviet conduct in Manchuria with that in Korea, where there was practically no capital removal or destruction of industry, and suggested that the former was deliberately designed to create conditions of chaos and instability.[23] This can hardly have been welcomed by the Chinese Communists either.

It is probably safe to assume, however, that the Soviet Union was much more concerned with American policy than with the susceptibilities of the Chinese Communists. The published records of the Moscow conference of foreign ministers in December 1945 show that the Russians were greatly preoccupied by the presence of United States troops in north China, and they proposed the simultaneous withdrawal of Soviet and American forces by mid-January 1946. Byrnes refused to agree to a fixed deadline, on the grounds that he could not predict when the American troops would have completed their mission of disarming the Japanese in north China; nonetheless, the Russians eventually withdrew their forces from Manchuria unilaterally in April and May.[24] During the first few months of 1946, moreover, Stalin made various overtures to Chiang Kai-shek, in which, according to the latter, he "not only asked China to bar third powers from Manchuria but also expressed the hope that China would adopt an "independent policy." He criticized the United States for helping Japan to recover and asked China to take positive measures together with Soviet Russia for joint defense against Japan." As the Russian dictator also stressed the desirability of a coalition with the Chinese Communists and the need for concessions to their point of view, Chiang regarded the overtures as no more than a ploy designed to make China "a Soviet satellite through 'peaceful transformation.'"[25] Up to a point, this was probably true, but if he had responded positively, it is by no means certain that Stalin would have favored his eventual elimination and replacement by Mao Tse-tung.

Stalin could afford to flirt with Chiang Kai-shek, for American policy ensured that the Chinese Communists could have no other external ally than the Soviet Union. At the beginning of the Marshall mission, it seems that they did make a somewhat self-conscious bid for American support. "We believe that the democracy to be initiated in China should follow the American pattern," the chief Communist negotiator, Chou En-lai, told General Marshall on 31 January 1946. "Since in present-day China, the conditions necessary to the introduction of Socialism do not exist, we Chinese Communists, who theoretically advocate Socialism as our ultimate goal, do not mean, or deem it possible, to carry it into effect in the immediate future. In saying that we should pursue the American path, we mean to acquire U. S. style democracy and science, and specifically to introduce to this country agricultural reform, industrialization, free enterprise and development of individuality, so that we may build up an independent, free and prosperous China." Chou went on to say that it had been rumored that Mao Tse-tung was planning to visit Moscow. "On learning this," he claimed, "Chairman Mao laughed and remarked half-jokingly that if ever he would take a furlough abroad, which would certainly do much good to his present health condition, he would rather go to the United States, because he thinks that there he can learn lots of things useful to China."[26]

Since Mao is on record as having said, in August 1945, that "U. S. imperialism wants to help Chiang Kai-shek wage civil war and turn China into a U. S. dependency,"[27] his sense of humor may have been even more developed than Chou En-lai indicated, but if the Chinese Communists did entertain serious hopes of winning American support, they were soon disillusioned. By June 1946, Chou En-lai was accusing the United States of following a two-faced policy towards China. While Marshall followed the road of conciliation and cooperation, others took a different line.

In the Pacific [Chou went on], the U. S. has now made military dispositions. In China, they actively helped the Kuomintang before the Chinese Government was democratized. After victory over Japan, the U. S. still assisted the Kuomintang by providing supplies which were not for the purpose of fighting the Japanese any more. Troops were sent to North China and recently to Manchuria. . . .

Right now, war supplies in Manchuria were ample enough to last for another three months of war. These supplies were of course sent up by the U. S. Navy. In Manchuria, airplanes had been used extensively. . . . These planes undoubtedly were handed over to the Kuomintang through lend-lease—also fuel. Civil war in China had not been stopped. The U. S. Navy has sent two fleets to China . . . and has furnished the Chinese Navy with vessels, though the Ministry of Defense is completely controlled by the Kuomintang. There were incidents in which the U. S. Marines . . . had been provocative. . . .

General Chennault [the former U. S. army air force commander in China], on his way back to the United States, declared at Pearl Harbor that the Chinese Communist problem should be resolved by force. The U. S. Navy was still cooperating with [secret police chief] General Tai Li's office and was continuing to supply the Tai Li units. All these circumstances if viewed objectively tend to encourage the Kuomintang to wage civil war. If the Kuomintang received such assistance and felt that it was backed up, it would fear nothing.[28]

Marshall's personal immunity from criticism did not last much longer, and by the end of September, Mao Tse-tung would tell an American newspaper correspondent: "I doubt very much that the policy of the U. S. Government is one of 'mediation'. Judging by the large amount of aid the United States is giving Chiang Kai-shek to enable him to wage a civil war on an unprecedented scale, the policy of the U. S. Government is to use the so-called mediation as a smoke-screen for strengthening Chiang Kai-shek in every way and suppressing the democratic forces in China through

Chiang Kai-shek's policy of slaughter so as to reduce China virtually to a U. S. colony."[29] What finally led to Marshall's return to the United States was the refusal of the Communists to go on accepting him as a mediator.

Some of the Communists' charges were exaggerated. They were quite wrong in believing that the United States wanted a civil war in China, and they seem to have completely dismissed the various embargoes and sanctions that Marshall imposed upon the Nationalist government and of which they must have been fully aware even if not officially informed. Nevertheless, their basic assumption—that American policy was designed to support Chiang Kai-shek—was quite correct. This was hardly the foundation for a cordial relationship with the United States.

The failure of the Marshall mission would have compelled the United States to rethink its China policy in any case, but the process was accelerated by the marked deterioration in the military position of the Nationalists during the second quarter of 1947 and by the heightening global tension between the United States and the Soviet Union symbolized in the enunciation of the Truman Doctrine (March 1947) and the Marshall Plan (June). On 26 May, Marshall, who was now secretary of state, lifted the arms embargo imposed ten months previously, but this was not seen as enough in some quarters. In an important paper of 9 June, the Joint Chiefs to Staff argued that "the military security of the United States will be threatened if there is any further spread of Soviet influence and power in the Far East" and that, given the fact that Japan was disarmed and occupied, "the only Asiatic government at present capable of even a show of resistance to Soviet expansion in Asia is the Chinese Nationalist Government." The chiefs recommended, therefore, that "United States assistance to those nations on the periphery of Soviet-controlled areas in Eurasia should be given in accordance with an over-all plan. This plan should take into account the necessity for the maintenance of the Chinese National Government and should eventually provide sufficient assistance to that Government to eliminate all communist armed opposition, the latter in accordance with the priorities established by the over-all plan."[30]

To be fair to the chiefs, they did not believe much military assistance would be necessary—"in large part merely ammunition and replacement parts for American equipment furnished the National Government forces during and immediately following the recent war"[31]—but their recommendation was potentially open-ended and, moreover, contradicted the previous official position that there could be no military solution to the Communist problem in China. For the State Department, John Carter Vincent opposed the chiefs' proposals, "because such a course (1) would lead inevitably to direct intervention in China's civil war; (2) would provoke the USSR to similar intervention on the side of the Chinese

Communists; (3) would be inconclusive unless we were prepared to take over direction of Chinese military operations and administration and remain in China for an indefinite period; (4) would invite formidable opposition among the Chinese people; and (5) would constitute a strategic commitment in China inconsistent with [an earlier JSC assessment] which examines the problem of United States assistance to other countries from the standpoint of 'urgency of need and importance to the national security of the United States' and places 'China very low on the list of countries which should be given such assistance.'" His office believed, he concluded "that a USSR-dominated China is not a danger of sufficient immediacy or probability to warrant committing ourselves to the far-reaching consequences which would ensue from our involvement in the Chinese Civil War on the side of the National Government."[32]

In order to resolve the difference of opinion among his advisers, or perhaps simply to postpone having to come to terms with it, President Truman, at Marshall's suggestion, resorted to the time-honored bureaucratic device of sending a committee of enquiry to China to examine the situation at first hand. The mission was headed by General Wedemeyer, and its report was submitted to the president on 19 September 1947. In essence, it adopted the approach of the Joint Chiefs of Staff, proposing an increase in military assistance, considerable expansion of the size and role of the U. S. military advisory groups,[33] and a five-year program of economic aid. At the same time, the report recognized that maladministration and corruption had caused a loss of confidence in the Nationalist government and that without far-reaching economic and political reforms, no aid program could achieve its objectives.[34]

Much to Wedemeyer's annoyance, the administration simply sat on his report. At a meeting with the secretary of defense, James Forrestal, on 3 November 1947, General Marshall

said that the State Department was actively working on the report and that particular attention was being given to the military phase as well as the financial phase. . . . He summarized by saying that apparently everyone is in agreement that we wish to prevent Soviet domination of China and that we wish to provide for a stable government there, but there is no unanimity on the way in which assistance can be rendered. He said that the immediate problem is to determine what we can do effectively. He said that we must recognize that we have the problem of prolonging the agonies of a corrupt government, and that we probably have reached the point where we will have to accept the fact that this government will have to be retained in spite of our desire to change its character. He said that he was of the opinion that we cannot afford to make the Wedemeyer Report public as to do so would do much more harm than good.[35]

Apart from the problem of how one could provide effective aid to "a corrupt government," there was growing doubt in Washington as to whether what happened in China was all that important anyway. The key figure in this reappraisal of China's role seems to have been George Kennan, who was appointed director of the new policy planning staff in the State Department in May 1947 and who wielded considerable influence in the formulation of American foreign policy during Marshall's term as secretary of state. The core of Kennan's approach was "that there were only five regions of the world—the United States, the United Kingdom, the Rhine valley with adjacent industrial areas, the Soviet Union, and Japan—where the sinews of modern military strength could be produced in quantity; ... that only one of these was under Communist control; and ... the main task of containment, accordingly, was one of seeing to it that none of the remaining ones fell under such control." By this token, Japan and not China was the country in the Far East most vital to the United States security, as indeed Kennan argued in a paper on the global situation presented to Marshall at the end of February 1948. A corollary of this was that the United States should "liquidate unsound commitments in China and try to recover our detachment and freedom of action with relation to that situation."[36]

When Marshall went before Congress in February 1948 to present the administration's proposals for limited aid to the Nationalist government, his statement to the House Committee on Foreign Affairs and the Senate Committee on Foreign Relations bore the unmistakable imprint of Kennan's thinking. "China does not itself possess the raw material and industrial resources which would enable it to become a first-class military power within the foreseeable future," Marshall declared. "Furthermore, on the side of American interests, we cannot afford, economically or militarily, to take over the continued failures of the present Chinese Government to the dissipation of our strength in more vital regions where we now have a reasonable opportunity of successfully meeting or thwarting the Communist threat, that is, in the vital industrial area of Western Europe with its tradition of free institutions." Given the Chinese government's deficiencies, "any large-scale U. S. effort to assist [it] to oppose the Communists would most probably degenerate into a direct U. S. undertaking and responsibility, involving the commitment of sizeable forces and resources over an indefinite period. Such a dissipation of U. S. resources would inevitably play into the hands of the Russians, or would provoke a reaction which could possibly, even probably, lead to another Spanish type of revolution or general hostilities." In sum, not only would "the costs of an all-out effort to see Communist forces resisted or destroyed in China ... be impossible to estimate; but the magnitude of the task and the probable costs thereof would clearly be out of proportion to the results to be obtained."[37]

But if Kennan's views were so influential, it may be asked, why was any aid extended to China at all? One reason was given by Marshall in his statement. "We are already committed by past actions and by popular sentiment among our people," he said, "to continue to do what we can to alleviate suffering in China and to give the Chinese Government and people the possibility of working out China's problems in their own way. It would be against U. S. interests to demonstrate a complete lack of confidence in the Chinese Government and to add to its difficulties by abruptly rejecting its request for assistance. The psychological effects on morale in China would be seriously harmful."[38] Much more important, however, was the fact that China policy was developing into a political issue in the United States. The second half of 1947 saw the reemergence of a "China Lobby," both in Congress and outside, which criticized the administration's record on China and urged greater support for Chiang. It was not powerful enough to dictate the course of the government's policy, but its views could not be ignored.[39]

Truman's unexpected victory in the presidential election of November 1948 marked a setback for the China Lobby, but it seems to have prevented the administration from disengaging itself from the crumbling Nationalist government in 1949 as completely as it would have wished. Thus, while no new military assistance was supplied beyond that already voted in the China Aid Act of 1948, the unexpended portion was not cut off at the expiration of the act, and economic aid continued. The United States, therefore, was still associated with support for Chiang Kai-shek.

This was a pity, for the administration evidently wished to keep its options open in respect of China. An important factor underlying this desire was the possibility that Mao Tse-tung might become another Tito. When the Cominform published its resolution condemning Yugoslavia at the end of June 1948, the U. S. embassy in Moscow immediately noted that it had "extremely interesting implications" for the Chinese Communists and that "parallels in agrarian background [of the] two parties and applicability [of] certain criticisms in document to Chinese party policies cannot fail to impress Chinese C. P. leaders." On 15 June, the U. S. ambassador in China, John Leighton Stuart, reported on a recent six-hour conversation between his Soviet colleague and the Chinese minister of the interior in which the latter "sensed a certain distrust of the Chinese Communists" on the part of the Russians, who apparently feared that "they might take a course of action similar to that of Tito."[40]

By early 1949, an authoritative series of articles in the *New York Times* showed that the administration was taking the Titoist possibility very seriously. The Chinese Communists, it was pointed out, were irritated by Soviet attempts to foster separatism in north China and, more recently, in Sinkiang, where the Russians had just begun negotiations with the Nationalist authorities. In south China, it was argued, the Russians might even favor the establishment of a non-Communist Chinese state in order to reduce Mao's influence still further and to prevent the Chinese Communists from coming into direct contact with the Moscow-led Communist movements of Southeast Asia. This may have been the reason that the Soviet bloc ambassadors followed the Nationalist government to Canton in February 1949 while those of the United States and the other western powers remained in Nanking. Apart from these considerations, it was felt that Mao's independence might well develop more rapidly than Tito's since no pan-Slav mystique linked the Chinese to the Russians and Mao, unlike the Yugoslav leaders, had never been a completely indoctrinated agent of the Comintern.[41]

There was clearly some basis for these beliefs. Mao himself has stated that the Russians did indeed fear that he would become another Tito[42] and at least one reputable scholar has presented evidence, from what he describes as "a reliable source," to suggest that Moscow endeavored to forestall the Communist conquest of Sinkiang by setting up a separatist government there.[43] It is even true that the Russians did advocate the establishment of separate governments in north and south China at this time, although the reason advanced in favor of such a step was, hardly surprisingly, not the same as that adduced by the American government's analysts. In a commentary on Mao Tse-tung's poem "The PLA Occupies Nanking," published in the official Chinese Communist Party newspaper in January 1964, Kuo Mo-jo wrote: "Before and after the campaign against Nanking [the city fell to the Communists on 23 April 1949], there were some well-meaning friends both inside and outside the country who proposed that China should be left with separate governments in the north and the south, and that it was better not to provoke the interference of imperialism, especially American imperialism."[44]

Regardless of the misgivings with which the Russians evidently viewed their imminent victory, the Chinese Communists were not about to exchange membership in the socialist camp for the perils of neutrality, and still less for a rapprochement with the power that had consistently, if ineffectually, opposed them since 1945. "The forty years' experience of Sun Yat-sen and the twenty-eight years' experience of the Communist Party," Mao Tse-tung declared on 30 June 1949, "have taught us to lean to one side, and we are firmly convinced that in order to win victory and consolidate it we must lean to one side. In the light of the experience accumulated in these forty years and these twenty-eight years, all Chinese without exception must lean either to the side of imperialism or to the side of socialism. Sitting on the fence will not do, nor is there a third road.... Internationally, we belong to the side of the anti-imperialist front headed by the Soviet Union, and so we can turn only to this side for genuine and friendly help, not to the side of the imperialist front."[45]

In part, at least, this declaration must have been designed to reassure Stalin. It was a pity, therefore, that the United States took it so literally. In the letter under cover of which he transmitted the China White Paper to President Truman on 30 July, Dean Acheson, who had succeeded Marshall as secretary of state in January 1949, wrote:

The Communist leaders have foresworn their Chinese heritage and have publicly announced their subservience to a foreign power, Russia, which during the last 50 years, under czars and Communists alike, has been most assiduous in its efforts to extend its control in the Far East. In the recent past, attempts at foreign domination have appeared quite clearly to the Chinese people as external aggression and as such have been bitterly and in the long run successfully resisted. Our aid and encouragement have helped them to resist. In this case, however, the foreign domination has been masked behind the facade of a vast crusading movement which apparently has seemed to many Chinese to be wholly indigenous and national. Under these circumstances, our aid has been unavailing. . . .
[Nevertheless] we continue to believe that, however tragic may be the immediate future of China and however ruthlessly a major portion of this great people may be exploited by a party in the interest of a foreign imperialism, ultimately the profound civilization and the democratic individualism of China will reassert themselves and she will throw off the foreign yoke. I consider that we should encourage all developments in China which now and in the future work toward this end.[46]

This attack upon the legitimacy and patriotism of the Chinese Communists, coupled with the barely disguised threat that the United States would support, albeit in some ill-defined way, efforts to rid China of their presence, can only have served to strengthen Mao in his prejudices.[47]

The proclamation of the Chinese People's Republic (CPR) on 1 October 1949 brought with it two immediate problems for the United States: diplomatic recognition and the Chinese seat in the United Nations. With regard to recognition, Tang Tsou showed quite clearly more than ten years ago that, in spite of rumors at the time and various allegations since, the United States never came close to recognizing the CPR during the period preceding the outbreak of the Korean War. One of the main reasons was the new government's harsh treatment of American diplomats and the seizure of American property in China. As Acheson told the United Nations secretary-general, Trygve Lie, on 21 January 1950, "the whole Peking regime was an improvisation that scarcely knew what it was doing, or what repercussions its acts had internationally. He went on to recall the recent seizure of American properties, the closing of the American Consular Offices and the kidnapping of American citizens. The United States would certainly not recognize Peking in such circumstances. . . ."[48]

Acheson went on to say that the United States also opposed the admission of the CPR to the United Nations. But since the American representative on the Security Council had said on 10 January that the United States would accept a simple majority vote of that body and would not use its veto, Lie, who favored the CPR's admission, believed for some time that it might be possible to arrange something with the other members of the council. Unfortunately, the Chinese Communists chose this very moment to recognize the rebel regime of Ho Chi Minh in Vietnam, and this not only cut short French plans to recognize the CPR, but also led them to oppose its admission to the United Nations. Moreover, after the signature of the Sino-Soviet treaty on 14 February, the American attitude hardened; and Lie was reliably informed that the State Department had begun to exert pressure on one of the Latin American countries that had hitherto favored the CPR's admission to reverse its stand.[49] Supporters of the CPR's admission to the United Nations would have to wait twenty-one years to secure the necessary number of votes.

Although the Soviet Union was ostentatiously boycotting the Security Council at this time, on the grounds that it could not recognize the credentials of the Chinese Nationalist delegate, some highly placed Western observers believed that it did not really want the CPR to be admitted to the United Nations because an isolated China would be more amenable to Russian influence and control. It was even suggested that some of the actions that had so damaged the CPR's cause, such as the recognition of Ho Chi Minh's regime, might have been suggested by the Russians with precisely this end in view.[50] We do not, of course, know the truth of these allegations. But Mao Tse-tung had revealed that the negotiations for the Sino-Soviet treaty, which so upset the Americans, "involved a hard struggle" and that Stalin "did not want to sign it." This does not indicate the close relationship between the Chinese Communists and the Russians that the United States assumed throughout this period and upon which its policy was based.[51]

Refusal to recognize the CPR and opposition to its admission to the United Nations did not automatically resolve the problem of the United States' relations with the rump Nationalist government on the island of Formosa. The position at the end of 1949 was clearly set out in a draft report submitted to the National Security Council on 23 December:

It is not believed [it stated] that denial for Formosa to the Chinese Communists can be achieved by any method short of actual U. S. military occupation. As a CIA Intelligence estimate of October 19, 1949 (. . . concurred in by the intelligence organizations of the Departments of State, Army, Navy and Air Force) states: "Without major armed intervention, U. S. political, economic, and logistic support of the present Nationalist island regime cannot insure its indefinite survival as a non-Communist base. Communist capabilities are such that only extended U. S. military occupation and control of Taiwan can prevent its eventual capture and subjugation by Chinese Communist forces. Failing U. S. military occupation and control, a non-Communist regime on Taiwan probably will succumb to the Chinese Communists by the end of 1950."

. . . In the light of the foregoing, and in view of the estimate of the JCS, reaffirmed in NSC 37/7 of August 22, 1949, that "the strategic importance of Formosa does not justify overt military action . . . ," it is believed that U. S. military occupation of Formosa, which would require concurrent responsibility for the administration of the Island, would not be in the U. S. national interest.

But although their assessment of Formosa's strategic importance had not changed, the Joint Chiefs of Staff did believe that "a modest, well-directed and closely supervised program of military advice and assistance to the anti-Communist Government in Formosa would be in the security interest of the United States, and should be integrated with a stepped-up political, economic and psychological program pursued energetically in extension of present United States programs there."[52] "I objected to this toying with the mousetrap," Dean Acheson wrote subsequently; "the National Security Council supported my view; and the President endorsed it." In other words, as Truman made plain in a statement on 5 January 1950, the United States was not going to give any kind of military assistance in order to prevent the Chinese Communists from seizing Formosa.[53]

In retrospect, the announcement on 27 June 1950, after the outbreak of the Korean War, that the Seventh Fleet would prevent a Communist invasion of Formosa and vice versa marked a decisive turning point in United States policy towards Chiang Kai-shek's regime; this was so in spite of the fact that the announcement was sheer bluff[54] and that administration spokesmen pointed out that it was a temporary measure occasioned by the fighting and was not intended to prejudge the future of the island. Now American support for Chiang began to pick up, a process that was accelerated after the Chinese Communists entered the Korean War at the end of October. Arms shipments to the Nationalist regime were renewed in August and stepped up in January and February 1951. In March, it was agreed to send a military advice and assistance group to Formosa. As William Bueler has written, "These steps signaled unqualified U. S. support for the Nationalist authorities as the rightful government of Taiwan, and, since that government never claimed to be just the government of Taiwan but rather the legitimate government of all China, this major commitment of U. S. aid implied that the United States was even willing to acquiesce in the Nationalist claim to legitimacy over all China."[55] Even more noticeable than the shift in government policy was that of public opinion. Whereas in January 1950, fewer than 20 percent of those asked favored extending financial and military aid to Chiang Kai-shek, a year or so later, no fewer than 58 percent thought he should be given the wherewithal to invade the mainland![56] It all went to show that the American blood being shed in Korea, much of it at Chinese Communist hands, was a great deal thicker than the water that had flowed under the bridge since the Marshall mission of 1945/46.

\* \* \*

During the last year of the Second World War, some "old China hands" in the State Department actually suggested that the United States should support the Chinese Communists rather than Chiang Kai-shek. But, as President Roosevelt's confidant, Harry Hopkins, explained to one of them, this was out of the question. "I have no doubt that the picture you give is largely correct," he said. "But the only Chinese that most Americans have ever heard of is Chiang Kai-shek. And they [i.e., Chiang's opponents] call themselves Communists."[57] The proposal was never put forward again. But while it may have been impossible, on account of the public opinion to which Hopkins alluded, for the United States to have backed the Communists in the Chinese civil war, especially after the deterioration of U. S. relations with the Soviet Union, support for Chiang was not the only alternative. Indeed, it could be argued that a policy of genuine neutrality would have served American interests far better than the ineffectual assistance extended to the Nationalists. In this respect, the Soviet Union played a much more skillful game than its rival. Although the Russians gave strong verbal support to the Chinese Communists, they seem to have provided no material assistance after their withdrawal from Manchuria in early 1946; and they were prepared, as we have seen, to accept a non-Communist regime in south China as late as April 1949.

For various reasons—of which public opinion does not appear to be one[58]—the United States did not adopt a similarly flexible approach. To begin with, at the time of the Marshall mission, American policymakers evidently gave much more importance to China and their Chinese protégés than did their Soviet counterparts. Later, when they sought to disengage, they ran into the opposition of a vocal minority in Congress. Finally, despite all the talk about Titoism, the American leaders were unable, when it came to the point, to differentiate between the Chinese Communists and the Soviet imperialism they felt they were confronting throughout the rest of the world. No one can pretend that relations between a regime led by a dedicated group of Marxist-Leninist revolutionaries and the world's most powerful capitalist nation would ever have been easy. But for the factors mentioned above, however, they might have been somewhat less bitter and antagonistic.

# 9

# FDR, TRUMAN, AND INDOCHINA, 1941-1952: The Forgotten Years

In a front page story of the Sunday *New York Times,* published on June 13, 1971, the American reading public was apprised by correspondent Neil Sheehan that a massive study of how the United States went to war in Indochina, conducted by the Pentagon three years previously, demonstrated that four administrations (Truman, Eisenhower, Kennedy and Johnson) had developed progressively a sense of commitment to a non-Communist Vietnam, a readiness to fight the North to protect the South, and an ultimate frustration with this effort—all to a much greater extent than their public statements had acknowledged at the time. Covering the period from 1945 to May 1968, the latter date marking the start of the Paris peace talks after President Johnson had imposed limits on future military commitments and had revealed his decision to retire from public life, the *New York Times* version of the so-called Pentagon Papers reached a number of tentative conclusions. The most important of these were, first, that President Truman's decision to provide military assistance to France in her colonial war against the Communist-led Vietminh had "directly involved" the United States in Vietnam and set the course of American foreign policy in the region for years to come; second, that President Eisenhower's decision to rescue South Vietnam from a Communist coup and to undermine Ho Chi Minh's regime in the north had given the administration a direct role in the ultimate breakdown of the Geneva settlement in 1954; third, that President Kennedy, though spared from major escalation decisions by his death, had transformed a policy of "limited risk," which he had putatively inherited, into a relatively "broad commitment" that left the Johnson administration with the restricted options of either escalating or withdrawing; fourth, that President Johnson, though himself reluctant to make a final decision on the matter, had intensified the covert war against North Vietnam and had begun planning in the spring of 1964 to wage an overt war, a full year before he publicly revealed the depth of his involvement; and fifth, and finally, that the campaign of growing clandestine military pressures through 1964, together with the expanded bombing of North Vietnam, had been initiated despite the judgment of the federal intelligence community that such measures would probably not cause Hanoi to cease its support of the Vietcong and that the bombing had been deemed militarily ineffective within a short period of time. Such stories of dissimulation in high places and governmental deception of the public fell on fertile ground. For, at the time, the Nixon administration, with its obsession with secret diplomacy and studied indifference to public reaction to, say, the American incursion into Cambodia and later the Watergate affair, generally reinforced the image conveyed by the Pentagon Papers.

For all of its timeliness and significance, the *New York Times* edition of United States–Vietnamese relations exhibited several serious flaws. Leslie H. Gelb, the chairman of the Vietnam Task Force that undertook the study, found the *Times* in error with regard to the principal piece of evidence relied upon to establish its case against the government. "First," he wrote in September 1971, "they should have stated explicitly that President Johnson before the 1964 election was not part of the general consensus in our government to bomb North Vietnam. Our studies do not show that he was, and indeed depict him as quite resistant to this course."[1] "Second," continued Gelb, "they give a misleading view of CIA findings. [For] while the CIA was arguing that the bombing of the North was having the opposite of the desired effects . . . it was not nearly as pessimistic about the war in the South." Gelb, in essence, argued that taken by themselves the documents tended to distort the true picture of events.

The Pentagon Papers, in whatever form they appeared (in addition to the *New York Times* edition, there were the four-volume Senator Gravel and the official twelve-volume Defense Department editions) failed to reconstruct the total framework in which America's Vietnamese policy evolved. For while the compilers had full access to Defense files and CIA materials, the Task Force had had only limited access to State Department cables and memoranda and none at all to those of the White House. Moreover, they were expressly forbidden to interview any of the principal participants, a defect that has partly been remedied. Even the 548-page study of the Vietnam War ordered by then National Security adviser Henry Kissinger in January 1969 added little to what was already well known. (Incidentally, the Kissinger study was subsequently made available to the *New York Times* in the spring of 1972, very likely to indicate to the *Times*'s editors that there were no hard feelings on the part of the Nixon administration in its abortive attempt to censor material in advance of publication.)

All these studies of America's Vietnamese policy, then, despite their wealth of information, failed to take into consideration what social scientist Robert F. Berkhofer, Jr., has called the "situational" approach to history, that is to say, the concept of studying concrete actions in relation to a process of ever-changing situations. According to Berkhofer, the situational approach to history includes for subjects of study "the attitudes people possess about how to act toward one another; how to utilize their physical environment; [and] how they should judge the good, the true and the beautiful."[2] Nor did these studies emphasize the growth and evolution of the Cold War mentality under which policymakers acted out their roles and, in fairness to them, met their own responsibilities as they perceived them. Consideration of these factors would have taken place in what historian of science Thomas S. Kuhn has termed "paradigm" analysis, an analysis that includes the study of "the entire constellation of beliefs, values, and techniques and so on shared by members of a given community," the mental sets and unspoken assumptions "that for a time provide model problems and solutions to a community of practitioners."[3] Finally, and perhaps more importantly in an era when issues of public morality have come to play a prominent role in political life, the Pentagon Papers failed to indicate whether or not there were moral alternatives to decisions taken, or even the remote possibility that any had been contemplated. In the search for possible moral alternatives, and this is the principal thrust of this essay, an understanding of the origins and evolution of American involvement in Vietnam is utterly unintelligible considered apart from the climate of opinion and from the far larger foreign policy considerations and requirements of the United States during World War II, the early Cold War period, and the Korean War.

In an examination of these factors, it will be argued that Franklin D. Roosevelt's Indochinese policy served on the whole both as a function of his overall policy to accelerate the liberation of colonial peoples (where possible) on one side and his efforts to punish the French by depriving them of their Southeast Asian colonial empire on the other side. Under Harry S. Truman, whose administration in time virtually overturned FDR's policies in the area, America's Vietnamese policy served as a function of HST's larger policy of containing first Soviet and then Sino-Soviet imperialism in Korea and Southwest Asia. From the impact of the Korean experience onward, successive American presidents—Eisenhower, Kennedy, Johnson, Nixon, and then Ford—increasingly came to view the Vietnam theater as an internationalized testing ground of rival great powers and ideological claims and never seriously bothered to consider the political realities of that part of Asia, which were from time to time dimly perceived, separately from larger policy considerations. When the Nixon trips to Peking and Moscow inaugurated a period of détente with America's erstwhile rivals, in any case a legacy of dubious value, the nation's Vietnam policy stood alone for a season and appeared, at least to those who had forgotten their own history (or worse, never knew it), basically absurd if not evil. The official arguments that the United States presence there gave credibility to the nation's international commitments and determination to stand by those commitments (and subsequent arguments for continued economic and military assistance to South Vietnam) merely highlighted this absurdity.

In what may properly be called the first phase of United States–Vietnamese relations, Vietnam (and Indochina generally) was seen by the Roosevelt administration as one part of its overall strategy both to accelerate the decolonization of the Far East and to punish the French (de Gaulle?) by depriving them of their Southeast Asian empire, although by the end of World War II there remained the distinct possibility that France herself would be permitted to liberate her own colonies under specified conditions. Recent scholarship has suggested that FDR's determination to prevent the resumption of French colonial rule in Indochina and to establish in its place an international trusteeship that would ultimately gain its independence foundered, in the words of Gary R. Hess, on "Roosevelt's reluctance to risk a rupture in the wartime coalition and utilize fully his military and diplomatic power."[4] Still others have argued that under the combined pressure of the British and the French, FDR had totally abandoned his plans for a liberated Indochina by mid-1944; this thesis, however, has been undermined by revelations in the recently declassified wartime messages between Roosevelt and Churchill, which provide evidence that as late as March 1945, the president and the prime minister shared very different views on the matter.[5] Both judgments, whatever their merits, seem to overlook the alternative hypothesis that FDR's apparent diplomatic weakness *and*, at least in this instance, principal strength lay in his ostensible vacillation; for until the Axis powers were completely defeated it would surely have been unreasonable on his part, a possibility perhaps overlooked by his critics, to take a fixed position on such peripheral issues. The central point here is that the general direction of President Roosevelt's policy, i.e., the liberation and ultimate independence of the Indochinese peoples, was constantly in the same direction.

"From time to time," recalled Secretary of State Cordell Hull of FDR's Indochinese policy, "the President had stated forthrightly to me and to others his view that French Indo-China should be placed under international trusteeship after the end of the war, with a view to its receiving full independence as soon as possible." As a correlative to this goal, FDR appeared to have been equally motivated by his desire to see the French punished for what he regarded as their moral turpitude in the face of danger. "The French dependency," continued Hull, "stuck in his mind as having been the springboard for the Japanese attack on the Philippines, Malaya, and the Dutch East Indies. He could not but remember the devious conduct of the Vichy Government in granting Japan the right to station troops there, without consultation with us but with an effect to make the world believe we approved."[6]

The occasions on which FDR discussed the possibility of an international trusteeship were both numerous and well documented. Hull related that in March 1943 he attended a White House conference at which British Foreign Secretary Eden and Ambassador Halifax heard the president indicate his hope to see an international trusteeship in the region. The British, who would later be accused of using their own opposition to the dissolution of the French Far Eastern empire as a "stalking horse" with regard to theirs, were furious. After finding some support from Under Secretary of State Sumner Welles, Eden cabled Churchill that "the President was being very hard on the French, from which the strongest opposition was to be expected. He [FDR] admitted this but said that France would no doubt require assistance for which consideration might be the placing of certain parts of her territory at the disposal of the United Nations."[7] One cannot help thinking that Eden must surely have suspected that FDR had counted on the British, too, to "require assistance for which consideration might be the placing of certain parts of her territory at the disposal of the United Nations."

At the Anglo-American conference (Trident) at Washington in May 1943, which was principally devoted to global strategy planning and the opening of a second front in Europe, Roosevelt personally called Churchill's attention to the fact, as he saw it, that the French had renounced their claims to Indochina in favor of the Japanese fully six months before Pearl Harbor. Then, according to the Wallace diary, FDR continued by saying, "I believe that after the Japs are driven out, the French have no longer any claim to French Indo-China and I am sure that the Chinese will not want French Indo-China." The prime minister retorted, "Of course, the Chinese will want it." Never one to refrain from twisting the lion's tail, Roosevelt characteristically replied: "Well, you are speaking for Britain which has been for centuries an imperialistic power and you have several generations of imperialist ancestors behind you. You have never refused a square mile anywhere that you could lay your hands on."[8]

In early October 1943, Hull attended another White House conference with Admiral William Leahy and State Department officials. At this time FDR reaffirmed the idea of an international trusteeship for Indochina, as well as the same probability for the Dutch East Indies; he also discussed the possibility, to quote Hull, that "the British might, as a gesture of generosity, return Hong Kong to China while China might, in turn, immediately declare Hong Kong a free port under international trusteeship." Such suggestions doubtless gave the British anxious moments. In January 1944, Ambassador Halifax called on the secretary of state for clarification; two weeks later Hull notified FDR of the British inquiry; ten days later, on January 24, 1944, FDR informed Hull of a recent discussion with Halifax on the subject. "I," Hull quoted FDR as having said, "saw Halifax last week and told him quite frankly that it was perfectly true that I had, for over a year, expressed the opinion that Indo-China should not go back to France but that it should be administered by an international trusteeship." The president's estimate of the French was severe: "France has had the country—thirty million inhabitants—for nearly one hundred years, and the people are worse off than they were at the beginning." After noting that he had already secured the support of Chiang Kai-shek and Stalin, he added that he saw "no reason to play in with the British Foreign Office in this matter." Roosevelt contended further that "the only reason they seem to oppose it is that they fear the effect it would have on their own possessions and those of the Dutch. They have never liked the idea of trusteeship because it is, in some instances, aimed at future independence"—a thought, one could imagine, of no small discomfiture to Prime Minister Churchill. After conceding that each case must be judged on its own merits, FDR concluded that the case of French Indochina was clear: "France has milked it for one hundred years. The people of Indo-China are entitled to something better than that."[9] From this basic assumption FDR never departed.

Nonetheless, and in spite of his preference for an international arrangement for Indochina, Roosevelt officially hesitated to discuss hard and fast plans relative to the implementation of the trusteeship. For, as late as November 1944, FDR still seemed uncertain about the political future of Southeast Asia. "We have made no final decision on the future of Indo-China. This should be made clear."[10] Yet, on the eve of that same Presidential election, Harry Hopkins could confidently predict that in contrast to the Republicans, who would have posed no serious obstacles to British territorial planning "you will find him [Roosevelt] right in on all these questions with his own views and you will have to pay attention to them."[11] Then, moving on to specific instances, Hopkins continued:

Take Indo-China. I know what French rule has meant in Indo-China. It is going to be American and British boys who will die to take it back from the Japanese. Why would we let the French walk in again on their own terms when it is we and not they who will have made all the sacrifices?

Nonetheless, in early January 1945, FDR again demonstrated his reluctance to commit himself officially too soon to what was an obviously fluid situation. Consequently, he wrote in a memorandum to the secretary of state, "I still do not want to get mixed up in any Indochinese situation. It is a matter for postwar."[12] The president's logic seemed both unexceptional and unexceptionable. "From both the military and civilian point of view," he concluded, "action at this time is premature." Historical critics have understandably seized on such comments as sufficient proof of Roosevelt's indecisiveness and general weakness in planning for the postwar world. But in point of fact, it was only on details, implementation, etc., that FDR was prepared to keep his options open. Again, the thrust of his anti-French policy remained on course and in fact never failed to make a profound impact on those most concerned with the area.

For example, FDR indicated beyond peradventure that the French should have as little as possible to do with liberating Indochina. "The President orally expressed the view to Mr. Stettinius," wrote James C. Dunn, the director of the Office of European Affairs, in March 1944, "that no French troops should be used in Indo-China. He added that in his view the operation should be Anglo-American in character and should be followed by the establishment of an international trusteeship over the French colony."[13] Moreover, United States armed forces were ordered not to interfere with the Japanese eviction of the remaining French troops there. General Chennault of the Fourteenth Air Force Group stationed in south China recalled that he had been under explicit orders "to proceed with 'normal action' against the Japanese provided it did not involve supplying French troops." Chennault recounted in his memoirs that "apparently it was American policy that French Indo-China would become a mandated territory after the war and not be returned to the French." The Roosevelt administration hoped that the postwar separation of Indochina from the French empire could more easily be achieved if the French were first ejected from the area. Chennault, the consummate soldier, carried out his orders despite his own reservations about their wisdom. "I carried out my orders to the letter," concluded Chennault, "but I did not relish the idea of leaving Frenchmen to be slaughtered in the jungle while I was forced officially to ignore their plight."[14] Their plight was being closely observed by General de Gaulle, however,

In the context of the American ambassador's being told that French troops still resisting the Japanese in Indochina had futilely appealed to

American military authorities in China and that the United States government had refused to provide transport for an expeditionary force to Indochina, de Gaulle remarked that he was deeply disturbed by the American attitude. "This worries me a great deal," Ambassador Jefferson Caffery quoted the general as having said, "and it comes at a particularly inopportune time." Undoubtedly pretending to be puzzled, de Gaulle then launched into what was to become a standard French diplomatic blackmail motif for the rest of the decade. "What are you driving at?" he earlier had demanded of Harry Hopkins. "Do you want us to become... one of the federated states of the Russian aegis?" Developing his case further, de Gaulle tied the issue of Indochina to the fate of France in Europe. "If the public here comes to realize that you are against us in Indo-China," he went on to say, "there will be terrific disappointment and nobody really knows to what that will lead. We do not want to become Communist; we do not want to fall into the Russian orbit, but I hope that you do not push us into it."[15] By January 1945, the French government insisted that the principle of its reestablishment in Indochina was no longer susceptible to discussion. French policymakers sought, with now almost complete disregard for American opinion, "to go forward with the integration of the colonies into an Empire system; that is to say, as fast as their education, etc., allows, they will advance toward complete equality with Metropolitan France—politically and otherwise."[16]

Despite the French repudiation of American influence in the region, probably further exacerbated by FDR's quarrel the previous year with General de Gaulle over the proposed postwar American use of bases in the French empire, Roosevelt continued to pursue his own plans for the eventual liberation and independence of Indochina. At a presidential press conference on 23 February 1945, in response to a reporter's query as to which nation would be liberating French Indochina, Roosevelt, off the record, reiterated his concern about Indochina and his discussion of the matter with Chiang Kai-shek and Stalin at Teheran. According to the president, Chiang and Stalin both agreed that Indochina should not be returned to the French. FDR's characterization of French rule was both characteristic and consistent: "They [the French] have been there over a hundred years and have done nothing about educating them. For every dollar they have put in, they have taken out ten."[17] After recalling the possibility of establishing an international trusteeship, Roosevelt then added:

Stalin liked the idea. China liked the idea. The British don't like it. It might bust up their empire, because if the Indo-Chinese were to work together and eventually get their independence, the Burmese might do the same thing to the King of England. The French have talked about how they expect to recapture Indo-China, but they haven't got any shipping to do it with. It would only get the British mad. Chiang would go along, Stalin would go along. As for the British, it would only make the British mad. Better to keep quiet just now.

Such comments and the reiteration of his views shortly after Yalta suggest Roosevelt's strongly held views on the subject, as well as his predictable cautionary note, "Better to keep quiet just now."

In March 1945, the month before he died, Franklin Roosevelt continued to evidence a growing and acute sensitivity to the needs and minimum political requirements of the colonial peoples of the Far East in general and those of Indochina in particular. "The President," wrote State Department adviser Charles Taussig of a recent discussion with FDR, "said he was concerned about the brown people in the East. He said that there are 1,100,000,000 brown people. In many Eastern countries they are ruled by a handful of whites and they resent it."[18] Having made a realistic estimate of the situation, FDR then noted prophetically that "our goals must be to help them achieve independence—1,100,000,000 potential enemies are dangerous." With regard to the Indochinese problem, Roosevelt was under no particular illusions about the rough sledding ahead with the French; but he was still confirmed in his belief "that French Indo-China . . . should be taken from France and put under a trusteeship." In what might be considered his last thoughts on the subject, he conceded, however, that he might be persuaded to retreat somewhat, if the French were prepared to make a number of appropriate and formal concessions. "If we can get the proper pledge from France to assume for herself the obligations of a trustee, then . . . [he] would agree to France retaining these colonies with the proviso that independence was the ultimate goal . . . and you can quote me in the State Department." The president died a short time afterwards, on April 12.

At this juncture, traditional historical scholarship, as well as plainly partisan accounts, concluded that the Indochina trusteeship plan went to the grave with FDR, and that Harry S. Truman, faced with a new set of circumstances, mainly the threat of Soviet imperialism in Europe, either declined to meddle in French affairs or, worse, supported them. There is, of course, some truth in this judgment, for which the usual documentation may be cited.[19]

A number of American policymakers bitterly resented Truman's apparent reversal of FDR's plans for Indochina. On May 29, 1945, Patrick J. Hurley, the United States ambassador to China and the man most on the scene, urgently cabled Washington for instructions, offering the observation that there seemed to be a shift away from the administration's inherited anticolonial views. Complaining that "the French Ambassador and Military Missions have become exacting in their demand for American support. . . . and war supplies as a matter of right," he went on to recall:

> In my last conference with President Roosevelt I informed him fully on the Indo-China situation. I told him that the French, British and Dutch were cooperating to prevent the establishment of a United Nations trusteeship for Indo-China. The imperialist leaders believe that such a trusteeship would be a bad precedent for the other imperialistic areas in Southeast Asia. I told the President also that the British would attempt with the use of our Lend Lease supplies and if possible our man power to occupy Indo-China and reestablish imperial control.[20]

At this point Hurley then related how he had earlier asked FDR for a written directive for General Wedemeyer, chief of staff to Chiang Kai-shek, and himself; the president had replied that at the coming San Francisco conference a United Nations trusteeship would be set up aimed at allowing the Indochinese to choose their own form of government. Specifically, continued Hurley, the behavior of "the American Delegation at San Francisco seemed to support the theory of imperial control of colonies and dependent nations by the separate or combined imperialistic nations, not by a United Nations trusteeship," all of which "seemed to indicate a change in American policy." The one-time secretary of war and lawyer from Oklahoma was furious and added his own judgment:

> If American policy is not opposed to imperialism in Asia it is in conflict with the Hull policy. It is in conflict with the principles of the Atlantic Charter. It is in conflict with the principles of the Iran Declaration. It is in conflict with the policy to which all the nations including the imperialistic nations gave support when they were asking the United States to join the fight for liberty and democracy. It is in conflict with the policy that the United States invoked as our reason for the defeat and destruction of Japanese imperialism.

In reply to Hurley's previous request that month for disclosure of any secret arrangements worked out at Yalta, the State Department responded on May 18: "No Yalta decision relating to Indo-China known to Department. Military and political papers now under consideration will be transmitted for your secret information when approved." No message was sent. On 6 June 1945, Hurley apprised State, in what must have been a sense of exasperation, "This morning I received definite information through another source that the State Department advised the War Department of a change in policy in regard to Indo-China."[21] It was thus painfully obvious, at least to Hurley, that Roosevelt's hope for an international trusteeship had been more or less jettisoned for the sake of Franco-American relations, in itself a policy shift of some complexity and one effected with obvious reluctance.

When fighting broke out between the French and the Vietnamese in 1946, the Truman administration found itself in a difficult position. On the one hand, it believed that "as a general principle, the United States should support the armed forces of France with military supplies; on the other hand, it does not . . . desire to strengthen the hand of the French Government in its current attempt to restore by force the pre-war position of France in Indo-China."[22] During the last months of 1945 and throughout 1946, Franklin Roosevelt's policy towards Indochina became gradually transformed in the hands of Truman into a policy that attempted to accomplish two things simultaneously: first, to contribute towards the liberation and ultimate independence of the Indochinese people, albeit now within a prescribed French framework; and, second, to coordinate Allied support against what was perceived as a Soviet threat to Western Europe, a not unreasonable perception given Soviet activities in Eastern and Central Europe. There can be no doubt with regard to the sincerity of the United States' intention to understand and improve, so far as it could, the conditions of the Indochinese peoples. In a State position paper dated 22 June 1945, Acting Secretary of State Joseph C. Grew pointed out that inasmuch as America had an interest in the Pacific, "there should be a progressive enlargement of the political responsibilities, both as individuals and as groups, of all the peoples of this region in order that they may be prepared and able to assume the responsibilities of natural freedom as well as to enjoy its rights."[23] Correlative to this desire was the concern and difficult task of how best to support colonial peoples without at the same time alienating the colonial powers whose support was needed in Europe, i.e., to construct a united front to check Soviet ambitions. The problem thus revolved around the question, How to secure the cooperation of France and Britain in Europe while supporting the increasingly insistent demands of their colonies for a greater share of political and economic freedom? The policy finally adopted, which by its nature was probably foredoomed, was to harmonize the two goals if possible but in the last instance to abandon the colonial peoples if necessary.

These judgments were based, again, on a relatively realistic analysis of political conditions in the area. The State Department accurately predicted in 1945 that "the Indochinese independence groups, which have been working against the Japanese, will quite probably oppose the restoration of French control." Independence sentiment was on the rise, and there could be little doubt that its advocates were prepared to fight and die for it. (This particular observation was supposed to have been one of the "great lessons" of United States involvement in Vietnam in the 1960s.) "It is believed," noted Grew, "that the French will encounter serious difficulty in over-coming this opposition and in re-establishing French Control." And again it was hoped that a large measure of self-government, generously bestowed by the French, presumably, would be the best immediate remedy. At the same time, and here was the rub, it became increasingly apparent that "French policy toward Indo-China will be dominated by the desire to re-establish control in order to reassert her prestige in the world as a great power."

By the summer of 1945, then, the official policy of the United States was to recognize French sovereignty over Indochina, with the hopeful expectation that the French "would allow colonial peoples an opportunity to prepare themselves for increased participation in their own government with eventual self-government as the goal." In this manner, and to an extent that has been virtually ignored, the Truman administration, in part, attempted to execute FDR's last will and testament on Indochina. Within a short period of five years, however, American policymakers systematically abandoned the Indochinese to the tender mercies of the French and in so doing sacrificed Vietnamese aspirations and dreams to the larger considerations of Cold War policy, falling into the trap that Walter Lippmann predicted would befall the executors of a containment blindly pursued.

As is well known, wartime United States-Vietnamese relations unofficially originated in late 1944, when the Vietminh assisted in the rescue of an American pilot shot down over Tonkin. After personally aiding in the return of the pilot to his base in South China, Ho Chi Minh shortly established contact with the Office of Strategic Services and was soon recruited to organize rescue teams for American flyers and was even provided with arms and munitions, presumably with the understanding that they were to be used against the Japanese and not the French. With the Japanese coup in March 1945, in which the Japanese eliminated the French opposition, the Vietminh received additional military supplies and radio equipment from the OSS. In May, several OSS units, which were apparently impressed with Ho's determination to realize independence, parachuted into Tonkin and proceeded for the next several months to work closely with the Vietminh.

In the wake of the Japanese surrender, Ho utilized the OSS to transmit messages to the State Department in what was to be the beginning of a futile effort to secure the aid and recognition of the United States. Ho Chi Minh early hoped and, to a degree, expected that America would take special interest in his country. Between October 1945 and February 1946,

Ho addressed a series of messages to the Truman administration, a fact generally unknown by the public for more than twenty-five years. In the summer of 1945, Ho requested that Vietnam be accorded the same status as the Philippines—i.e., tutelage followed by independence; in November 1945, he wrote Acheson requesting the invitations of a cultural exchange; and in February 1946, he wrote to President Truman to defend Vietnamese independence, pointing to the gracious granting of independence to the Philippines.[24] Ho, who seemed to be confronted with a host of obstacles, worked hard in attempting to warm up the Americans. For example, in proclaiming Vietnamese independence on 2 September 1945, Ho invoked the spirit and indeed the very words of the United States Declaration of Independence: "All men are created equal; they are endowed by the Creator with certain inalienable rights; among them are Life, Liberty, and the pursuit of Happiness." Ho's borrowing was obviously open, intentional, and, unfortunately for the course of American history, of marginal impact.

The last and perhaps the most significant appeal of Ho Chi Minh to the Truman administration occurred in September 1946, while Ho was in Paris attempting to negotiate a modus vivendi with the French. According to George M. Abbott, first secretary of the United States Embassy, who spoke with him at the request of Ambassador Caffery, Ho "emphasized his admiration for the United States and the respect and affection for President Roosevelt which is found even in the remote villages of his country."[25] He made particular reference, continued Abbott, "to our policy toward the Philippines and pointed out that it was only natural that his people, seeing an independent Philippines on one side and India about to gain its freedom on the other, should expect France to understand that similar measures for Indo-China are inevitable." Ho also "took up the question of his supposed Communist connections which he, of course, denied," pointing out "that there are no Communist ministers in his government and that the Viet-Nam constitution opens with a guarantee of personal liberties and the so-called rights of man and also guarantees the right to personal property," although he admitted "that there are Communists in Annam. . . ." Finally, Ho spoke to Abbott of the aid that he might acquire for his country. And then, what must seem in retrospect very odd behavior for a presumably dedicated revolutionary, he went on to mention attractive investment opportunities to be found in Southeast Asia. "He explained," Abbott quoted Ho as having said, "that the riches of his country were largely undeveloped, [and] that he felt that Indo-China offered a fertile field for American capital and enterprise." To further interest the Americans, with their traditional preoccupation with a freely trading "open door" world, Ho made it clear that the French could no longer rely on all their previously held special privileges in the region, inasmuch as "he resisted and would continue to resist the French desire for a continuation of their former policy of economic monopoly." In any case, Ho's parting wish was the hope "that through his contacts with the Embassy the American public would be informed of the true situation in Indo-China." That Ho's message remained obscured from the general public for more than twenty-five years must surely be one of the larger ironies of history.

In a telegram sent 5 December 1946, before large-scale fighting broke out between the French and the Vietminh, Assistant Secretary of State Dean Acheson cautioned a special Department of State representative in Indochina that in future reporting he should "keep in mind Ho's clear record as agent international communism, absence evidence recantation Moscow's affiliations, confused political situation France and support Ho receiving French Communist Party."[26] Hardening Cold War attitudes gradually produced an intolerable tension in the Truman administration's two-tier policy of pursuing the political independence of the Vietnamese people on the one hand and of guaranteeing its allies on the other hand. The increasing reliance on the French in Europe caused United States policymakers ultimately to sacrifice the once avowed interests of the Indochinese people. American analyses of the situation in Southeast Asia became decidedly one-dimensional and subordinated to anti-Soviet foreign policy considerations.

And yet there were nagging doubts. In early February 1947, Secretary of State George C. Marshall observed that while the United States recognized French sovereignty in Indochina, "we cannot shut our eyes to the fact that there are two sides to this problem and that our reports indicate both a lack [of] French understanding of other side . . . and continued existence [of a] dangerously outdated colonial outlook and method in [the] area."[27]

Nonetheless, and indicative of the extent to which the nation's Vietnam policy remained a function of anti-Soviet communism in general, Marshall underscored the real danger in Vietnam. "We do not lose sight [of the] fact," he noted, "that Ho Chi Minh has direct Communist connections and it should be obvious that we are not interested in seeing colonial administrations supplanted by philosophy and political origin emanating [from] and controlled by [the] Kremlin." The peculiar realities of Vietnam became less and less important in and of themselves. "[The] fact does remain, however," observed Marshall, pointing out the broad implications for Vietnam, "that a situation does exist in Indo-China which can no longer be considered, if it ever was considered, to be of a local character." The problem remained of course in proving Ho's connection with Moscow, at that time a difficult proposition. As late as July 1948, Marshall wrote that the State Department had "no evidence of [a] direct link between Ho and Moscow but *assumes* it exists."[28]

Further doubts with respect to Ho's presumed Soviet source of support were reinforced in a survey of Communist influence in Southeast Asia conducted by the Department of State's Office of Intelligence Research in the fall of 1948. "If there is a Moscow-directed conspiracy in Southeast Asia," observed the report, "Indo-China is an anomaly so far."[29] The analysis of the possible reasons for this situation is revealing. Among the possibilities given were, first, "no rigid directives have been issued by Moscow"; second, "the Viet-Nam government considers that it has no rightist elements that must be purged"; third, "the Viet-Nam Communists are not subservient to foreign policies pursued by Moscow"; and, fourth and finally, "a special dispensation for the Viet-Nam government has been arranged in Moscow." Having said that, the report then concluded that of these possibilities the most likely were that Moscow had both not issued rigid directives and also had provided a special dispensation to Ho's government. The third possibility—i.e., that Ho was independent of the Kremlin— had apparently no support.

By the spring of 1949, and with the "loss" of China facing the Truman administration squarely in the face, such differentiations had become academic. Or, as Acheson put it in May 1949: "Question whether Ho as much nationalist as Commie is irrelevant. All Stalinists in colonial areas are nationalists. With achievement nat[ionalist] aims (i.e. independence) their objective necessarily becomes subordination state to commie purposes and ruthless extermination not only opposition but all elements suspect even slightest deviation."[30]

Nonetheless, and despite Acheson's growing concern with communism in general and Vietnamese communism in particular, some American policymakers still realistically viewed the situation. Such State Department officials as Abbot Low Moffat, Chief of the Division of Southeast Asian Affairs, observed in early 1947 that the only alternative to an independent Vietnam was a "gigantic armed colonial camp."[31] The problem was, of course, that the name of Ho Chi Minh had become anathema. A State Department position paper, dated September 1948, frankly admitted that the Truman administration's greatest difficulty lay in its "inability to suggest any particular solution to the Indo-China problem, as we are all too well aware of the unpleasant fact that Communist Ho Chi Minh is the strongest and perhaps the ablest figure in Indo-China and that any suggested solution which excludes him is an expedient of uncertain outcome."[32] Or, as Marshall himself conceded a year earlier, "Frankly we have no solution of [the] problem to suggest."[33] In any case, American planners found themselves caught on the horns of a dilemma. "We are naturally hesitant," continued the position paper, "to press the French too strongly or to become deeply involved so long as we are not in a position to suggest a solution or until we are prepared to accept the onus of intervention."[34] Equally important, and part of the recurring motif of the United States-Vietnamese-French triangle throughout the 1940s, was the recognition that American considerations were "complicated by the fact that we have an immediate interest in maintaining in power a friendly French government, to assist in the furtherance of our aims in Europe"; further, "this immediate and vital interest has in consequence taken precedence over active steps looking toward the realization of our objective in Indo-China." Such considerations, although not always for the same reasons, survived well into the decade of the 1950s.

The triumph of Mao in China in 1949, together with other events, perceived to be related, of that and the previous year—the Communist purges in Czechoslovakia, the Berlin Blockade, and especially the Soviet detonation of an atomic device—irrevocably began to alter United States policy considerations in Southeast Asia. For it was at this time American planners resolved to draw the line from which the United States could no longer retreat. In a draft of a National Security Council position paper, dated 23 December 1949, United States policymakers contended that it was "now clear that southeast Asia is the target of a co-ordinated offensive directed by the Kremlin." Further, and much more ominously, the paper went on "the extension of communist authority in China represents a grievous political defeat for us; if southeast Asia is also swept by communism we shall have suffered a major political rout the repercussions of which will be felt throughout the world, especially in the Middle East and in a then critically exposed Australia."[35]

As a solution to this predicament, the study called for the "gradual reduction and eventual elimination of the preponderant power and influence of the USSR in Asia to such a degree that the Soviet Union will not be capable of threatening from that area the security of the United States or its friends." Among the study's recommendations, the most important was that "the United States should now . . . scrutinize more closely the development of threats from Communist aggression, direct or indirect, and be prepared to help within our means to meet such threats by providing political, economic, and military assistance and advice where clearly needed to supplement the resistance of the other governments in and out of the area which are more directly concerned."[36] At the Fiftieth Meeting of the National Security Council, held in late December 1949, the report's recommendation became the official policy of the Truman administration.

Thus, in much the same manner as United States Vietnamese foreign policy had been subordinated to larger American considerations in the immediate postwar period, United States Vietnamese foreign policy was now subordinated to the American preoccupation with communist threats everywhere. Forced to employ the vulgarized language of containment concepts, which had been implied in the Truman Doctrine message of March 1947 and, rightly or wrongly, attributed to Kennan's "X" article of the following July, American planners overwhelmingly tended to think and formulate policy in those terms. In this way, America's Vietnamese policy, as well as its foreign policy in general, metamorphosed itself into a form that bore little or no resemblance either to Roosevelt or earlier Truman policy.

In early February 1950, after the French parliament had ratified agreements with Bao Dai and the other Associated States of Indochina, the United States officially recognized (South) Vietnam, Laos, and Cambodia. And, as a correlative, the Truman administration considered what specific steps might be taken to prevent what was perceived to be externally fostered dissension in the region. At the same time, the State Department professed alarm at the Soviet recognition of the government of North Vietnam. For Soviet recognition at this point provided the administration with conclusive, and until then elusive, proof that Moscow was the source of Ho's strength. "The recognition by the Kremlin of Ho Chi Minh's Communist movement in Indo-China," wrote Secretary of State Acheson in a curious sentence, "comes as a surprise."[37] Having assumed for a number of years that Ho was under orders from Moscow, Acheson skillfully utilized Soviet recognition to confirm publicly something he had previously not the slightest doubt about: "The Soviet acknowledgement of this movement should remove any illusion as to the 'nationalist' nature of Ho Chi Minh's aims and reveals Ho in his true colours as the mortal enemy of native independence in Indo-China." Thus the last part of the Vietnamese paradigm that was to serve successive American administrations during the 1950s and 1960s was fitted into place.

On 16 February 1950, the French government made an appeal to the Americans for direct military and economic aid for Indochina, asserting that previous efforts had been "such a drain on France that a long-term program of assistance was necessary and it was only from the United States that it could come."[38] Then, engaging in the diplomatic blackmail that had been going on since late 1945, Paris reluctantly suggested the alternative: "Otherwise . . . it was very likely that France might be forced to reconsider her entire policy with the possible view to cutting her losses and withdrawing from Indo-China." Up to that time, and in accordance with the spirit, if not always the letter, of its traditional anticolonialist policy, the United States had officially refused to supply military equipment directly to Indochina, although the State Department had had no great doubts that military shipments sent to French ultimately found their way to Indochina. For, according to one observer, "This policy has been limited in its effects as we have allowed the free export of arms to France, such exports thereby being available for reshipment to Indo-China or for releasing stocks from reserves to be forwarded to Indo-China."[39] Now, in response to the French request, the United States abandoned all efforts to disguise the shipment of arms directly to France in Vietnam. Or, as Acheson phrased it: "The United States Government, convinced that neither national independence nor democratic evaluation exist in any area dominated by Soviet imperialism, considers the situation to be such as to warrant its economic and military equipment to the Associated States of Indo-China and to France in order to assist these states to pursue their peaceful and democratic evolution."[40] From this position further plans evolved, contributing to the incremental involvement of the United States in the destiny of Southeast Asia.

Several weeks later, in a National Security Council study on Indochina, American planners theorized that "in the present state of affairs, it is doubtful that the combined native Indochinese and French troops can successfully contain Ho's forces should they be strengthened by either Chinese Communist troops . . . or Communist supplied arms and material in quantity from outside Indo-China."[41] To bolster the French and to prevent such a situation, the study further reasoned that it was "important to United States security interests that all practicable measures be taken to prevent further communist expansion in Southeast Asia." Moreover, the study went on, in a manner adumbrating the much-used domino image of the 1950s, "Indo-China is a key area of Southeast Asia and is under imminent threat. The neighbouring countries of Thailand and Burma could be expected to fall under Communist domination if Indo-China were controlled by a Communist-dominated government. The balance of Southeast Asia would then be in grave hazard." From this proposition, it was argued that "the Departments of State and Defense should prepare as a matter of priority a program of all practicable measures designed to protect United States security interests in Indo-China."

A similar analysis by the Joint Chiefs of Staff was equally emphatic, arguing that for a number of reasons, including the protection of "major sources of certain strategic materials required for the completion of United States stockpile projects," the mainland states of Southeast Asia were of current critical importance.[42] The JCS scenario in the event of the fall of Indochina evoked what today has become a haunting melody in the American military establishment. "The fall of Indo-China," concluded the

JCS in 1950, "would undoubtedly lead to the fall of the other mainland states of Southeast Asia." Furthermore, continued the report, the fall of Southeast Asia would require, inter alia, "changing the Philippines and Indonesia from supporting positions in the Asian off-shore island chain to front-line bases for the defense of the Western Hemisphere." Additionally, it would "bring about almost immediately a dangerous condition with respect to the internal security of the Philippines, Malaya, and Indonesia, and would contribute to their probable eventual fall to the communists." In sum, predicted the JCS, "the fall of Southeast Asia would result in the virtually complete denial to the United States of the Pacific littoral of Asia."

In any case, when the North Koreans invaded South Korea on 25 June 1950, the Truman administration simply *assumed* that the North Korean attack marked the opening of a preparatory, wide-scale attack on the whole of Southeast Asia. "The attack upon Korea," declared Truman on 27 June 1950, in a statement to the American people, "makes it plain beyond all doubt that communism has passed beyond the use of subversion to conquer independent nations and will now use armed invasion and war."[43] Indicative of the administration's linking of Southeast Asia with putative Soviet- and Chinese-inspired aggression, which is another story, the president in his initial Korean strategy both accelerated the supply of military assistance to the French and to the Associated States in Indochina and dispatched a military mission to the area to coordinate working relations. In effect, Ho Chi Minh's North Vietnamese government became identified with the North Korean aggression and, by implication, with the international Communist conspiracy operated and managed by Moscow and Peking.

The outbreak of the Korean War and the American reaction to it, more than any other single event, crystallized the Cold War mentality that had been more or less in a state of fluidity from 1945 to 1950. As part of this process, American understanding and appreciation of Indochinese realities and aspirations, which had briefly been embraced during and immediately after 1945, were transformed into an almost unrecognizable body of knowledge, which in turn was then processed through a Cold War prism. With the North Korean invasion across the 38th Parallel, Indochina came to be seen mainly as an aspect of the larger problem of coping with the Soviet and Chinese Communist conquest of the Free World. Or, as Truman put it: "We were seeing a pattern in Indo-China timed to coincide with the attack in Korea as a challenge to the Western world . . . a challenge by the Communists alone, aimed at intensifying the smouldering and anti-foreign feeling among most Asian peoples."[44]

Accordingly, the legacy of the Cold War paradigm that portrayed the

Indochina conflict as but a functional aspect of worldwide Communist aggression was passed on intact to the Eisenhower administration. The Korean War, argued President Eisenhower unequivocally, was "clearly part of the same calculated assault that the aggressor is simultaneously pursuing in Indo-China."[45] And, conversely, the working out of a settlement of the Korean War would presumably have a lasting impact on Indochina as well as on other nations in the region. That John F. Kennedy thought and acted upon the same assumptions can hardly be open to question. For in his words: "Viet-Nam represents the cornerstone of the Free World in Southeast Asia, the Keystone of the arch, the finger in the dike. Burma, Thailand, India, Japan, the Philippines and, obviously, Laos and Cambodia are among those whose security would be threatened if the red tide of Communism overflowed into Viet-Nam. . . . Moreover, the independence of Free Viet-Nam is crucial to the free world in fields other than military. Her economy is essential to the economy of all of Southeast Asia; and her political liberty is an inspiration to those seeking to obtain or maintain their liberty in all parts of Asia—and indeed the world." For these reasons, then, added JFK, "The fundamental tenets of this nation's foreign policy, in short, depend in considerable measure upon a strong and free Vietnamese nation."[46]

President Lyndon B. Johnson, like his predecessor, could not escape the conclusion that Vietnam, by whatever justification, was *the* test case of American determination to hold the line against further Communist incursions, thus continuing the obstruction of a clearer view of Vietnamese realities. As Johnson noted in his memoirs relating to the period from late 1961 to 1965: "It became increasingly clear that Ho Chi Minh's military campaign against South Viet-Nam was part of a larger, much more ambitious strategy being conducted by the Communists."[47] The president's perception is revelatory. "What we saw taking shape rapidly," recalled Johnson, "was a Djakarta–Hanoi–Peking–Pyongyang axis, with Cambodia probably to be brought in as junior partner and Laos to be merely absorbed by the North Vietnamese and Chinese." Given the presumed correctness of these assumptions, the argument concluded: "the members of this new axis were undoubtedly counting on South Viet-Nam's collapse and an ignominious American withdrawal. . . . The entire region would have been ripe in the plucking."

Similarly, Richard M. Nixon's policy of détente with the Soviet Union and China failed appreciably to alter the image of Vietnam as a vital test case and an aspect of a larger problem. "An American defeat in Viet-Nam," declared former President Nixon on May 8, 1972, in a message to the American people explaining his decision to mine the entrances to North Vietnamese ports, "would encourage this kind of aggression all over the world.... small nations, armed by their major allies, could be tempted to attack neighbouring nations at will, in the Mid-East, in Europe and other areas."

Finally, there would have been no reason to expect a change in the attitude of Gerald Ford's administration. For in his formal and fore-doomed request to Congress in 1975 for continued military aid to South Vietnam (and Cambodia), President Ford reminded his recent colleagues that "U. S. unwillingness to provide adequate assistance to allies fighting for their lives would seriously affect our credibility as an ally." In con-clusion, one can only wonder what Franklin Roosevelt would have thought of such logic, a logic more than distant, indeed divorced from his original vision of a free and independent Indochina.

# NOTES

Chapter One
*Australia and the Cold War*
Glen St. John Barclay

1.  Alfred Deakin to Lord Crewe, Sept. 27, 1909, Foreign Office file 800/91, Public Records Office.
2.  Prime Minister of Australia to Prime Minister, United Kingdom, Mar. 10, 1939, Commonwealth Record Series (CRS) A816, file 19/301/437, "U. K.– Defense, 1935–1938," Australian Commonwealth Archives Office (hereafter cited as ACAO).
3.  G. Hermon Gill, *Australia in the War of 1939–45: Royal Australian Navy, 1939–42, Australian War Memorial* (Canberra, 1957), p. 43.
4.  Memorandum for the Prime Minister from the Minister of External Affairs, Dec. 18, 1938, External Affairs II, Correspondence Files, item 15, USA, CRS A981, ACAO.
5.  Records of the Council of Defense, 1935–39, file CRS AA1971/216, ACAO; for this aspect in general see G. St. J. Barclay, "Singapore Strategy," *Military Affairs* (1975).
6.  Memorandum for the Prime Minister from the Minister of External Affairs, file CRS A981, item Australia 205, pt. 2, ACAO.
7.  Lord Lothian to Lord Halifax, Nov. 10, 1939, in *Documents Relating to New Zealand's Participation in the Second World War* (Wellington, 1963), III, 534.
8.  Stanley Bruce to Prime Minister of Australia, Dec. 1, 1941; John Curtin to Reginald G. Casey, Dec. 2, 1941, in Paul C. Hasluck, *The Government and the People, 1939–1942,* (Canberra, 1965), I, 554–555.
9.  See Raymond A. Esthus, "President Roosevelt's Commitments to Britain to Intervene in a Pacific War," *Mississippi Valley Historical Review,* 50 (1963), 28-38.
10. Eggleston Diary, Dec. 8, 1941, file MS 423/9/1051, Eggleston Papers, National Library of Australia, Canberra.
11. Lewis H. Brereton to George C. Marshall, Jan. 26, 1942, in Alfred D. Chandler, ed., *The Papers of Dwight David Eisenhower: The War Years* (Baltimore, 1970), I, 78, n. 2.
12. Maurice Matloff and Edwin M. Snell, *Strategic Planning for Coalition Warfare, 1941-1942* (Washington, D. C., 1962), p. 160.

13. Record of conversation between Curtin and his press secretary, Dec. 30, 1942, file MS 4675(44), Curtin Papers, National Library of Australia, Canberra; also G. St. J. Barclay, "Australia looks to America," accepted for publication in the *Pacific Historical Review*, 1976.

14. Herbert V. Evatt to John Curtin, May 20, 1944, file CRS A989, item 44/80/1/67/2, ACAO.

15. Cordell Hull to Nelson T. Johnson, Feb. 1, 1944, in U. S. Dept. of State, *Foreign Relations of the United States (FRUS) 1944: The British Commonwealth and Europe* (Washington, D. C., 1965), III, 177.

16. Memorandum of a conversation by the Secretary of State, Apr. 19, 1944, *FRUS* 1944, III, 191-92.

17. Sir Alan Watt to John Hood, Feb. 29, 1944, file CRS A989, 43/950/5/1, ACAO.

18. *Commonwealth Parliamentary Debates,* House of Representatives, Jun. 22, 1949.

19. Ibid., Jun. 17, 1948.

20. Ibid., Mar. 9, 1950.

21. *Sydney Morning Herald*, Mar. 21, 1950.

22. *CPD*, H. of R., Sep. 24, 1947.

23. *Sydney Morning Herald*, Aug. 7, 1950.

24. Ibid.

25. *New York Times*, Aug. 2, 1950.

26. *CPD*, H. of R., Feb. 21, 1951.

27. *Sydney Morning Herald*, Apr. 30, 1952.

28. *CPD*, H. of R., and Senate, Jan. 12, 1951.

29. *CPD*, H. of R., Jan. 20, 1955.

30. Ibid., Aug. 5, 1954.

31. *Sydney Morning Herald*, Sep. 23, 1950.

32. *CPD*, H. of R., Oct. 16, 1951.

33. Ibid., Aug. 5, 1954.

34. R. Murray, *The Split: Australian Labor in the Fifties* (Melbourne, 1970), p. 279.

35. Australia, Department of External Affairs, *Current Notes on International Affairs*, vol. 26, Feb.–Mar. 1955.

36. *Sydney Morning Herald*, Jan. 26, 1955.

37. *CPD*, H. of R., Sep. 19, 1957.

38. Ibid., Apr. 4, 1957.

39. Imperial Conference, 1926, 15.11.26, file CAB 32-46, Public Records Office.

40. *CPD*, H. of R., Feb. 23, 1950.

41. Ibid., Jan. 8, 1950.

42. *Sydney Morning Herald*, Mar. 2, 1961.

43. *CPD*, H. of R., May 22, 1963.

44. Ibid., May 6, 1965.

45. R. Aitchison, *Thanks to the Yanks?* (Melbourne, 1972), p. 92.

46. *Times* (London), Jan. 5, 1966.

47. *CPD*, H. of R., Mar. 8, 1966.

48. *The Australian*, Jul. 1, 1966.

49. Australian Department of Foreign Affairs, *Current Notes on International Affairs (CNIA)*, 37 (Jul. 1966), 455.

50. Hughes, op. cit., pp. 100-107.

51. I. Bellamy and J. Richardson, "Australian Defence Procurement," *Canberra Papers on Strategy and Defence*, no. 8, Australian National University, 1970.

52. Ibid., p. 36.

53. Aitchison, op. cit., p. 96.

54. Hughes, op. cit., p. 124.

55. *CNIA*, vol. 39, Jun. 1968, p. 256.

56.  G. St. J. Barclay, "Problems in Australian Foreign Policy, July–December 1968," *Australian Journal of Politics and History,* 15 (1969), 3.
57.  *The Australian,* Oct. 11, 1968.
58.  *CPD,* H. of R., Feb. 25, 1969.
59.  Ibid.
60.  *Sydney Morning Herald,* Nov. 27, 1963.
61.  Also see Donald T. Brash, "Australia as a Host to the International Corporation," in C. P. Kindleberger, ed., *The International Corporation,* (Cambridge, Mass., 1970), 295-318.
62.  *Sydney Morning Herald,* Jun. 16, 1974; also G. St. J. Barclay, "Problems in Australian Foreign Policy, July–December, 1974," *Australian Journal of Politics and History,* 21 (1975).
63.  *The Australian,* Jun. 21, 1973.
64.  *CPD,* H. of R., Sep. 24, 1947.

## Chapter Two
### *Italy and the Cold War*
### Vincent P. DeSantis

1.  Giovanni Gronchi, "Italians As Builders and Pioneers," *The Atlantic Monthly,* 202 (Dec. 1958), p. 118.
2.  The estimate of 25 percent was made by former Minister of the Budget Ugo La Malfa in an address to the national congress of the Republican Party on March 29, 1965; quoted from Norman Kogan, *A Political History of Postwar Italy* (New York, 1966), p. 158.
3.  For a discussion of the historiographical debate surrounding the literature of the Cold War, consult Joseph M. Siracusa, *New Left Diplomatic Histories and Historians: The American Revisionists* (New York, 1973), pp. 76-103.
4.  Luzzato Fegiz, *Il Volto Sconosciuto,* pp. 675, 739; quoted from Norman Kogan, *The Politics of Italian Foreign Policy* (New York, 1963), pp. 24-25. In addition to this study by Kogan on postwar Italy, see his *A Political History of Postwar Italy* (New York, 1966) and *Italy and the Allies* (Cambridge, Mass., 1956).
5.  Lloyd A. Free and Renzo Sereno, *Italy: Dependent Ally or Independent Partner* (Princeton, N. J., 1957), p. 121; quoted from Kogan, *Politics of Italian Foreign Policy,* p. 26.
6.  *L'unita,* Sept. 29, Oct. 1, 1957.
7.  Truman quotation is from Kogan, *Italy and the Allies,* p. 206.
8.  Congressional Special Committee to Study the Foreign Aid Program, *Survey No. 4, Western Europe* (Washington, D. C., 1957), pp. 1327-28; Kogan, *Politics of Italian Foreign Policy,* p. 120.
9.  Polls taken in March 1958 by the *Isituto italiano dell' opinione pubblica;* quoted from Kogan, *Politics of Italian Foreign Policy,* p. 27.
10. Kogan, *Political History of Postwar Italy,* p. 52.
11. Giuseppe Mammarella, *Italy After Fascism: A Political, 1943-1965* (Notre Dame, Ind., 1965), p. 192.

## Chapter Three
### *Belgium and the Cold War*
### Frans Govaerts

1.  This can be derived from a note of Mr. Ch. De Visscher, Belgian representative at the San Francisco Conference, written on 11 June 1945, in which he said: "We will nevertheless sign the Charter: First of all, because it seems politically

impossible to do otherwise. U. S. support for a possible defense of our country has been offered on the condition that we accept the Charter" (F. Van Langenhove, *La Sécurité de la Belgique: Contribution à l'histoire de la période 1940-1950* [Brussels, 1971], p. 164).

2. Belgium, *Parlementaire Handelingen, Kamer* (cited hereafter as *Parl. Hand., Kamer*), 1944-45, October 31, 1945, p. 1210. An interesting analysis of Belgium's policy with regard to the UN is also made in Royal Institute for International Relations, *La Belgique et les Nations Unies* (New York, 1958); and in O. De Raeymaeker, "Regionale accoorden en wettige zelfverdediging," *Politica* (Louvain), VII, no. 3 (July, 1957), 193-213.

3. See, e.g., the government's declaration of 14 February 1945 in Belgium, *Parlementaire Handelingen, Senaat* (cited hereafter as *Parl. Hand., Senatt*), 1944-45, 14 February 1945, p. 91. Same in the government's declaration of 7 August 1945 in: *Parl. Hand., Kamer*, 1944-45, August 7, 1945, p. 630.

4. See, for Belgium's foreign policy in the interwar period, O. De Raeymaeker, *België's internationaal beleid 1919-1939* (Brussels, 1945); P. Van Zuylen, *Les Mains Libres: Politique extérieure de la Belgique, 1914-1940* (Brussels, 1950); J. K. Miller, *Belgian Foreign Policy between Two Wars, 1919-1940* (New York, 1951); and D. O. Kieft, *Belgium's Return to Neutrality: An Essay in the Frustrations of Small Power Diplomacy* (Oxford, 1972).

5. P. H. Spaak, *Combats Inachevés: De L' Indépendance à l'Alliance* (Paris, 1969), p. 157. See also "Planning for the Postwar Period" in my contribution, "Belgium, Holland and Luxembourg," to O. De. Raeymaeker, (ed.), *Small Powers in Alignment* (Louvain University Press, Belgium, 1974).

6. Van Langenhove, op. cit., p. 138. Moreover, Belgium's selling of Congolese uranium to the Americans and British in December 1944 facilitated the production of nuclear weapons by 1945, a fact that certainly did not stimulate Belgo-Soviet relations. See Spaak, op. cit., pp. 177-78.

7. Van Langenhove, loc. cit.

8. Ibid.

9. *Parl. Hand., Kamer*, 1944-45, 6 December 1944, pp. 90-93.

10. This rise in the Communist Party's popularity was mainly due to their active part in the resistance.

11. Except for a few days between 13 March and 19 March 1946, they had taken part in it from the end of the war onward.

12. R. Steel, *Pax Americana* (London, 1967), p. 33. The Italian elections were held on 18 April 1948.

13. Spaak, op. cit., p. 216.

14. See, on Belgium's role in the creation of the Brussels Treaty, Van Langenhove, op. cit., pp. 205-15; and Spaak, op. cit., pp. 251-61.

15. H. S. Truman, *Memoirs: Years of Trial and Hope* (New York, 1956), p. 243.

16. *Parl. Hand., Kamer*, 1947-48, 28 April 1948, pp. 21-22; and *Parl. Hand., Senaat*, 1947-48, 24 March 1948, p. 781.

17. US, *Congressional Record*, vol. 94, part 3, p. 2997, quoted in M. M. Ball, *NATO and the European Union Movement* (London, 1959), p. 11.

18. *Parl. Hand., Kamer*, 1948-49, 4 May 1949, p. 13; and *Parl. Hand., Senaat*, 1948-49, 12 May 1949, p. 1448.

19. W. Laqueur, *Europe since Hitler* (Harmondsworth, England, 1972), p. 129.

20. *Parl. Hand., Kamer*, 1951-52, 22 January 1952, p. 4.

21. It was ratified by the House of Representatives on 26 November 1953, some 18 months after its signing, with a majority of 148 votes. Forty-nine representatives voted against and three abstained. In the Senate the result was: 125 in favor, 40 against and 2 abstentions. Among the reasons for this long delay were certainly fear of a German rearmament, the fact that for a lot of people EDC membership would create a constitutional problem, and oppositional tactics against the Christian-Democratic government.

22. T. Luykx, *Politieke Geschiedenis van België* (Brussels, 1964), pp. 542-43.
23. See Table 2.
24. See, for a thorough analysis of this embargo policy: G. Adler-Karlsson, *Western Economic Warfare, 1947-1967: A Case Study in Foreign Economic Policy* (Stockholm, 1968). Most of the facts with regard to the embargo policy are taken from this very revealing publication.
25. Ibid., pp. 40-45.
26. Ibid., p. 45.
27. G. Myrdal in his foreword to Adler-Karlsson, op. cit., p. xii.
28. Ibid.
29. US, Congress, House, *US Overseas Loans and Grants and Assistance from International Organizations: Obligations and Loan Authorizations, July 1, 1945-June 30, 1965*. Special Report prepared for the House Foreign Affairs Committee (Washington D. C., USGPO), p. 117.
30. See Spaak, *Combats Inachevés: De L'Espoir aux Déceptions* (Paris, 1969), pp. 322-25.
31. L. Colot, "La politique Belge en matière de détente et de coopération en Europe," *Chronique de Politique Etrangère*, XXII, (January, 1969), 107-109.
32. Ibid., 110-113.
33. At the ministerial NATO council meeting at Paris on December 15-16, 1966.
34. *Parl. Hand., Senaat*, 1966-67, n. 18, 17 January 1967, p. 416. See also M. Vincineau, "La position belge sur la sécurité européenne," *Politique Etrangère*, no. 6, 1972, 733-63.
35. *Keesings Historisch Archief*, 1955-56, 12835.
36. Ibid.; also *Tijdschrift voor Politiek* (Brussels), VI, no. 6, February 1957, 516-17.
37. Spaak, *Combats Inachevés: De l'Espoir aux Déceptions* (Paris, 1969), p. 328.
38. *Cepess-dokumenten 1969* (Brussels), no. 1, 1969, 44 and 54.
39. *Parl. Hand., Senaat*, 1968-69, 15 January 1969.
40. Luykx, op. cit., p. 473. On 3 September 1960 the Soviet Union provided substantial military equipment with which P. Lumumba hoped to attack the secessionist Kasai and Katanga provinces (see W. Geerts, *Binza 10. De eerste tien onafhankelijkheidsjaren van de Demokratische Republiek Kongo* [Gent-Leuven, 1970], p. 89).
41. Luykx, op. cit., p. 473.
42. Geerts, op. cit., pp. 92-93. According to the same source, General Mobutu had also the sympathy of the Kennedy family (p. 93).
43. See M. Vincineau, "Le Parlement Belge devant la crise de l'alliance atlantique," *Chronique de Politique Etrangère* (January, 1968), 89-164.
44. *Cepess-dokumenten* (Brussels), *Verkiezingsprogramma's en regeringsverklaring 1972*, X, 1971, nos. 3-4, 44 and 209.
45. *The Military Balance*, 1963-64 and 1965-66; and *De Landsverdediging in Cijfertaal* (Brussels: Ministry of Defense, 1971), Table 2.
46. *The Military Balance*, 1961-62; and *De Landsverdediging in Cijfertaal*, Tables 7 and 8.
47. See General Vivario, "La Défense de la Belgique," *Eeuwfeest Krijgsschool-Centenaire Ecole de Guerre 1870-1970* (Brussels, 1971), p. 173.
48. See chapter 2, "The Price of Security: Benelux Defense Efforts" in my contribution, "Belgium, Holland and Luxembourg," to O. De Raeymaeker's (ed.), *Small Powers in Alignment* (see n. 5 above).

**Chapter Four**
*Germany and the Cold War: Historiographical Consequences*
John A. Moses

1. Examples containing extensive bibliographies are: Hans-Peter Schwarz, *Vom*

*Reich zur Bundesrepublik* (Neuwied and Berlin, 1966); Klaus Mehnert, *Der deutsche Standort* (Stuttgart, 1967); Waldemar Besson, *Die Aussenpolitik der Bundesrepublik* (Munich, 1970); and Heinrich End. *Zweimal deutsche Aussenpolitik* (Cologne, 1973).

2. Klaus Erdmenger, *Das folgenschwere Missverständnis* (Freiburg im Breisgau, 1967), p. 14.

3. Cf. Friedrich Meinecke, *Die deutsche Katastrophe* (Wiesbaden, 1946); Gerhard Ritter, *Machstaat und Utopie* (Munich, 1940); *Europa und die deutsche Frage* (Munich, 1948). These works went through several editions and changes, both in content and title.

4. See John A. Moses, "The Crisis in West German Historiography—Origins and Trends," *Historical Studies* 13 (April 1969), pp. 445-59, which attempts to gain perspective on developments in West Germany from a more or less liberal viewpoint. The chief authority on this subject is Georg G. Iggers, *The German Conception of History* (Middletown, 1968).

5. Early examples of West German writing that indicated this were collected by Hans Kohn and published in English under the title *German History: Some New German Views* (London, 1954).

6. In 1965 a group of leading East German historians produced a succinct outline of their view of historiographical developments in the Federal Republic. See Werner Berthold, Gerhard Losek and Helmut Meier, "Grundlinien und Entwicklungstendenzen in der westdeutschen Geschichtsschreibung von 1945 bis 1964," *Wissenschaftliche Zeitschrift der Karl Marx Universität Leipzig*, 14, 1965.

7. Ibid., p. 609.

8. Ibid.

9. Ibid.

10. Cf. 3d ed., London, 1957, p. 32.

11. In addition to the works mentioned above (n. 3) by Meinecke and Ritter, see also Hans Rothfels, *Zeitgeschichtliche Betrachtungen* (Göttingen, 1959).

12. See below, n. 35. The reference here to "paradigms" is, of course, taken from *The Structure of Scientific Revolutions* (2d ed., Chicago, 1970) by Thomas S. Kuhn. The Marxist historians of East Germany were sufficiently familiar with the components of the long-established "orthodox" set of concepts about German history to identify the "paradigm" most accurately. Like Kuhn, they (the East Germans) recognized the "entire constellation of beliefs, values, techniques, and so on, shared by the members of a given community"—in this case, the "guild" of German history professors. See David A. Hollinger, "T. S. Kuhn's Theory of Science and Its Implications for History," in *American Historical Review* 78 (April 1973), p. 73, n. 10.

13. See the two-part article on Meinecke by Gerhard Losek, "Friedrich Meinecke—ein Stammvater der NATO-Historiker in Westdeutschland," *Zeitschrift für Geschichtswissenschaft* 10 (1962), vols. 7 & 8.

14. Werner Berthold, *Grosshungern und Gehorchen—Zur Entstehung und politischen Funktion der Geschichtsideologie des westdeutschen Imperialismus untersucht am Beispiel von Gerhard Ritter und Friedrich Meinecke* (Berlin, 1960), p. 9.

15. Ibid., p. 10.

16. Leo Stern, ed., *Der Antikommunismus in Theorie und Praxis des deutschen Imperialismus* (Halle/Wittenberg, 1963).

17. Ibid., p. 18.

18. Ibid.

19. Ibid., p. 19.

20. Ibid., p. 37.

21. Ibid., p. 40.

22. Gerhard Losek, "Über Wesen und Funktion der Totalitarismus—Doktrin in

der imperialistischen westdeutschen Geschichtsschreibung" in Leo Stern, ed., op. cit., p. 95.

23. Ibid., pp. 95-96.
24. Ibid.
25. Ibid., p. 105.
26. J. C. G. Röhl, *From Bismarck to Hitler* (London, 1970), p. xii.
27. Werner Berthold, "Zur Reacktion auf die politisch-historische Konzeption der Geschichtswissenschaft der DDR in der reaktionären westdeutschen Geschichts-ideologie und zu positiven Erscheinungen im westdeutschen Geschichts-denken," in Leo Stern, ed., op. cit., p. 64.
28. Ibid., p. 65.
29. Ibid., p. 66. The author did, however, proclaim the support of East German historians for all "positive forces" (such as Fischer and Geiss) in West Germany.
30. This volume, with the subtitle *Handbuch zur Auseinandersetzung mit der westdeutschen bürgerlichen Geschichtsschreibung* (East Berlin, 1970), was published subsequently in Cologne under the title *Kritik der bürgerlichen Geschichtsschreibung*. The editors are Gerhard Losek, Helmut Meier, Walter Schmidt and Werner Berthold. References here are to the second edition, published in East Berlin in 1971.
31. Ibid., p. 18.
32. Ibid., p. 19.
33. Ibid.
34. Ibid., pp. 20, 21.
35. Ibid., p. 32.
36. Ibid., p. 27.
37. Ibid., p. 30.
38. Ibid., p. 31.
39. Ibid., p. 32.
40. Ibid., p. 47.
41. Ibid.
42. Ibid., p. 77.
43. Ibid., p. 78.
44. Ernst Nolte, "Über das Verhältnis von 'bürgerlicher' und 'marxistischer' Geschichtswissenschaft," *Aus Politik und Zeitgeschichte*, vol. 31/73, 4 August 1973, p. 14.
45. Ibid., p. 11. Nolte's published paper is a slightly shortened form of his in-augural lecture to a chair in the Friedrich Meinecke Institute of the Free University in West Berlin. He was appointed to this post in the summer se-mester of 1973. In the view of the present writer, Nolte's paper is a mile-stone in the East-West German historians' debate.
46. Ibid.
47. Ibid., p. 17.
48. Ibid., pp. 19-20.
49. Ibid., p. 21.
50. A more recent development among West German historians and social scientists of the postwar generation is not only the acceptance of Marxist-Leninist categories but the loud insistence that only these are scientific. Representative articles revealing this state of mind among comparatively young German his-torians are found in *Das Argument—Zeitschrift für Philosophie und Sozial-wissenschaften*, published in West Berlin.

### Chapter Five
*Nigeria: Wars Cold and Hot, and Lukewarm Ideas*
I. F. Nicolson

1. J. A. Hobson, *Imperialism: A Study* (London, 1902), influenced both Marxists

and non-Marxists in its diagnosis of an economic or capitalist "taproot" in the new imperialism, but his prescription for the disease (reform, not revolution) was one that only non-Marxists could, and did, more or less follow.

2.  The point is made, or the claim staked, in the very title of Lord Caradon's autobiography, *A Start in Freedom* (Sir Hugh Foot, London, 1964). For a sober, authoritative memoir of the period 1955-60, the period of his governor-generalship, see Sir James Robertson, *Transition in Africa* (London, 1974). Also, I. F. Nicolson, *The Administration of Nigeria, 1900-1960* (Oxford, 1969), describes in some detail the British administrative contribution to decolonization in Nigeria, particularly in the period 1948-60.

3.  Sir Bryan Sharwood-Smith, *But Always as Friends* (London, 1969, published in the United States by Duke University under the title *Recollections of British Administration in the Cameroons and Northern Nigeria, 1921-57*), may fairly be taken as representative of the more conservative school in the northern administration; conservative certainly, but Biggles rather than Blimp in his Britishness: and he alone (pp. 277-78) suggested "covert fostering" by communism of dissidents might represent a threat to "established authority."

4.  Ruth Schachter Morgenthau, *Political Parties in French-Speaking West Africa* (Oxford, 1964); also, "Communism in Tropical Africa" (pp. 75-100) in S. Hamrell and C. G. Widstrand, *The Soviet Bloc, China and Africa* (London, 1964); and Martin Staniland, "Single-Party Régimes and Political Change" (pp. 135-75) in Colin Leys, ed., *Politics and Change in Developing Countries* Cambridge, 1969).

5.  Charles Malik, "Developing Leadership in New Countries" (an address to CIOS XIII in New York, 1963, reprinted in *The Manager*, February, 1964).

6.  Colin Legum, citing Garvey, points out (in "Pan-Africanism and Communism," in Hamrell and Widstrand, op. cit., p. 11) that Garvey thought communism "the greatest abomination ever inflicted on mankind" and criticized the white world for denying to Africa the chance to produce "its black Rockefeller, Rothschild and Henry Ford." There is evidence, indeed, that Ford was one of Zik's "models," since Zik heads one of the chapters of his autobiography (p. 402) with a saying attributed to Henry Ford: "An idealist is a person who helps other people to be prosperous."

7.  Nnamdi Azikiwe, *Zik: A Selection from the Speeches of Nnamdi Azikiwe* (Cambridge, 1961), p. 58.

8.  Nnamdi Azikiwe, *My Odyssey* (London, 1970), p. xi.

9.  Ibid., p. 211.

10. Obafemi Awolowo, *Awo: The Autobiography of Chief Obafemi Awolowo* (Cambridge, 1960), pp. 110-111.

11. Ibid., p. 135.

12. Obafemi Awolowo, *Thoughts on Nigerian Constitution* (Ibadan, 1966), p. 10.

13. John Gunther, *Inside Africa* (London, 1955), p. 759.

14. Alhaji Sir Ahmadu Bello, Sardauna of Sokoto, *My Life* (Cambridge, 1962), p. 111.

15. Ibid., p. 75.

16. Ibid., p. 227.

17. Ibid., pp. viii, 236-38.

18. Outside observers' accounts of the Nigerian tragedy of 1966-70, the story of mutinies, murders, massacres, military rule and civil war, include J. P. Mackintosh, et al., *Nigerian Government and Politics* (London, 1966); A. H. M. Kirk-Greene, *Crisis and Conflict in Nigeria: A Documentary Source-Book*, 2 vols. (London, 1971); and John St. Jorre, *The Nigerian Civil War* (London, 1972). These cite or list the many Nigerian/Biafran writings published, including Okoi Arikpo, *The Development of Modern Nigeria* (London, 1967); Amino Kano, *Politics and Administration in Post-War Nigeria* (Lagos, 1968); R. Uwechue, *Reflections on the Nigerian Civil War*, rev. ed. (New York, 1971); and, of course, the writings and addresses of the two surviving protagonists of the political era, Zik and Awo, during and since the war.

## Chapter Six
### Argentine Foreign Policy in the Cold War
#### Carlos Juan Moneta

1. Carlos J. Moneta, *Argentina and Black Africa: Cooperation through Autonomy* (Ediciones Corregidor, Buenos Aires, 1974), chapter 12 passim.
2. Carlos J. Moneta, "The Struggle for Control of the International System: From Semiflexible Bipolarity to Concerted Condominium" (ILADE, Buenos Aires, 1974).
3. See Conil Paz–Ferrari, *Argentine Foreign Policy* (Ediciones Huemul, Buenos Aires, 1964), p. 157.
4. Along with the intention of Cuba to secede, according to its policy of heterodox autonomy, there had to be a readiness on the part of the Soviet Union to accept Cuba's affiliation to the Communist Bloc. This fundamental requirement has not existed in other cases—even in Latin America—so that secession or even autonomy has not been possible. The range of action of a middle or small power is thus restricted in cases where the USSR either is a long way away or recognizes limits imposed upon the support it can offer.
5. J. C. Puig, *Outlines of Foreign Policy* (ILADE, Buenos Aires, 1970).
6. Ibid.
7. J. C. Puig, *Outline of a New National Project* (National University of Tucuman, Argentina, 1971), p. 242.
8. Bryce Wood, *The Good Neighbor Policy* (Uteha, Mexico, 1967), pp. 319ff.
9. Herbert Goldhamer, *The Foreign Powers in Latin America* (Princeton University Press, 1972).
10. Argentine-Brazilian-North American exchanges in this period are analyzed in Carlos J. Moneta, "The Foreign Policy of Brazil," in *From Dependency to Liberation: The Foreign Policy of Latin America* (Bastilla, Buenos Aires, 1973), pp. 102-104.
11. Sherry Margan, "Report from Argentina," *Fortune,* April 1974; and Garcia Lupo, *Argentina and the World Scene* (Ediciones Corregidor, Buenos Aires, 1973), p. 98.
12. O. Edmund Smith, "Yankee Diplomacy: U. S. Intervention in Argentina," pp. 123-24, in R. Ciria, *The United States Looks at Us* (Edition La Bastilla, Buenos Aires, 1973).
13. Richard Pattee, "The Argentine Question: The War Stage," *The Review of Politics,* vol. 8, no. 4, October, 1946, p. 493.
14. See, for example, the White and Blue books on General Perón after his accession to power, and the Blue Book of the U. S. Department of State on the activities of Braden and his attempts to demonstrate the existence of a Nazi regime in Argentina.
15. Sumner Welles, *Where Are We Heading?* (Random House, New York, 1946), cited in Paz–Ferrari, op. cit., p. 161.
16. Helio Jaguaribe, *Models of Economic and Political Development* (Conference of the Institute Torcuato di Tella, Buenos Aires, 1968).
17. The Counselor of Embassy in Argentina (Ray) to the Ambassador in Uruguay (Briggs), February 20, 1948, in *Foreign Relations of the United States, 1948,* vol. 9, *The Western Hemisphere* (hereafter referred to as *FRUS*).
18. Donghi Halperin, *Contemporary History of Latin America* (Alianza Editorial, Madrid, 1969), p. 392.
19. Di Tella, and M. Zymelman, *Argentine Economic Cycles* (Paidos, Buenos Aires, 1973), chapter 12.
20. Ibid.
21. *Report of the Central Bank, 1946,* p. 9, cited in Di Tella and Zymelman, op. cit., pp. 356-57.
22. Ibid., p. 50.

23. Ibid., p. 5.
24. Republic of Argentina, *Reports of the Ministry of Foreign Affairs*, vols. 1945-46, 1946-47, 1947-48, 1948-49 and 1949-50. Argentina established agreements in this period, in addition to those mentioned in the text, with the following countries: France, Canada, Denmark, the United States, Norway, Spain, the Netherlands, Sweden, Switzerland, South Africa, Venezuela, the Military Government of the Occupying Powers in Germany, Japan, Peru, Australia, Austria, Hungary, Rumania.
25. Paz-Ferrari, op. cit., pp. 193-94.
26. Di Tella and Zymelman, op. cit., p. 355.
27. Paz-Ferrari, op. cit., p. 159.
28. Ibid., year 1950-51.
29. Ibid.
30. Memorandum by Mr. Henry Dearborn of the Division of River Plate Affairs, November 10, 1948, *FRUS*.
31. The Ambassador in Argentina (Bruce) to the Secretary of State, April 28, 1948, *FRUS*.
32. J. Remorino, *Argentine Foreign Policy, 1951-55*, Buenos Aires, 1968, vol. 1, pp. 326, 329, 366.
33. Tenth Inter-American Conference, *Speech of the Argentine Foreign Minister and Head of Delegation*.
34. Ibid.
35. Remorino, op. cit., pp. 353-54.
36. Fourth Extraordinary Meeting of the International Conference of American States, *Speech of the Minister of Commerce, Dr. Cafiero, President of the Argentine Delegation* (Quitandinha, Brazil, 1954).
37. J. D. Perón, "Address to the National Military Academy," in Perón, *Latin America: Now or Never* (Ed. Sintesis, Buenos Aires, 1973), p. 85.
38. Memorandum of Henry Dearborn, January 1, 1948, *FRUS* 1948, vol. 9.
39. Abadie-Aircardi, *The Plate Basin*, dissertation (Uruguay, 1973), p. 35.
40. See Moneta, *Argentine Foreign Policy*, op. cit.
41. See A. Carella and C. J. Moneta, "Pluralism in Latin America," in Petros, Cook, and others, *Politics of Power in Latin America* (Ed. Pleamar, Buenos Aires, 1974).
42. The Treaty of New York, signed between the Argentine and Brazilian governments, contained principles that were recognized in Resolution 2995 of the Twenty-seventh General Assembly of the UN. Essentially, it provided that states should not occasion any seriously harmful effects to territories under their national jurisdiction by way of exploration, exploitation or the development of natural resources.
43. Paz-Ferrari, op. cit.
44. See p. 101.
45. Bruce to Marshall, April 28, 1948, *FRUS*.
46. Paz-Ferrari, op. cit., pp. 166-67.
47. Ray to Marshall, September 13, 1948, *FRUS*.
48. Bruce to Marshall, op. cit.
49. Ibid.
50. Ibid.
51. Dearborn to Armour, January 20, 1948, *FRUS*.
52. Bruce to Marshall, op. cit.
53. Forrestal to Marshall, January 21, 1948, *FRUS*.
54. Marshall to Forrestal, February 3, 1948, *FRUS*.
55. Lenin, *Imperialism: The Last Stage of Capitalism*, in Lenin, *Complete Works* (Institute of Marxism-Leninism, 1962), vol. 27, p. 383.
56. "Sixth Congress of the Comintern," *International Press Correspondence*, December 1928.

57.   League of Nations, *Journal*, February 1936.
58.   Article published in *Voina i Rabochni Klas*, no. 16, Moscow, August 1944.
59.   *Documents of the Conference on the International Organization of the United Nations*, San Francisco, 1945.
60.   Cordell Hull, *Memoirs*, cited in D. Horowitz, *The United States Faces the World Revolution* (Ed. de Cultura Popular, Barcelona, 1968), p. 41.
61.   See *New York Times*, June 12, 1945 (article by James Reston); May 2, 1945 (article by Arthur Krock); and *New Times* of June 1, 1945 (article by L. Volinsky).
62.   *Pravda*, June 9, 1946.
63.   Bruce to Marshall, op. cit.
64.   Ibid.
65.   Republic of Argentina, *Report of the Ministry of Foreign Affairs*, 1950–51.
66.   Bruce to Marshall, op. cit.
67.   Republic of Argentina, Report of the Ministry of Foreign Affairs: *Position of Argentina in the Fourth General Assembly of the UN*, 1949–50.
68.   On the outbreak of the Korean War (25 June 1950), the Security Council adopted various methods to persuade the member countries to help reestablish peace in that country. Argentina agreed to assist in "deterring aggression and alleviating the condition of the Korean people." (See *Report of the Ministry of Foreign Affairs*, 1950–51.) The government of Argentina affirmed its intention to support the UN as one means of bringing about an effective and permanent peace (ibid., p. 71). In the event, Argentina provided various foodstuffs, valued at 2,500,000 pesos.
69.   *Report of the Ministry of Foreign Affairs*, loc. cit.
70.   Ibid.

## Chapter Seven
### *Yugoslavia and the Cold War*
### Phyllis Auty

1.   On Tito's relations with the great powers during and immediately after the Second World War, the following are useful: P. Auty, *Tito: A Biography* (London, 1970); J. C. Campbell, *Tito's Separate Road: America and Yugoslavia in World Politics* (New York, 1967); W. F. D. Deakin, *The Embattled Mountain* (London, 1971); M. Djilas, *Conversations with Stalin* (London, 1962); I. Ionescu, *The Politics of the European Communist States* (London, 1967); F. Maclean, *Disputed Barricade* (London, 1957); W. R. Roberts, *Tito, Mihailovic and the Allies, 1941–1945* (New Brunswick, N. J., 1973); W. Vucinich, ed., *Contemporary Yugoslavia* (Berkeley, Cal., 1969); M. Woodhouse, *British Foreign Policy Since the Second World War* (London, 1961).
2.   Among the many general works about the Cold War and its phases in international politics, the following have been found useful: P. Calvercoressi, *World Politics Since 1945* (London, 1968); C. O. Lerche, *The Cold War and After* (Englewood Cliffs, N. J., 1965); and E. Luard, ed., *The Cold War: A Reappraisal* (London, 1964).
3.   For the concept of self-management in Yugoslavia, see M. J. Broekmeyer, *Yugoslav Workers' Self-Management* (Dordrecht, Holland, 1970); B. Horvat, *Essay on Yugoslav Society* (New York, 1969); R. Moore, *Self-Management in Yugoslavia*, Fabian Research Pamphlet 281 (London, 1970); A. Sturmtahl, *Workers' Councils* (Cambridge, Mass., 1964).
4.   There are a number of very useful and informative articles on all aspects of contemporary Yugoslavia in *American Universities Field Reports: South East Europe Series*, articles by D. I. Rusinov, 1963–1973.
5.   See Tito's speech at Jajce on November 29, 1968 in *New York Times*,

November 30, 1968. For translations of excerpts from Tito's speeches on domestic and international affairs for the earlier part of the period dealt with in this article, consult J. B. Tito, *Selected Speeches and Articles* (Zagreb, 1963).

6.  A. Z. Rubinstein, *Yugoslavia and the Non-Aligned World* (Princeton, N. J., 1970); Vucinich, op. cit., 189-97.
7.  Broadcast of Polish Radio at the time of the Lusaka Conference. See also L. Mates, *Non-Alignment in Theory and Practice* (Belgrade, 1972).
8.  Yugoslav Survey, special issue (in English), *Yugoslav-Soviet Relations, 1955-1969* (Belgrade, 1972).
9.  For a detailed discussion of Yugoslav-Soviet economic relations, see *Komunist*, July 25, 1973.
10. See Rusinov, "Yugoslavia Reaps the Harvest of Coexistence," *American Universities Field Reports: South East Europe Series*, vol. 16, no. 1 (Yugoslavia).

## Chapter Eight
### America, Russia, China and the Origins of the Cold War, 1945-1950
#### Geoffrey Warner

1.  The most brilliant analysis I have seen along these lines—and all the more devastating for being so brief—is in Gen. Charles de Gaulle, *Mémoires de Guerre*, vol. 2, *L'Unité 1942-1944* (Paris, 1956), pp. 237-38.
2.  Sumner Welles, *Seven Major Decisions* (London, 1951), p. 151.
3.  Wedemeyer tel., 23 November 1945, United States Department of State, *Foreign Relations of the United States 1945*, vol. 7, *The Far East: China* (Washington, 1969), p. 665. Citations to this continuing series of U. S. government documents will be in the form *FRUS*, followed by the year and volume number.
4.  Unsigned minutes of meeting of the secretaries of state, war and the navy, 27 November 1945, ibid., pp. 685-86.
5.  The flamboyant Hurley had resigned on 27 November amid charges, which were to become depressingly familiar in later years, that his mission had been sabotaged by pro-Communist and pro-imperialist foreign service officers. A politically shrewd member of the Truman cabinet suggested that Marshall be appointed as Hurley's successor, on the grounds that it "would take the headlines away from Hurley's resignation the following day." (Walter Millis, ed. *The Forrestal Diaries* [New York, 1951], p. 113.)
6.  Marshall memo., 14 December 1945, *FRUS* 1945, 7, p. 770.
7.  The texts of these agreements may be found in Lyman P. Van Slyke, ed., *The China White Paper, August 1949* (Stanford, 1967), pp. 609-26. This is a reprint of the volume originally issued by the State Department under the title *United States Relations with China: With Special Reference to the Period 1944-1949*. It will be cited hereafter as *China White Paper*.
8.  Marshall memo., 10 March 1946, *FRUS* 1946, 9, p. 528.
9.  Smyth tel., 12 April 1946, ibid., 10, p. 980; Byrnes tel., 13 April 1946, ibid., p. 981, Cummins letter, 23 August 1946, ibid., p. 757; Marshall tel., 22 July 1946, ibid., p. 753; Marshall tel., 11 August 1946, ibid., p. 782; Caughey memo., 27 September 1946, ibid., p. 761.
10. See, for example, Anthony Kubek, *How the Far East Was Lost: American Policy and the Creation of Communist China, 1941-1949* (Chicago, 1963), ch. 14, "Marshall Makes Matters Worse."
11. Vincent memo., 9 September 1946, *FRUS* 1946, 10, p. 164.
12. John Robinson Beal, *Marshall in China* (Garden City, N. Y., 1970), p. 246.
13. Notes on meeting between General Marshall and Generalissimo Chiang Kai-shek, 1 December 1946, *FRUS* 1946, 10, p. 577.
14. Stuart dispatch, 31 October 1946, ibid., pp. 455-56; John F. Melby, *The*

*Mandate of Heaven: China 1945–49* (London, 1968), p. 98. Melby was second secretary in the U. S. embassy in China.

15. Vladimir Dedijer, *Tito Speaks* (London, 1953), p. 331.

16. "Liu Shao ch'i pao-kao shih-chu wen-ti (chiho-p'ing min-chu hsin chieh-tuan pao-kao)" [Liu Shao-ch'i's report on problems of the current situation (report on the new stage of peace and democracy)], 1 March 1946. I am greatly indebted to Fred Teiwes for drawing my attention to this document and for providing me with a summary translation of it.

17. Tang Tsou, *America's Failure in China, 1941–50* (Chicago, 1963), p. 414, n. 45.

18. Charles B. McLane, *Soviet Policy and the Chinese Communists, 1931–1946* (New York, 1958), pp. 253-55, 260-61.

19. It should be emphasized, however, that the Nationalist armies obtained far more Japanese weapons than the Communists, albeit not from the Russians. Tang Tsou gives the figures (*America's Failure in China*, p. 331, n. 168). They show that it is impossible to argue that Russian delivery of these weapons gave the Communists a decisive military advantage over their opponents, especially when American deliveries to the Nationalists are also taken into account.

20. Full details of Russian support for the Chinese Communists can be found in A. M. Dubinsky, *The Far East in the Second World War* (Moscow, 1972), pp. 355-59. Dubinsky's account is based mainly upon Soviet military archives.

21. Harriman tels., 30 January, 1 February 1946, *FRUS* 1946, 10, pp. 1100-1102; 1102; 1103-1104; Melby, *Mandate of Heaven*, p. 93.

22. Melby, *Mandate of Heaven*, p. 94.

23. *China White Paper*, p. 603.

24. See the documents on the Moscow discussions concerning China in *FRUS* 1945, 7, pp. 829-50.

25. Chiang Kai-shek, *Soviet Russia in China* (London, 1957), pp. 150-51.

26. Marshall tel., 1 February 1946, *FRUS* 1946, 9, pp. 151-52.

27. Speech to Party cadres, 13 August 1945, in Mao Tse-tung, *Selected Works*, vol. 4 (Peking, 1967), p. 20.

28. Minutes of meeting between General Marshall and General Chou En-lai, 3 June 1946, *FRUS* 1946, 9, pp. 952-53.

29. Mao Tse-tung, *Selected Works*, vol. 4, p. 109.

30. Enclosure to Lalor memo., 9 June 1947, *FRUS* 1947, 7, pp. 842, 845.

31. Ibid., p. 843.

32. The estimate to which Vincent referred was drawn up in April 1947 in connection with discussion on military assistance arising out of the formulation of the Truman Doctrine. See *FRUS* 1947, 1, pp. 736-50. See, in particular, pp. 745-46, 749.

33. No figure for the proposed number of military advisers is to be found in the published documents concerning the Wedemeyer mission. At the MacArthur Hearings in 1951, Wedemeyer said that about 10,000 officers and NCO's would have been needed to bring the level of U. S. military advisory assistance up to that obtaining in Greece, but it is not clear whether he advocated such a parallel in 1947. There were only just over 800 American military advisers in China on 1 October 1947. See Forrestal memo., 15 November 1947, *FRUS* 1947, 7, p. 919.

34. The text of the Wedemeyer report may be found in *China White Paper*, pp. 764-814.

35. Wedemeyer memo., 13 October 1947; minutes of the meeting of the committee of two, 3 November 1947; *FRUS* 1947, 7, pp. 892-93, 911.

36. George F. Kennan, *Memoirs, 1925–1950*, Boston, 1967, pp. 359, 374-75, 381.

37. *China White Paper*, pp. 383-84. It seems that Kennan actually drafted Marshall's statement. See Butterworth memo., 24 January 1948, *FRUS* 1948, 8, p. 461.

38. *China White Paper*, p. 383.
39. For the growth and activities of the China Lobby in this period, see Tang Tsou, *America's Failure in China*, pp. 447-51, 462-77; Bradford H. Westerfield, *Foreign Policy and Party Politics: Pearl Harbor to Korea* (New Haven, 1955), pp. 259-66; Ross Y. Koen, *The China Lobby in American Politics* (New York, 1960), pp. 100-106.
40. Smith tel., 1 July 1948; Stuart tel., 15 July 1948; *FRUS* 1948, 7, pp. 333-34, 360.
41. See the series of articles by Cyrus L. Sulzberger in the *New York Times*, 11, 15, 18 and 21 February 1949. These were based upon briefings by John Paton Davies, the China specialist on Kennan's policy planning staff. See Cyrus L. Sulzberger, *A Long Row of Candles: Memoirs and Diaries, 1934-54* (London, 1969), pp. 384-87.
42. Speech by Mao Tse-tung at the Tenth Plenum of the Eighth Central Committee of the Chinese Communist Party, 24 September 1962, *Chinese Law and Government*, Winter 1968/69, p. 89. The text of this speech became available during the Cultural Revolution.
43. Allen S. Whiting and General Sheng Shih-ts'ai, *Sinkiang: Pawn or Pivot?* (East Lansing, Mich., 1958), p. 117.
44. *Jen-min Jih-pao*, 4 January 1964. I am greatly indebted to my former colleagues, Ian Adie and Sally Borthwick, for the reference and the translation respectively.
45. Mao Tse-tung, *Selected Works* vol. 4, pp. 415, 417.
46. *China White Paper*, p. xvi.
47. A National Security Council statement of 29 December 1949 repeats an earlier, undated formulation to the effect that "the United States should exploit, through appropriate political, psychological and economic means, any rifts between the Chinese Communists and the USSR and between Stalinists and other elements in China, while scrupulously avoiding the appearance of intervention. Where appropriate, covert as well as overt means should be utilized to achieve these objectives." It also appears that non-Communist elements in China were to be granted American support provided they were willing to resist Communism in any case and provided the support would result in "reasonable resistance to the Communists and contribute to the over-all national interests of the United States." See Enclosure to Souers memo., 30 December 1949, United States Department of Defense, *United States-Vietnam Relations, 1945-1967*, vol. 8, Washington, 1971, p. 270.
48. Tang Tsou, *America's Failure in China*, pp. 513-19; Trygve Lie, *In the Cause of Peace* (New York, 1954), p. 255.
49. Trygve Lie, *In the Cause of Peace*, pp. 255-61; Jean Chauvel, *Commentaire*, vol. 2, *D'Alger à Berne* (Paris, 1972), pp. 242-44. Chauvel was the French representative on the Security Council.
50. Lie, *In the Cause of Peace*, pp. 258, 270-71; Chauvel, *D'Alger à Berne*, pp. 244-45.
51. Mao Tse-tung, Speech to the Tenth Plenum of the Eighth Central Committee of the Chinese Communist Party, 24 September 1962, *Chinese Law and Government*, Winter 1968/69, p. 89.
52. Enclosure to Souers memo., 23 December 1949, *United States-Vietnam Relations, 1945-67*, vol. 8, pp. 245-46.
53. Dean Acheson, *Present at the Creation: My Years in the State Department* (New York, 1969), p. 350; *Public Papers of the Presidents: Harry S. Truman, 1950* (Washington, 1965), pp. 11-12.
54. See Robert Simmons, "Comment: The Korean War," *China Quarterly* no. 54, April/June 1973, pp. 358-61.
55. William M. Bueler, *U. S. China Policy and the Problem of Taiwan* (Boulder, Col., 1971).
56. A. T. Steele, *The American People and China*, New York, 1966, pp. 35-36, 47.

57. John S. Service, *The Amerasia Papers: Some Problems in the History of US-China Relations* (Berkeley, 1971), p. 165, n. 45.
58. A public opinion poll taken at the end of August 1946 showed that only 57 percent of those asked had even heard of the conflict in China. Well over half of these favored a policy of noninvolvement. Only about a quarter supported positive action of one kind or another. (See H. Cantril and M. Strunk, *Public Opinion, 1935-1946* [Princeton, 1951], p. 953.) What is so interesting about this poll is that it was taken after American public opinion had begun to turn sharply against the Soviet Union.

## Chapter Nine
### FDR, Truman, and Indochina, 1941-1952: The Forgotten Years
Joseph M. Siracusa

I should like to express my personal gratitude to the Harry S. Truman Library Institute for National and International Affairs and to the Australian Research Grants Committee for financial assistance and the opportunity to conduct overseas research necessary for the revision of my earlier work on this subject.

1. Leslie H. Gelb, "Today's Lessons from the Pentagon Papers," *Life* (September 17, 1971), 34.
2. Robert F. Berkhofer, Jr., *A Behavioral Approach to Historical Analysis* (New York, 1969), p. 33.
3. Thomas S. Kuhn, *The Structure of Scientific Revolutions*, 2d ed. (Chicago, 1970), ch. 7, p. 175.
4. Gary R. Hess, "Franklin Roosevelt and Indochina," *Journal of American History*, LIX (September, 1972), 354.
5. Edward R. Drachman, *United States Policy toward Vietnam, 1940-1945* (Rutherford, N. J., 1970). See also the exchange between Roosevelt and Churchill on March 17 and 22, 1945, in *The Messages between Franklin D. Roosevelt and Winston S. Churchill, 1939-1945* (Microfilm edition, reel 5), Franklin D. Roosevelt Library, Hyde Park. N. Y.
6. Cordell Hull, *The Memoirs of Cordell Hull*, 2 vols. (New York, 1948), II, 1955.
7. Earl of Avon, *The Memoirs of Anthony Eden, Earl of Avon: The Reckoning* (Boston, 1965), p. 438.
8. An account of this exchange is found in *The Price of Vision: The Diary of Henry A. Wallace, 1942-1946*, ed. John Morton Blum (Boston, 1973), pp. 307-308.
9. Hull, *Memoirs*, II, 1596-97.
10. "Memorandum by President Roosevelt to the Under Secretary of State," November 3, 1944, Department of State, *Foreign Relations of the United States, Diplomatic Papers: 1944* (Washington, 1965), III, 780. (Hereafter this source will be referred to as *FRUS*.)
11. For FDR's personal views on Indochina on the eve of the presidential election of 1944, consult the Hopkins conversation in the Prime Minister's Confidential Files (PREMIER 4), File 27, Folder 7, 476-77, Public Record Office, London.
12. "Memorandum by President Roosevelt for the Secretary of State," January 1, 1945, *FRUS 1945*, VI, 293.
13. "The Director of the Office of European Affairs (Dunn) to the Director of the Civil Affairs Division, War Department (Hildering)," March 14, 1944, *FRUS 1944*, V, 1205-1206.
14. Claire Lee Chennault, *Way of a Fighter: The Memoirs of Claire Chennault* (New York, 1949), p. 342.
15. "The Ambassador in France (Caffery) to the Secretary of State," March 13, 1945, *FRUS 1945*, VI, 300.

16. "The Ambassador in France (Caffery) to the Secretary of State," January 30, *FRUS* 1945, VI, 668.
17. *Complete Presidential Press Conferences of Franklin D. Roosevelt*, 25 vols. (New York, 1972), XXV, 70-71.
18. "Memorandum of Conversation by the Adviser on Caribbean Affairs (Taussig)," March 15, 1945, *FRUS* 1945, I, 124.
19. See particularly "The Acting Secretary of State (Grew) to the Ambassador in France (Caffery)," May 9, 1945, *FRUS* 1945, VI, 307; and "The Acting Secretary of State (Acheson) to the Chargé in China (Robertson)," October 5, 1945, ibid., 313.
20. Cable, Ambassador Patrick J. Hurley to President Truman, May 29, 1945, White House Map Room File (Incoming Messages), Top Secret File, 1945–April–May, Truman Papers, Harry S. Truman Library, Independence, Mo. (hereafter cited as White House Map Room File).
21. Cable, Ambassador Patrick J. Hurley to Acting Secretary of State (Grew), White House Map Room File (Incoming Messages), Top Secret File, 1945–June. It is interesting to note that in two conversations, one a half-hour interview, in the first week of March, 1945, with Secretary of War Stimson, Hurley did not broach the subject of Indochina. Henry Lewis Stimson Diaries, L: 156, 171 (Microfilm edition, reel 9), Manuscripts and Archives, Yale University Library, New Haven, Conn.
22. "Report by the Subcommittee on Rearmament to the State–War–Navy Co-ordinating Committee," March 21, 1946, *FRUS* 1946, I, 1154.
23. "Policy Paper Prepared in the Department of State," June 22, 1945, *FRUS* 1945, VI, 557-58, 567-68.
24. U. S. Department of State, *United States-Viet-Nam Relations*, I, sec. I, C-4, C-60, C-62, C-96, C-97.
25. Abbott Memorandum, September 12, 1946, *United States-Viet-Nam Relations*, I, sec. I, C-103.
26. Acheson Tel., December 5, 1946, *United States-Viet-Nam Relations*, VIII, 85.
27. "The Secretary of State to the Embassy in France," February 3, 1947, *FRUS* 1947, VI, 67-68 (hereafter cited as "Marshall Memo").
28. Marshall Tel., July 2, 1948, *United States-Viet-Nam Relations*, VIII, 127 (italics mine).
29. Ibid., I, sec. I, A-50.
30. Acheson Tel., May 20, 1949, ibid., VIII, 196-97.
31. "The Consul General at Singapore (Josselyn) to the Secretary of State," January 7, 1947, *FRUS* 1947, VI, 55.
32. "Department of State Policy Statement of Indo-China," September 27, 1948, *United States-Viet-Nam Relations*, VIII, 145, 148-49 (hereafter referred to as "Indo-China Statement").
33. "Marshall Memo."
34. "Indo-China Statement."
35. "The Position of the United States with respect to Asia," December 23, 1949, ibid., 248.
36. "Report by the National Security Council on the Position of the United States with respect to Asia," December 30, 1949, ibid., 266-67.
37. *Department of State Bulletin*, XX (February 13, 1950), 244.
38. Paris Tel., February 22, 1950, cited in *United States-Viet-Nam Relations*, I, sec. IV A.2, 7, 22.
39. Ibid., VIII, 145-46.
40. *Department of State Bulletin*, XX (May 22, 1950), 821.
41. "The Position of the United States with respect to Indo-China," February 27, 1950, *United States-Viet-Nam Relations*, VIII, 285.

42. "The Position of the United States with respect to Indo-China," December 21, 1950 (Enclosure "B"), ibid., 411.
43. Harry S. Truman, *Memoirs: Years of Trial and Hope*, 2 vols. (Garden City, N. Y., 1956), II, 380.
44. Ibid.
45. *Presidential Papers: Dwight D. Eisenhower, 1953* (Washington, 1960), I, 16. For another, ironically more "realistic," view see John Foster Dulles, *War or Peace* (London, 1950), p. 231.
46. John F. Kennedy, "America's Stake in Vietnam," *A Symposium on America's Stake in Vietnam* (New York, 1956), 10; quoted in Chester L. Cooper's *The Lost Crusade: America in Vietnam* (New York, 1970).
47. Lyndon Baines Johnson, *The Vantage Point: Perspectives of the Presidency, 1963-1969* (London, 1971), pp. 134, 136.

# INDEX

# THE CONTRIBUTORS

**Phyllis Auty**, Reader in South Slav History at the School of Slavonic and East European Studies, Univeristy of London. Author of *Tito: A Biography;* "Yugoslavia and Bulgaria since 1945," in R. R. Betts, ed., *Central and Southeastern Europe;* and other volumes.

**Glen St. John Barclay**, Reader in International Relations, University of Queensland, Australia. Author of *Commonwealth or Europe?; Struggle for a Continent,* and *The Empire Is Marching.*

**Vincent P. DeSantis**, Professor of History, University of Notre Dame. Author of a number of works, including *The Shaping of Modern America, 1877-1914; Roman Catholicism and the American Way of Life;* and "The United States and Italy," in O. DeRaeymaeker, ed., *American Foreign Policy in Europe.*

**Frans Govaerts**, Research Fellow of the National Foundation for Scientific Research and Assistant to the Department of Political Science (International Relations), Catholic University of Louvain, Belgium. Author of "Belgium, Holland, and Luxembourg," in O. DeRaeymaeker, ed., *Small Powers in Alignment,* and a forthcoming study on Switzerland and the Common Market.

**Carlos Juan Moneta**, Professor of Contemporary International Politics, University of El Salvador, Argentina. Author of *1970: Dangerous Relations; From Dependency to Liberation;* and *Power Politics in Latin America* (original titles in Spanish).

**John A. Moses**, Reader in German History, University of Queensland, Australia. Author of *The War Aims of Imperial Germany: Professor Fritz Fischer and His Critics; The Politics of Illusion: The Fischer Revolution in German Historiography;* and numerous articles.

**I. F. Nicolson**, Reader in Public Administration, University of Queensland, Australia. Author of *The Administration of Nigeria, 1900-1960,* related chapters in J. P. Mackintosh, ed., *Nigerian Government and Politics,* and in L. F. Blitz, ed., *The Politics and Administration of Nigerian Government,* and other works in the fields of Asian and comparative government and public administration.

**Joseph M. Siracusa**, Senior Lecturer in American Diplomatic History, University of Queensland, Australia. Author of *New Left Diplomatic Histories and Historians: The American Revisionists; The American Diplomatic Revolution: A Documentary History of the Cold War, 1941-1947;* and (with Glen Barclay) *Australian-American Relations Since 1945.*

**Geoffrey Warner**, Professor of European Studies, University of Hull, United Kingdom. Author of *Pierre Laval and the Eclipse of France* and various articles on United States foreign policy and the origins of the Cold War.